Culture and Customs of Tanzania

Recent Titles in
Culture and Customs of Africa

Culture and Customs
of Tanzania

KEFA M. OTISO

Culture and Customs of Africa
Toyin Falola, Series Editor

 GREENWOOD

AN IMPRINT OF ABC-CLIO, LLC
Santa Barbara, California • Denver, Colorado • Oxford, England

Library of Congress Cataloging-in-Publication Data

Otiso, Kefa M.
    Culture and customs of Tanzania / Kefa M. Otiso.
        p. cm. — (Culture and customs of Africa)
    Includes bibliographical references and index.
    ISBN 978–0–313–33978–3 (hardcopy : alk. paper) — ISBN 978–0–313–08708–0 (ebook)
1. Tanzania—Civilization. 2. Tanzania—Social life and customs. I. Title. II. Series: Culture and customs of Africa.
DT442.5.O85   2013
967.8—dc23   2012035630

ISBN: 978–0–313–33978–3
EISBN: 978–0–313–08708–0

17 16 15 14 13   1 2 3 4 5

This book is also available on the World Wide Web as an eBook.
Visit www.abc-clio.com for details.

Greenwood
An Imprint of ABC-CLIO, LLC

ABC-CLIO, LLC
130 Cremona Drive, P.O. Box 1911
Santa Barbara, California 93116-1911

This book is printed on acid-free paper (∞)

Manufactured in the United States of America

To the Great People of Tanzania

Mumethubutu, Mumeweza, na Mnazidi Kusonga Mbele!

"You have dared, you have overcome, and you have kept moving forward!"
I cannot wait to see you take your next step forward.

Contents

Series Foreword

Africa is a vast continent, the second largest, after Asia. It is four times the size of the United States, excluding Alaska. It is the cradle of human civilization. A diverse continent, Africa has more than fifty countries with a population of over 700 million people who speak over 1,000 languages. Ecological and cultural differences vary from one region to another. As an old continent, Africa is one of the richest in culture and customs, and its contributions to world civilization are impressive indeed.

Africans regard culture as essential to their lives and future development. Culture embodies their philosophy, worldview, behavior patterns, arts, and institutions. The books in this series intend to capture the comprehensiveness of African culture and customs, dwelling on such important aspects as religion, worldview, literature, media, art, housing, architecture, cuisine, traditional dress, gender, marriage, family, lifestyles, social customs, music, and dance.

The uses and definitions of "culture" vary, reflecting its prestigious association with civilization and social status, its restriction to attitude and behavior, its globalization, and the debates surrounding issues of tradition, modernity, and postmodernity. The participating authors have chosen a comprehensive meaning of culture while not ignoring the alternative uses of the term.

Each volume in the series focuses on a single country, and the format is uniform. The first chapter presents a historical overview, in addition to information on geography, economy, and politics. Each volume then proceeds to examine the various aspects of culture and customs. The series highlights

the mechanisms for the transmission of tradition and culture across generations: the significance of orality, traditions, kinship rites, and family property
distribution; the rise of print culture; and the impact of educational institutions. The series also explores the intersections between local, regional,
national, and global bases for identity and social relations. While the volumes
are organized nationally, they pay attention to ethnicity and language groups
and the links between Africa and the wider world.

The books in the series capture the elements of continuity and change in culture and customs. Custom is represented not as static or as a museum artifact
but as a dynamic phenomenon. Furthermore, the authors recognize the current
challenges to traditional wisdom, which include gender relations, the negotia-
tion of local identities in relation to the state, the significance of struggles for
power at national and local levels and their impact on cultural traditions and
community-based forms of authority, and the tensions between agrarian and
industrial/manufacturing/oil-based economic modes of production.

Africa is a continent of great changes, instigated mainly by Africans but also
through influences from other continents. The rise of youth culture, the pen-
etration of the global media, and the challenges to generational stability are some
of the components of modern changes explored in the series. The ways in which
traditional (non-Western and nonimitative) African cultural forms continue to
survive and thrive—that is, how they have taken advantage of the market system
to enhance their influence and reproductions—also receive attention.

Through the books in this series, readers can see their own cultures in a different perspective, understand the habits of Africans, and educate themselves
about the customs and cultures of other countries and people. The hope is
that the readers will come to respect the cultures of others and see them not
as inferior or superior to theirs but merely as different. Africa has always been
important to Europe and the United States, essentially as a source of labor,
raw materials, and markets. Blacks are in Europe and the Americas as part
of the African diaspora, a migration that took place primarily because of the
slave trade. Recent African migrants increasingly swell their number and vis-
ibility. It is important to understand the history of the diaspora and the newer
migrants as well as the roots of the culture and customs of the places from
where they come. It is equally important to understand others in order to
be able to interact successfully in a world that keeps shrinking. The accessible
nature of the books in this series will contribute to this understanding and
enhance the quality of human interaction in a new millennium.

Toyin Falola
Frances Higginbothom Nalle Centennial Professor in History
The University of Texas at Austin

Preface

Tanzania is the largest and most diverse country in East Africa. It is larger than the combined area of its immediate neighbors, Kenya, Uganda, Burundi, and Rwanda. Aside from its more than 130 indigenous ethnic groups, it also has a sprinkling of people groups from other parts of the world. Most of its people are practitioners of Christianity, Islam, and various African traditional religions. Yet despite this diversity, Tanzania is one of Africa's most politically stable countries. How has Tanzania managed to do this? Why is it one of Africa's fastest growing economies? What do Tanzanians like to eat? What do they do for fun? What music do they like to listen to? What are their family relations like? I explore these and other fascinating aspects of Tanzania in this book.

As my goal is to give you, the reader, a broad overview of the country, I have mainly captured the country's most important social, cultural, political, economic, historical, and geographic features and illustrated these with a few select examples. While it is not possible to capture the full scope of the country's immense physical and social diversity in a volume of this size, I trust that you will enjoy reading it.

Acknowledgments

I wish to thank Professor Toyin Falola for inviting me to contribute to the Culture and Customs of Africa series. Many others have, however, helped to bring this volume to fruition. I thus wish to thank Doris Mrutu, Wellington Kamala, Alvera Byabato, Bruce Edwards, and Naftali Mandi for teaching me a thing or two about Tanzania. I am grateful to the Achokis for making it possible for me to visit the interior of Tanzania long before I decided to work on this book. The insights I gained from the trip have been invaluable in the preparation of this manuscript.

Thanks to ABC-CLIO's Kaitlin Ciarmiello, Erin Ryan, James Dare, and Michelle Scott and to PreMedia Global's Bhuvaneswari Rathinam for patiently shepherding the book to fruition.

I thank Kemunto, Moraa, and Meroka for making this whole project worthwhile. I also wish to show appreciation for my parents, Hezron and Priscilla Otiso, and grandparents, Naomi Kemunto Meroka, Meroka Okemwa, Dinah Kemunto Nyambega, and Nyambega "Kahawa" Tigo, for letting me stand on their shoulders so I can see further. I am also grateful to my Cornerstone Church family for its steadfast love and support over the years.

I appreciate Bowling Green State University for giving me a great professional opportunity and environment. I am grateful to my extended family, friends, and work colleagues for their companionship in the journey of life.

As with any acknowledgment list, this is bound to be incomplete. I, therefore, thank the many helpers whom I have not managed to thank by name. But ultimately, thanks be to God for this and other blessings. Like the Psalmist, I often wonder, "What is man that you are mindful of him, the son of man that you care for him?" (Psalms 8:4, NIV).

Chronology

3.6 million years BP	Early humans (hominids) emerge and roam in present-day northern mainland Tanzania.
3 million years BP	*Homo habilis* ("handy man") evolves in the general vicinity of contemporary Kenya and mainland Tanzania.
0.5–1 million years BP	*Homo erectus* emerges and makes use of tools like axes, some of which have been unearthed near lakes near Olduvai Gorge and Iringa. *Homo sapiens* emerges soon after with more advanced tool-making skills.
50,000 years BP	Sparse groups of hunter-gatherers inhabit Tanzania and live in some of the rock shelters near Kondoa. Contemporary Sandawe and Hadza are thought to be descendants of these hunter-gatherers.
c. 3,000 BP	Cushitic peoples such as the Iraqw move in from the northeast, though they are subsequently absorbed by waves of Nilotic peoples such as the modern-day Maasai.
1000–1 BC	Bantu migrants enter mainland from north and south and bring pottery and iron-working skills. They absorb the area's hunter-gatherers.

40–70 AD	Greek guidebook *Periplus of the Erythraean Sea* mentions Rhapta, a trading center on the coast of Azania (East Africa) where Arabs exchange ivory, rhinoceros horn, tortoise shell, and coconut oil for hatchets, daggers, lances, glass vessels, wheat, and cloth. Coastal people of "piratical habit, very great stature, and under chiefs" are later confirmed by Ptolemy in his *Geography* to be dark, tall, and noted for their oratory and fighting spirit and are called the Zenj. They later lend their name to modern Zanzibar.
700	Arab settlers begin building towns on Zanzibar, Mafia, and Kilwa islands and bring Islam to East Africa.
1107	First mosque in East Africa is built in the city of Kizimkazi in southwest Zanzibar.
1200	Shirazi descendants of the Shiraz in Persia settle in Zanzibar and create new dynasties. Their intermarriage with locals gives birth to the Swahili people. Trade develops with interior peoples.
1330	Ibn Battuta visits Kilwa Sultanate and is impressed by the humility and religion of its ruler, Sultan al-Hasan ibn Sulaiman, as well as the layout of Kilwa.
1300s–1700s	Salt is extracted from the springs at Uvinza in Kigoma and Ivuna in Mbeya and becomes a key commodity in early trade.
1400s	Kilwa gains control of gold trade from Sofala, a port to the south of the Zambezi River, and this wealth helps create probably the grandest Islamic architecture in sub-Saharan Africa.
1498	Vasco da Gama, Portuguese explorer and first European to round the Cape of Good Hope and to sail along the East African coast, finds Kilwa to be a large city with 12,000 people and good buildings of stone and mortar with terraces. Soon afterward, Portuguese colonize East Africa and use it as a refueling stop on their way to the Middle East and India. They try to trade with Africans, but their cruelty (which prompts Africans to refer to them as *Afriti*, or devils) undermines their success.

1631	Pemba rebels against Portuguese, but the rebellion is ruthlessly suppressed.
1652	Omani Arabs plunder Zanzibar.
1698	Omani Arabs capture Mombasa, Kenya, and end Portuguese colonial rule in East Africa. By this time, the Portuguese have been weakened by Turkish raids. Nevertheless, the Portuguese leave a legacy of a few words lent to the Swahili language, some forts (e.g., Kenya's Fort Jesus), and the introduction of bullfighting on Pemba.
1811	Captain Thomas Smee visits Zanzibar and finds it large, populous, dirty, and unhealthy.
1818	Clove trees, indigenous to the Molucca Islands in the South Pacific, are introduced to Pemba and Zanzibar. Together, the two islands become the world's largest producers of cloves.
1829	Sakalava cannibals from Madagascar plunder Mafia and eat most of their victims.
1832	Sultan Sayyid Said of Muscat, Oman, makes Zanzibar his home. He encourages trade with Arabia, Persia, and India and signs commercial treaties with the United States, France, and Britain. He ensures good relations with the indigenous Hadima people and their chief, Mwenyi Mkuu (Great Lord). He trades in slaves, ivory, hides, cowrie, gum copal, and cloves.
1845	Ahamed bin Mohamed bin Hassan el Alawi builds a magnificent palace with a mosque at Dunga, Zanzibar. The complex is now in ruins.
1848	German missionary Johann Ludwig Krapf visits King Kimweri of Usambara.
1848	German missionary Johannes Rebmann reaches the foot of Mount Kilimanjaro.
1856	Zanzibar becomes a separate state from Oman.
1857–1858	Richard Burton and John Hanning Speke travel along the caravan routes to the great lakes near northwestern Tanzania.

1858	David Livingstone explores eastern and central Africa for the British government.
1866	David Livingstone sets off from Zanzibar on his last expedition through mainland Tanzania.
1868	The Sultan of Zanzibar allows Fathers of the Holy Ghost to establish the first Catholic mission in East and Central Africa at Bagamoyo.
1871 (October 27)	Henry Stanley, on a mission to find Livingstone, finds him in the town of Ujiji on the shores of Lake Tanganyika.
1872	Richard Francis Burton, who has been exploring the interior of Africa from Zanzibar, publishes the two-volume set *Zanzibar: City, Island and Coast*.
1873	Sultan Sayyid Barghash prohibits slave exports from Zanzibar at the behest of the British navy.
1874 (February 24)	David Livingstone's companions, Abdulla Susi and James Chuma, reach Bagamoyo with David Livingstone's dry body. They have carried it for 11 months and 1,500 miles from Chitambo, Zambia, where he had died on May 4, 1873. He is eventually buried at Westminster Abbey, London.
1883	Sultan Sayyid Barghash builds the House of Wonders in Zanzibar.
1884	Southern parts of East Africa come under German rule.
1888 (April 28)	Dr. Karl Peters acquires (for his German East Africa Company) the right to administer the coastal strip from the Sultan of Zanzibar. Abushiri bin Salim leads local Africans, Asians, and Arabs in a revolt against German rule. Eventually, the revolt is crushed with the aid of more German troops under Major von Wissmann.
1890	The Sultan of Zanzibar cedes the coastal strip for a paltry amount of gold. German East Africa Company is disbanded as Tanganyika officially becomes German East Africa. This is met with much African resistance from, for instance, the

	Yao under Machemba and the Hehe under Chief Mkwawa.
1894	Chief Mkwawa's fortified capital of Kalenga falls to Germans after a long battle.
1897	Slavery is abolished in Zanzibar, though domestic slavery continues until 1917.
1897	Anglican Bishop Steere starts building the Cathedral Church of Christ on the old slave market in Zanzibar. It gets a small crucifix made from the chitambo tree under which Dr. David Livingstone died in 1873.
1905	Germans introduce a poll tax and forced labor to compel Africans to become part of the money economy. They use them to create large sisal, cotton, coffee, and rubber plantations.
1905	Harsh German labor and economic measures trigger the Maji Maji rebellion, which costs some 75,000 African lives. While the Germans manage to suppress it, it succeeds in uniting Africans to start agitating for independence.
1914 (December)	British occupation of German East Africa begins on Mafia Island and is resisted by mobile German troops until November 14, 1918.
1915	Mafia hosts the first airplane flights in Africa. The flights are by assembled military planes used for reconnaissance in World War I.
1916 (May 19–September 18)	Belgians occupy northwest parts of German East Africa.
1919 (May 30)	Belgian-British Treaty grants contemporary Rwanda and Burundi to Belgians as of March 1921.
1920 (January 10)	Kionga triangle, south of Ruvuma River, under Portuguese occupation since 1918, is ceded to Portuguese Mozambique.
1922 (July 20)	League of Nations (precursor of United Nations) gives Britain mandate to administer Tanganyika as a trust territory.

1922–1929   Birth of nationalist movement as educated Afri-
                         cans organize into mutual advancement societies
                         like the Tanganyika Territory African Civil Service
                         Association in Tanga (1922) and the Tanganyika
                         African Association in Dar es Salaam (1929); eth-
                         nic organizations like the Bukoba Bahaya Union
                         are also formed to challenge the colonial chiefs.

1925   Tanganyika is divided into provinces (led by com-
                         missioners that are responsible to the governor)
                         for ease of administration. A consultative Legisla-
                         tive Council, with no Africans, is appointed.

1926   Governor Donald Cameron, fearful of growing
                         nationalism in India, adopts the policy of indirect
                         rule with stronger traditional authorities led by
                         chiefs. He also establishes native courts and treas-
                         uries. A divide-and-rule policy that is anchored
                         around the tribe is established.

1946 (December 11)   Tanganyika becomes a UN trust territory ruled
                         by Britain. Trusteeship limits British colonial
                         power in Tanganyika, unlike in neighboring
                         Kenya. However, this also limits British settle-
                         ment and investment in the country.

1954   Tanganyika African Union becomes more politi-
                         cal and changes its name to Tanganyika African
                         National Union (TANU) under the leadership of
                         Nyerere. It launches its *Uhuru na Umoja* (Free-
                         dom and Unity) slogan and starts to pressure the
                         United Nations for freedom. The government
                         launches its own United Tanganyika Party (UTP).

1958   TANU routs UTP in the 1958 elections, and five
                         of its representatives become ministers.

1960   TANU scores another resounding electoral vic-
                         tory that peacefully ushers Tanganyika to
                         independence.

1961 (May 1)   Tanganyika achieves self-rule

1961 (December 9)   Tanganyika gains independence from UK-
                         administered UN trusteeship.

1962 (December 9)   Republic of Tanganyika is proclaimed and Julius
                         Kambarage Nyerere becomes president. He
                         remains in office until November 5, 1985.

1963 (December 19)	Zanzibar gains independence from the United Kingdom.
1964 (January)	Zanzibar revolution brings Afro-Shirazi Party to power, effectively ending centuries of Arab dynastic rule. It also ends the domination of Africans by Arabs in Zanzibar.
1964 (April 26)	Tanganyika unites with Zanzibar to form the United Republic of Tanganyika and Zanzibar.
1964 (October 29)	The Tanganyika-Zanzibar union becomes the United Republic of Tanzania.
1965	Tanzania becomes a one-party constitutional democracy.
1967	President Nyerere proclaims the Arusha Declaration on Socialism and Self-Reliance with the goals of justice, equality, and dignity. He nationalizes banks, trading houses, key industries, and estates.
1970–1975	China builds Tanzania-Zambia Railway (TAZARA) from Dar es Salaam to Zambia.
1972	Government is decentralized to foster more popular participation and self-management.
1972	Nyerere launches *Ujamaa* (familyhood) policy anchored on self-help and respect. Communal villages are established to maximize utilization of agricultural land and sharing of output.
1974–1975	Massive villagization is launched, and scattered rural population is resettled in villages with development with essential services.
1975	Ambitious industrialization policy is launched to complement self-reliance by providing basic industrial needs.
1977 (February 5)	President Nyerere merges the mainland's Tanganyika African National Union (TANU) party with the Zanzibar ruling party, the Afro-Shirazi Party (ASP), to form the *Chama cha Mapinduzi* or CCM (Revolutionary Party).
1978 (October)	President Idi Amin of Uganda invades Tanzania and occupies Kagera region.

1979	Tanzania counter-invades Uganda with the help of the Uganda National Liberation Front (UNLF), an umbrella organization of Ugandan exiles and anti-Amin forces including Yoweri Museveni. Amin is defeated and flees into exile in Saudi Arabia, where he eventually dies in 2003.
1984	Merger of TANU and ASP parties is reaffirmed.
1985	Julius Nyerere relinquishes power but retains chairmanship of CCM.
1985 (November)	Ali H. Mwinyi becomes president and governs until November 23, 1995. Mwinyi abandons the country's socialist economic policies and adopts capitalism.
1990	Nyerere resigns as chairman of CCM.
1990	Sections of Zanzibar demand independence referendum.
1995 (November 23)	Tanzania holds first ever multiparty elections. Benjamin William Mkapa wins and succeeds Mwinyi as president. Mkapa is later reelected and stays in office until December 21, 2005.
2000	Contested elections in Zanzibar lead to January 2001 massacre in which many protesters are killed or injured.
2005 (December 21)	Jakaya Mrisho Kikwete succeeds Mkapa as president.
2010 (November 5)	Kikwete is reelected president for a final term that will end in 2015.
2010	Zanzibar holds peaceful elections and creates government of national unity.
2011	Tanzania celebrates 50 years of independence.
2012 (May)	Unrest in Zanzibar in which Muslim extremists in Zanzibar town burn churches.

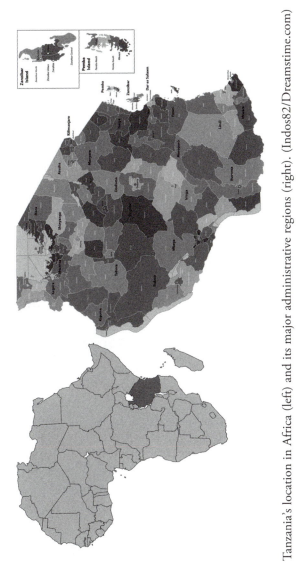

Tanzania's location in Africa (left) and its major administrative regions (right). (Indos82/Dreamstime.com)

1

Introduction

TANZANIA IS IN East Africa and is the largest country in the region both in terms of territory and population size. At 364,900 square miles, Tanzania is slightly over twice the size of the U.S. state of California or about half the size of Western Europe. Although Tanzania is larger than the combined land area of its immediate East African neighbors of Kenya, Uganda, Burundi, and Rwanda, its 2012 population of 45 million is slightly higher than that of Kenya's 43 million people—the second largest population in the region. Tanzania is one of the most politically stable countries in Africa despite its unusual history of colonial rule by the Germans and the British and its experimentation with African socialism for much of President Nyerere's presidency.

LAND

Territory

Tanzania's territory consists of 342,010 square miles (948,740 square kilometers) of land and 22,793 square miles (59,033 square kilometers) of water. This territorial size includes the Indian Ocean islands of Mafia, Pemba, and Zanzibar. The country is bordered by Kenya, Uganda, Mozambique, Zambia, the Democratic Republic of the Congo (DRC, formerly Zaire), Malawi, Burundi, Rwanda, and the Indian Ocean. The total length of its international land boundary is 2,394 miles (3,852 kilometers), with the longest segments being those that it shares with Kenya and Mozambique. Its Indian Ocean coastline is 883 miles (1,400 kilometers) long.

Water Resources

The country's 19,982 square miles of inland water resources, the largest of any African country, include Lakes Natron, Eyasi, Manyara, Mtera, and Rukwa. It also has the bulk of Lake Victoria (which it shares with Kenya and Uganda), Lake Tanganyika (which extends into Burundi, the DRC, and Zambia), and Lake Nyasa or Malawi (which forms its southwest boundary with Malawi), 13.8 regular miles (23 kilometers) of territorial sea, and an Indian Ocean exclusive economic zone of 230 regular miles (370 kilometers). Lakes Victoria and Tanganyika add to Tanzania's uniqueness because they are respectively the world's third largest freshwater lake (after North America's Lakes Michigan-Huron and Superior) and second deepest lake (after Russia's Lake Baikal). At about 420 miles (676 kilometers), Lake Tanganyika is also the world's longest freshwater lake as well as one of the narrowest major lakes, averaging between 10 and 45 miles (16 to 72 kilometers) wide. Tanzania's major rivers include Rufiji, Ruvuma, and the Great Ruaha, to name just a few. Because of its numerous surface-water resources, Tanzania is generally a well-watered country.

Location and Climate

Tanzania's location close to the equator gives the country a tropical climate whose rainfall and temperature characteristics are mainly influenced by elevation and local wind patterns. Thus, the narrow coastal lowland has a hot and humid tropical climate while the interior has a warm, drier tropical climate. At elevations exceeding 6,563 feet, temperate and polar climates exist on the upper slopes of the country's highest mountains, for instance, Gelai (9,650 feet), Rungwe (9,706 feet), Hanang (11,211 feet), Loolmalasin (11,965 feet), Meru (14,973 feet), and Kilimanjaro (19,340 feet).

Mountains and Valleys

Tanzania has Africa's highest peak and deepest lake. These are respectively Mount Kilimanjaro, which is 19,340 feet tall, and Lake Tanganyika, which is 4,708 feet deep. Lake Tanganyika is this deep because it lies in the Great Rift Valley, a substantial portion of which lies in Tanzania. Much of the rest of Tanzania falls between 0 and 6,562 feet above sea level.

Tanzania has two main mountainous regions, the northern Arusha and Kilimanjaro regions that include Mounts Kilimanjaro (19,340 feet) and Meru (14,980 feet) and the southern Rukwa, Mbeya, and Iringa regions that include the Poroto and Livingstone mountains. There are also extensive swampy or marshy areas including Bahi, Tendigo, Wembere, Usangu, Kibasira, and Sagara.

Tanzania's Mount Kilimanjaro is Africa's tallest mountain. (Gbuglok/Dreams-time.com)

Vegetation

Tanzania's vegetation patterns closely follow its climatic and relief patterns and include, in descending order of elevation, forest, woodland, bushland and thicket, wooded grassland, grassland, swamp, and desert and semidesert. The country has relatively limited forest cover, and much of what exists is found in the major moist upland areas of Arusha, Kilimanjaro, Tanga, Iringa, Shinyanga, and Kagera. Woodlands are, perhaps, the most common vegetation type in Tanzania, covering extensive areas of the moist southern half of the country.

Outside of the forested and wooded areas are the wooded grasslands, grass-lands, swamps, semideserts, and deserts. On the Zanzibar archipelago, wooded grasslands dominate on the moister western half while grasslands cover much of the less moist eastern half. Throughout the country, vegetation patterns are also increasingly affected by human activity and wildlife popula-tions. While Tanzania's growing human population is an increasing cause of deforestation and desertification in many areas the concentration of the country's wildlife in increasingly limited habitats is threatening the country's game parks and preserves.

PEOPLE

Tanzania has a current population of 45 million people, which represents a 10 million person increase since the 2002 census that pegged the country's population at nearly 35 million people (Table 1.1).[1] Tanzania's population consists of 99 percent Africans and 1 percent non-Africans. The African population consists of over 120 ethnic groups, about a dozen of which form the bulk of the country's population. The Sukuma are the country's largest ethnic group while the Chagga are probably the most Westernized and enterprising. The Sukuma, Chagga, Haya, and Nyamwezi each have more than 1 million people. Other large groups include the Hadzapi, Maasai, Gogo, Hehe, and Makonde. Because none of the country's major ethnic groups is dominant, there is limited ethnic conflict in the country, hence its remarkable political unity and stability.

Tanzania's African population is predominantly of Bantu stock with a limited number of Nilotic (e.g., Maasai and Luo) and Cushitic (e.g., Iraqw) groups. The tiny non-African population consists of Asians, Arabs, and Europeans. Tanzanians are multireligious with the main religions on the mainland being Christianity, Islam, and indigenous African beliefs. Nearly the entire population of the Zanzibar archipelago practices Islam.

The majority of Tanzania's population (97%) lives on the mainland (formerly known as Tanganyika) while the rest lives on the Zanzibar archipelago, which is dominated by the islands of Zanzibar and Pemba. In 2010, the country's most populated mainland regions were Shinyanga, Mwanza, Dar es Salaam, Mbeya, and Kagera while the least populated were Pwani and Lindi (Table 1.1). While the high populations of Mwanza, Shinyanga, Mbeya, and Kagera are partly the result of favorable environmental and cultural conditions, Dar es Salaam's high population is the result of high natural increase and rural-urban migration into the nation's premier urban center.

Regional variations are also evident in the number of total households, with many of the country's most populated regions also having the most households (Table 1.2). An important exception to this is Dar es Salaam, which leads in the number of households even though it ranks third in the country in total population. This situation arises because Dar es Salaam is an urbanized area with many single-person households. The total number of households in the Zanzibar archipelago is less than that of all mainland regions (Table 1.2).

While Tanzania has a modest national population density of 46 people per square kilometer (119 people per square mile), there are significant regional density variations based on land area, economic activity, level of economic

Table 1.1 Population by Census and Intercensal Growth Rates (Sorted by 2002 Census)

| Region | Actual Population from the Censuses | | | | 2010 (Estimate) | Growth Rates | | Sex Ratio |
	1967	1978	1988	2002		1978–1988	1988–2002	2002
Mwanza	1,055,883	1,443,379	1,876,635	2,942,148	3,566,000	2.6	3.2	98
Shinyanga	899,468	1,323,535	1,763,800	2,805,580	3,842,000	2.9	3.3	95
Dar es Salaam	356,286	843,090	1,360,850	2,497,940	3,118,000	4.8	4.3	102
Mbeya	753,765	1,079,864	1,476,278	2,070,046	2,662,000	3.1	2.4	92
Kagera	658,712	1,009,767	1,313,594	2,033,888	2,564,000	2.7	3.1	97
Morogoro	682,700	939,264	1,220,564	1,759,809	2,115,000	2.6	2.6	99
Tabora	502,068	817,907	1,036,150	1,717,908	2,349,000	2.4	3.6	97
Dodoma	709,380	972,005	1,235,328	1,698,996	2,112,000	2.4	2.3	94
Kigoma	473,443	648,941	856,770	1,679,109	1,814,000	2.8	4.8	93
Tanga	771,060	1,037,767	1,280,212	1,642,015	1,967,000	2.1	1.8	94
Iringa	689,905	925,044	1,193,074	1,495,333	1,737,000	2.7	1.5	90
Kilimanjaro	652,722	902,437	1,104,673	1,381,149	1,636,000	2.1	1.6	94
Mara	544,125	723,827	946,418	1,368,602	1,823,000	2.9	2.5	91
Arusha	610,474	926,223	744,479	1,292,973	1,665,000	3.8+	4	97
Rukwa	276,091	451,897	698,718	1,141,743	1,503,000	4.3	3.6	96
Mtwara	621,293	771,818	889,100	1,128,523	1,324,000	1.4	1.7	90
Ruvuma	395,447	561,575	779,875	1,117,166	1,375,000	3.4	2.5	95
Singida	457,938	613,949	792,387	1,090,758	1,367,000	2.5	2.3	95
Manyara	—	—	603,691	1,040,461	1,388,000	—	3.8	106
Pwani	428,041	516,586	636,103	889,154	1,063,000	2.1	2.4	98
Lindi	419,853	527,624	646,494	791,306	924,000	2	1.4	93

(continued)

Table 1.1 (Continued)

| Region | Actual Population from the Censuses | | | | | Growth Rates | | Sex Ratio |
	1967	1978	1988	2002	2010 (Estimate)	1978–1988	1988–2002	2002
Mainland	*11,958,654*	*17,036,499*	*22,455,193*	*33,584,607*	*41,914,000*	*2.8*	*2.9*	*96*
Urban West	95,047	142,041	208,571	391,002	483,000	3.8	4.5	95
North Pemba	72,015	106,290	137,189	186,013	254,000	2.6	2.2	96
South Pemba	92,306	99,014	127,623	176,153	247,000	2.6	2.3	95
North Unguja	56,360	77,017	96,989	136,953	177,000	2.3	2.5	96
South Unguja	39,087	51,749	70,313	94,504	113,000	3.1	2.1	102
Zanzibar	*354,815*	*476,111*	*640,685*	*984,625*	*1,274,000*	*3*	*3.1*	*96*
Tanzania	**12,313,469**	**17,512,610**	**23,095,878**	**34,569,232**	**43,188,000**	**2.8**	**2.9**	**96**

Source: http://www.nbs.go.tz/

Table 1.2 Population, Households, and Average Household Size by Region, 2002 (Ordered by Households)

Region	Population	Households	Average Household Size
Dar es Salaam	2,497,940	596,264	4.2
Mwanza	2,942,148	495,400	5.9
Mbeya	2,070,046	491,929	4.2
Shinyanga	2,805,580	445,020	6.3
Kagera	2,033,888	394,128	5.2
Morogoro	1,759,809	385,260	4.6
Dodoma	1,698,996	376,530	4.5
Tanga	1,642,015	356,993	4.6
Iringa	1,495,333	346,815	4.3
Kilimanjaro	1,381,149	297,439	4.6
Mtwara	1,128,523	293,908	3.8
Tabora	1,717,908	291,369	5.9
Arusha	1,292,973	286,579	4.5
Mara	1,368,602	246,600	5.5
Kigoma	1,679,109	242,533	6.9
Ruvuma	1,117,166	232,340	4.8
Rukwa	1,141,743	222,868	5.1
Singida	1,090,758	217,572	5
Pwani	889,154	200,919	4.4
Manyara	1,040,461	199,860	5.2
Lindi	791,306	190,761	4.1
Mainland	*33,584,607*	*6,811,087*	*4.9*
Urban West	391,002	74,363	5.3
North Pemba	186,013	33,019	5.6
South Pemba	176,153	29,776	5.9
North Unguja	136,953	27,854	4.9
South Unguja	94,504	19,937	4.7
Total Zanzibar	*984,625*	*184,949*	*5.3*
Total Tanzania	**34,569,232**	**6,996,036**	**4.9**

Source: http://www.nbs.go.tz/

development, culture, urbanization, and environmental conditions such as climate, water supplies, and soil fertility (Table 1.3).

The effect of limited land area on population density is, perhaps, best exemplified in the Zanzibar archipelago, where population density in three of its four rural regions—Urban West, South Pemba, North Pemba, and North Unguja—exceeds that of all mainland regions except Dar es Salaam. In fact, even South Unguja, which has the lowest population density on the archipelago, has a higher population density than all but two mainland regions, that is, Dar es Salaam and Mwanza. Population density in Urban

Table 1.3 Population Density by Region, 1967, 1978, 1988, 2002, and 2008

| | Land Area | | Density | | | | | | | | | |
| | | | 1967 | | 1978 | | 1988 | | 2002 | | 2008 | |
Region	km²	mi²	km²	mi²	km²	mi²	km²	mi²	km²	mi²	km²	mi²
Dar es Salaam	1,393	538	256	663	605	1,567	977	2,530	1,793	4,644	2,961	7,669
Mwanza	19,592	7,565	54	140	74	192	96	249	150	388	168	435
Kilimanjaro	13,309	5,139	49	127	68	176	83	215	104	269	121	313
Kagera	28,388	10,961	23	60	36	93	47	122	72	186	82	212
Mara	19,566	7,554	28	73	37	96	50	129	70	181	77	199
Mtwara	16,707	6,451	37	96	46	119	53	137	68	176	75	194
Tanga	26,808	10,351	29	75	39	101	48	124	61	158	70	181
Shinyanga	50,781	19,607	18	47	26	67	35	91	55	142	70	181
Kigoma	37,037	14,300	13	34	18	47	23	60	45	117	45	117
Dodoma	41,311	15,950	17	44	24	62	30	78	41	106	49	127
Arusha	36,486	14,087	-	-	-	-	20	52	35	91	44	114
Mbeya	60,350	23,301	12	31	18	47	25	65	34	88	42	109
Pwani	32,407	12,512	13	34	16	41	20	52	27	70	31	80
Iringa	56,864	21,955	12	31	16	41	21	54	26	67	29	75
Morogoro	70,799	27,336	10	26	13	34	17	44	25	65	28	73
Tabora	76,151	29,402	7	18	11	28	14	36	23	60	29	75
Manyara	45,820	17,691	-	-	-	-	13	34	23	60	28	73
Singida	49,341	19,051	9	23	12	31	16	41	22	57	26	67
Ruvuma	63,498	24,517	6	16	9	23	12	31	18	47	20	52
Rukwa	68,635	26,500	4	10	7	18	10	26	17	44	20	52
Lindi	66,046	25,500	6	16	8	21	10	26	12	31	13	34

Table 1.3 (Continued)

Region	Land Area		Density									
			1967		1978		1988		2002		2008	
	km²	mi²	km²	mi²	km²	mi²	km²	mi²	km²	mi²	km²	mi²
Mainland	*881,289*	*340,267*	*14*	*36*	*19*	*49*	*26*	*67*	*38*	*98*	*45*	*117*
Urban West	230	89	428	1,109	640	1,658	906	2,347	1,700	4,403	1,998	5,175
South Pemba	332	128	226	585	242	627	385	997	531	1,375	681	1,764
North Pemba	574	222	157	407	232	601	239	619	324	839	408	1,057
North Unguja	470	181	124	321	169	438	206	534	291	754	352	912
South Unguja	854	330	47	122	62	161	82	212	111	287	125	324
Zanzibar	*2,460*	*950*	*149*	*386*	*201*	*521*	*260*	*673*	*400*	*1,036*	*485*	*1,256*
Tanzania	**883,749**	**341,217**	**14**	**36**	**20**	**52**	**26**	**67**	**39**	**101**	**46**	**119**

Sources: National Bureau of Statistics, Population and Housing Censuses: 1967, 1978, 1988, 2002, 2012, http://www.nbs.go.tz/ National Bureau of Statistics, Ministry of Planning, Economy and Empowerment, *Tanzania Census 2002 Analytical Report* (Vol X), Dar es Salaam: United Republic of Tanzania, 2006, http://www.nbs.go.tz/takwimu/references/2002popcensus.pdf, accessed October 1, 2012.

Note: All mi² density figures are author estimations

West, the urbanized region of the archipelago, is the second highest in the country after that of the Dar es Salaam region (Table 1.3).

Age Structure

Tanzania's population is mostly young and in the reproductive ages. As a result, the country's population will be growing for many years to come. The country's proportion of males to females is within the normal range, namely, 98 males per 100 females.

Population Growth

In 2010, Tanzania's population was growing at an estimated 2 percent a year. Because the country's birth and death rates were 33 births and 12 deaths per 1,000 population while its net migration rate was nearly −1 migrants per 1,000 population, it is clear that much of its population change (in this case, growth) was natural (i.e., 21 more births than deaths per 1,000 population) rather than through migration. That the country had a negative net migration rate of nearly 1 person per 1,000 population means that more people left the country than came in. This points to the country's poor socioeconomic conditions, which force more people to leave than enter the country.

Another indicator of Tanzania's low socioeconomic situation in 2010 is its poor health conditions. For instance, its high total infant mortality rate of 68 deaths per 1,000 live births ranks the country 22nd in the world, compared to, say, the United States, which is ranked number 178 in the world—on this score, a lower rank means that a country is doing poorly. Also unlike in the United States, where the male and female infant mortality rates were almost equal in 2010, in Tanzania the male infant mortality rate was 15 times higher than the female infant mortality rate—a difference that points to Tanzania's poor maternal, neonatal (newborn child), and general health conditions. Consequently, Tanzania's total fertility rate is slightly over four children born per woman—a value that is twice that of the United States, where infant mortality is much lower. In other words, Tanzanian women, to some extent, give birth to more children than their U.S. counterparts to protect themselves from the prospect of being rendered childless by their country's high infant mortality rate.

Besides high infant mortality rates, Tanzania has a high vulnerability to infectious diseases, food- or waterborne diseases (e.g., bacterial diarrhea, hepatitis A, and typhoid fever), vector-borne diseases (e.g., malaria and plague), and water-contact diseases like bilharzias or snail fever. While the country's HIV/AIDS adult prevalence rate is about 6.2 percent, an estimated 1.4 million Tanzanians live with the disease while 96,000 die from it annually. Yet the ravages of HIV/AIDS pale in comparison to those of malaria, a common, age-old tropical disease that is transmitted by mosquitoes that thrive in Tanzania's nearly constant warm tropical climate. The disease afflicts almost half of all Tanzanians annually and kills nearly 100,000 of them every single year, making Tanzania one of the leading epicenters of this disease in the world. While the disease is preventable, treatable, and curable, high levels of poverty coupled with limited health facilities and personnel, poor transport infrastructure, tainted blood transfusions, and the relatively high cost of antimalarial drugs continue to allow the disease to ravage Tanzanians with significant negative impacts on their society and economy. Increased national and international attention on the disease is beginning to reverse the disease's devastating impact on Tanzania.[2]

LANGUAGES

The diversity of languages spoken in Tanzania mirrors the diversity of its population. Because each of the country's over 120 native ethnic groups has its own vernacular or local language, interethnic communication is frequently conducted in Swahili or English, the country's official languages. English is also the primary language of commerce, administration, and higher education. On the Zanzibar archipelago, Kiunguja (a dialect of Swahili) and Arabic are widespread. Because Swahili arose to facilitate interaction between local coastal Bantu peoples and Arab traders, it incorporates significant aspects of both peoples' language and culture. From its humble origins on the Kenya-Tanzania coastal region, Swahili has grown into the *lingua franca* of Eastern and Central Africa and has over time integrated vocabulary from a wider variety of sources, including English. In Central Africa, the language features vocabulary from many local languages, especially Lingala.

Of Tanzania's two official languages, Swahili is more widespread than English, which is generally acquired in the formal school system. Swahili is more widely spoken in the country because most Tanzanians are Bantus who have a natural advantage in learning the language because it is dominated by Bantu language structure and vocabulary. Moreover, Tanzania has since independence vigorously promoted the language in a bid to unify the country—a goal that has largely been achieved. Additionally, unlike many other indigenous languages in Tanzania, Swahili has been a written language since the thirteenth century and has an extensive literature that aids its development.

The adoption and promotion of Swahili as Tanzania's official and national language and the country's rapid modernization and increased population migration and intermixing are growing threats to the survival of many of the country's native languages, especially the smaller ones. Worryingly, some of the country's indigenous languages, such as Aasáx and Kw'adza, are now extinct.

EDUCATION

The provision of quality education is one of Tanzania's most important national priorities given its role in supplying skilled labor for the country's economy. In addition, Tanzania hopes that its educational sector will enable it to create a regionally and globally strong and competitive economy that can continue to meet the social, economic, and technological needs of its growing population. To ensure that the country's educational system lives up to expectations, Tanzania is committed to ensuring that its population has growing and equitable access to high-quality formal education and adult literacy. This it is doing by continuously expanding its educational facilities, increasing and maintaining a high level of efficiency, investing in continuous quality improvement, and maximizing the supply and use of resources. In 2003, Tanzania's literacy level—that is, population aged 15 and over who can read and write Swahili, English, or Arabic—stood at 78 percent, with male literacy being 86 percent and female literacy 71 percent.[3]

Tanzania's formal education structure consists of basic, secondary, and tertiary levels organized in a 2-7-4-2-3 structure. That is, two years of preprimary education and seven years of primary education (basic), four years of junior secondary or ordinary level, two years of senior secondary or advanced level (secondary), and three or more years of university or tertiary education. The basic education level also includes nonformal adult education while the tertiary level incorporates other nonuniversity higher-educational institutions like teacher training colleges.

The country's education sector is mainly managed by the Ministry of Education and Vocational Training (MoEVT), whose vision is "to have a Tanzanian who is well educated, knowledgeable, skilled, and culturally mature to handle national and international challenges in various political and social-economic fields by 2025."[4] The complementary Ministry of Communications, Science and Technology (MCST) seeks to create a knowledge-based Tanzanian society that has a high scientific and technological capacity and capability.[5] Although MCST works closely with Tanzania's universities, it is not in charge of them, and neither is MoEVT. Instead, the governance of the nation's tertiary educational system is legally anchored in the country's Universities Act of 2005, which also established the Tanzania Commission for Universities (TCU) to "recognize and accredit the country's university institutions and their programs; to approve relevant examinations regulations and determine the equivalence and hence recognize awards given by higher education institutions inside and outside Tanzania." Subordinate to this overall framework is the right of individual universities to govern themselves through their own charters.[6]

Tanzania's educational system uses Swahili and English as the languages of instruction. Swahili is used at the basic level and is a compulsory subject at the secondary level and an optional one at the tertiary level. Conversely, English is the medium of instruction at the secondary and tertiary levels and is a compulsory subject at the basic or primary level. While the country's dual-language policy enables its citizens to communicate and access their national cultural heritage through Swahili, English connects them to the larger global society. Overall, most Tanzanians are more proficient in Swahili than in English.

From independence to the mid-1990s, the government was the key player in the educational sector. But because of resource constraints, the government has since sought to facilitate the operation and expansion of the education sector by creating an enabling environment that can promote the provision of education by public, nonprofit (e.g., NGOs), and private entities. Bilateral financial, technical, and research assistance from friendly countries such as the United Kingdom and the United States is also helping to advance the development of Tanzania's educational sector.

Currently, there are 18 universities in Tanzania, including the University of Dar es Salaam (UDSM), Sokoine University of Agriculture (SUA), and Muhimbili University of Health and Allied Sciences (MUHAS). While 8 are public and 10 are private, most of the largest and oldest universities are publicly owned. There are also 15 major university colleges in Tanzania as well as other institutions of higher learning and training, including the Centre for Agricultural Mechanization and Rural Technology, the National Institute of Medical Research (NIMR), and the Serengeti Wildlife Research Institute.

About one-third (42,107, or 36%) of the 117,057 university students in the country in the 2009–2010 academic year were females while 74,950 (64%) were males. When broken down by type of institution, female students constituted 30 percent of students at public universities, 38 percent at private universities, and 43 percent at technical universities. This gender disparity in university enrollment is caused by many factors, including many families' preference for male children and investment in their education. Of the 18 universities in the country, only MUHAS enrolled more female than male students in the 2009–2010 academic year. This is because, in Tanzania, the nursing profession is generally seen as the preserve of women. The gender disparity in university student ratios is also reflected in these institutions' academic and administrative staff, where only 29 percent (1,467) of such workers are female.[7]

Despite the many tertiary institutions in Tanzania, the country is still far from satisfying its need for tertiary education because of a shortage of physical, human, and financial resources. Lack of physical facilities is responsible for growing overcrowding while a shortage of teachers is a major contributor to the worsening teacher-student ratio and declining educational standards. Moreover, many of the nation's tertiary institutions lack instructors with advanced training in their subject areas. UDSM is probably the only one in the country with enough qualified instructional staff as about 70 percent of its instructors have doctorates in their respective fields. Other universities in the country have a much smaller proportion of instructional staff with doctorate degrees.[8] The shortage of personnel is especially acute in the natural sciences. The other challenges of the Tanzanian tertiary education system include an aging teaching workforce, poor faculty salaries and retirement systems, and frequent student strikes and riots due to underfunding of tertiary institutions and substandard learning facilities. Many of these problems are also prevalent in the private universities, which are often more underresourced than their public counterparts.

CITIES

There are approximately 300 major urban areas in Tanzania. The largest of these are Dar es Salaam, Mwanza, Zanzibar, Arusha, and Mbeya (Table 1.4). As the table shows, Tanzania's cities vary widely in population size, ranging from the nearly 3 million people in Dar es Salaam to slightly over 64,000 in Mpanda. There are hundreds of smaller urban areas all over the country.[9]

Most of Tanzania's major urban areas are in the heavily populated part of the country, especially the mainland's Indian Ocean front, which contains the Dar es Salaam region and city, the regions around Lake Victoria (e.g., Mwanza, Shinyanga, and Kagera), and the regions in the southern part of the country, such as Mbeya. The areas around Lake Victoria have many urban areas because their favorable environmental conditions allow them to support high population densities (Tables 1.1, 1.2, and 1.3). As the nation's premier urban center, Dar es Salaam has for decades experienced rapid population growth due to high rural-urban migration (Table 1.4).

Despite their diverse histories and population sizes, Tanzanian cities have many similar challenges. These include rapid population growth, insufficient urban infrastructure such as roads, growing slum and squatter settlements due to lack of sufficient quantities of good-quality housing, inadequate sanitation,

Table 1.4 Major Urban Areas in Tanzania, 2008

Rank	City	Population	Rank	City	Population
1	Dar es Salaam	2,538,100	13	Musoma	114,500
2	Mwanza	400,300	14	Iringa	112,900
3	Zanzibar	372,400	15	Uvinza	111,700
4	Arusha	299,200	16	Katumba	105,000
5	Mbeya	271,600	17	Shinyanga	98,300
6	Morogoro	234,200	18	Mtwara	98,000
7	Tanga	220,900	19	Kilosa	93,200
8	Dodoma	168,500	20	Ushirombo	92,900
9	Kigoma	153,300	21	Sumbawanga	85,000
10	Moshi	152,700	22	Bagamoyo	75,400
11	Tabora	143,100	23	Bukoba	65,200
12	Songea	115,100	24	Mpanda	63,800
Population of the Major Urban Areas Shown Above					6,185,300
Total National Urban Population					10,419,287 (25%)
Total National Rural Population					30,726,997 (75%)
Total National Population					41,146,284 (100%)

Sources: MekaTroniks (2008), "Tanzania City & Town Population," http://www.tageo.com/index-e-tz-cities-TZ-step-4.htm; Tanzania Communications Regulatory Authority (2006), "Telecommunication Statistics as at 30th June 2008," http://www.tcra.go.tz/publications/telecom.html

and food scarcity, especially in the lower segments of society. Moreover, the cities suffer from high levels of unemployment and poverty, insufficient quantities of social amenities such as schools and hospitals, haphazard urban development as a result of insufficient land-use control, inadequate human resources to guide the nation's urban development, and continued reliance on colonial urban planning and housing standards that are inappropriate to local conditions.[10]

The following portraits of Dar es Salaam, Zanzibar, and Dodoma illustrate the diverse origins and characteristics of Tanzania's urban areas.[11]

Dar es Salaam

Dar es Salaam is the largest city in Tanzania. It is located on the Indian Ocean in the Dar es Salaam region of Tanzania. With a current population of 2.5 million, it is much larger than the country's second largest city of Mwanza (Table 1.4). But while Dar es Salaam is no longer the capital city of Tanzania, it is nevertheless the country's social, educational, diplomatic, and economic nerve center.

The city started about 1,000 years ago as a settlement for the Barawa people who had settled around the city's current Mbwa Maji, Kivukoni, Mjimwema, and Gezaulole areas. Sultan (Arabic for *king*) Seyyid Majid of Zanzibar, who had envisioned it as a fishing village and started its construction in about 1857,

A view of Tanzania's commercial capital, Dar es Salaam. (INSADCO Photography)

eventually gave it its current name, Dar es Salaam ("haven of peace" in Arabic) in 1866.

Under German and British colonial rule, it was a racially segregated city with three major areas: the European quarter (*Uzunguni*) in the Oyster Bay/ Msasani area, the Indian quarter (*Uhindini*) near the Upanga area, and the African quarter (*Uswahilini*) in Kariakoo (carrier corps), Kinondoni, Magomeni, and Temeke. Since that time, the quality of housing, urban infrastructure, and amenities has been highest in Uzunguni (though this is no longer the exclusive abode of whites) and lowest in Uswahilini. The city's unplanned settlements also emerged on the outskirts of the city in the colonial era and have since become large slums with a substantial population.

The city has a reasonable industrial base in food, beverages, oil, textiles, clothing, shoes, cement, aluminum products, and pharmaceuticals. Its superb beach hotels, such as The Kilimanjaro and Royal Palm, host many of the country's tourists.

Culturally, Dar es Salaam is very diverse. Besides its majority black population, the city also includes many people of Asian (Indian), Arabic, and European ancestry. Whereas much of the city's Indian and European population dates to the onset of colonial rule in the latter 1880s, its Arabic population is older, having started settling there since the founding of the city in the 1850s. Much of the Asian population consists of people from Indian and Pakistan while the white population consists of people from Britain, Germany, and the United States. Despite British capture of the country from Germans in World War I, significant German cultural and architectural influence over the city still remains. Tanzania's substantial tourist trade continues to contribute to the city's growing population diversity.

The city has a variety of museums under the auspices of the National Museum of Tanzania (NMT), which is a consortium of five museums across the country that seek to collect, conserve, display, and conduct research on all materials related to Tanzania's cultural and natural heritage. The NMT was conceived in 1934 and built in 1940. Two of NMT's branches, the Village Museum and the Museum and House of Culture, are based in Dar es Salaam. The Village Museum is noted for its 16 full-size and fully furnished traditional houses from various Tanzanian ethnic communities along with their material and crop cultures. Moreover, the museum has artists and craftsmen who produce various cultural artifacts for sale to locals and tourists. It also regularly holds traditional music-dance-drama performances from various Tanzanian communities. The Museum and House of Culture has permanent exhibitions on human evolution, the history of Tanzania, and the country's broad ethnic, plant, and animal diversity.

Zanzibar

Zanzibar is the third largest city in Tanzania and is the administrative capital of the semiautonomous archipelago of Zanzibar and Pemba that lies 22 miles (35 kilometers) from mainland Tanzania.[12] Zanzibar, which in Persian is *Zendji-Bar*, or "Land of Blacks," has a population of 372,400 people (Table 1.4).

Although it was founded as a trading depot by the Portuguese in the 1500s, it was not until Sultan Majid of Oman transferred his capital there in 1841 that it grew into a major Indian Ocean ivory- and slave-trading center that drew merchants from Southwest Asia, South Asia, the United States, Britain, and Germany. Later, when Britain became the dominant power in the area, Zanzibar became the capital of the British protectorate of Zanzibar in 1890 and subsequently became the capital of the independent republic of Zanzibar in 1963. In 1964, the city of Zanzibar reverted to its status as capital of Zanzibar and Pemba when the independent archipelago merged with the mainland territory of Tanganyika to create Tanzania.

Zanzibar is a scenic, sophisticated, and multicultural city with old, snaking streets that feature colorful markets and architecture, including that of its many mosques, the former sultan's palace, and Christian churches.[13] The city's economy depends on exports of clove, copra, and seaweed and on tourism. While cosmopolitan, Zanzibar is mainly an Islamic city.

Dodoma

Dodoma is Tanzania's political capital city as well as its eighth largest urban center. It started in the late 1800s as a stop on the arduous overland caravan route from the Indian Ocean to Lake Tanganyika. Its name, Dodoma, is derived from *Idodomya*, which means "the place where it sank" in the local Chigogo language (the dialect of the local Wagogo people). The name refers to an incident involving an elephant that came for a drink at the nearby Kikuyu stream and got stuck.

The city is located on a dry plateau at 3,658 feet above sea level and has a population of about 168,500 people (Table 1.4). Though it became the new capital in 1973 because of its central location in the country, the idea of relocating the capital there was first considered in 1915 and eventually endorsed by the colonial parliament in 1959. Nevertheless, only the Tanzanian legislature is based there while the rest of the government is still headquartered in Dar es Salaam.

The city's surrounding area has long specialized in the production of crops like millet, sorghum, maize, livestock, and wine. Its main industries include furniture, ceramics, bricks, tiles, and food and beverage processing. While the city is also home to the University of Dodoma and St. Johns University of Tanzania, its economic development is far below potential.

ECONOMY AND OCCUPATIONS

Tanzania had a purchasing-power-parity (PPP) gross domestic product (GDP) of nearly $62 billion in 2010, a figure that ranks the country 84th in the world in economic size despite its large natural resource base. In mid-2012, its stock market was valued at nearly US$8 billion and its currency, the Tanzanian shilling (Tsh) traded at 1,582 to US$1. The major contributors to the country's economy are agriculture and fishing (27%), industry and construction (21%), and services (52%). Although agriculture contributes about a third of Tanzania's GDP and provides 37 percent of the country's exports, it employs nearly 80 percent of Tanzania's workforce.[14]

Whereas Tanzania is a fairly large country, physical conditions have limited its crop agricultural sector to only 4 percent of its total land area. Much of its industry is agriculture based and is focused on the production of basic consumer goods. Its service sector is dominated by tourism, government, finance, retailing, and educational services. Collectively, the predominantly urban-based industrial and service sectors employ about 20 percent of the country's 21 million workers. Between 2000 and 2010, the economy grew by an average of 7 percent a year.

In 2010, the country's per capita income based on PPP was $1,500 against an estimated inflation rate of 7.2 percent. The proportion of Tanzanians below the poverty line in 2002 was approximately 36 percent. Although the country had a socialist economic policy until the end of President Julius Nyerere's rule in the mid-1980s, it has a relatively large family income gap (with a Gini index of about 35), although this is a little lower now than in the 1990s. Moreover, in 2009 the lowest 10 percent of Tanzanian households controlled only 2.9 percent of national household income while the top 10 percent controlled 27 percent. Neither figure changed much in the 1993–2009 period.

In 2011, Tanzania's government spent $6.1 billion and collected $4.6 billion in revenues. That year's deficit of $1.5 billion continued Tanzania's decades-old trend of annual budget deficits that have long been filled by the country's multilateral development partners such as the United States, the European Union, Japan, China, and the World Bank and IMF. Its foreign-exchange reserves in 2011 were nearly $3.7 billion while the external debt stood at nearly $9.5 billion, which ranked Tanzania 99th in the world in terms of size of its external debt. In that year, its overall public debt stood at nearly 36 percent of GDP while its current account balance had a deficit of $2.3 billion against nearly $5.4 billion worth of exports of mostly gold, coffee, cashew nuts, manufactures, and cotton to China (14%), India (10%), Japan (8%), Germany (7%), and United Arab Emirates (5%). Simultaneously, it had $8.7 billion worth of imports of consumer goods, machinery and transportation equipment, industrial inputs, and crude oil from India (20%), China (17%), South Africa (7%), Kenya (6%), and United Arab Emirates (5%). As with many other African countries, Tanzania's export and import partners have changed a bit since 2000 with China and India having replaced Western countries as its top export and import partners. South Africa and Kenya continue to be leading regional sources of imports.

Economic Natural Resources

Tanzania has a rich and diverse economic natural resource base. Its land area makes Tanzania the 13th largest country in Africa and the 31st largest in the world. Its key economic natural resources include fisheries (like lakes, rivers, and the Indian Ocean), major landforms such as mountains and rift valleys, commercial mineral deposits, wildlife, and forests.

Fisheries

In addition to providing drinking water, transportation, and leisure opportunities, Tanzania's water resources, which constitute about 7 percent of its territory and measure 23,938 square miles—excluding its 86,100-square-mile Indian Ocean exclusive economic zone—are a rich fishery and major source of livelihood.[15] Its main water resources include a 883-mile Indian Ocean shoreline; nearly 50 percent of Lake Victoria, 45 percent of Lake Tanganyika, 20 percent of Lake Nyasa; the three main inland lakes of Rukwa, Manyara, and Eyasi and many minor ones; dams, reservoirs, swamps, and ponds; and rivers such as the Rufiji, Ruvuma, and Ruaha that are all either natural fisheries or capable of supporting aquaculture—the natural or controlled cultivation of aquatic animals (e.g., fish) and plants (e.g., seaweed) in marine or freshwater environments.

The country's major water resources contain hundreds of edible and ornamental fish and plant species of variable commercial importance. The country's most important fish species are Nile perch, catfish, haplochromis, and tilapia. Much of the country's Nile perch (a high-meat-yielding fish that can grow to enormous sizes and weigh up to 530 pounds) and Nile tilapia catch comes from Lake Victoria. While many of Tanzania's major rivers are rich in tiger fish and catfish, they are not navigable enough to provide meaningful transport services. Tanzania's Indian Ocean waters offer a wide variety of shallow and deep-sea fish including kingfish, marlin, dolphin, horse mackerel, sailfish, rock cod, and great white sharks. Deep-sea fishing in Tanzania is still a very young industry.

Overall, Tanzania's annual fish catch weighs nearly 350,000 metric tons (772 million pounds). The industry directly employs about 80,000 people, most of whom are small-scale artisanal fishermen who, however, account for 90 percent of the catch with the rest coming from industrial fishing. While most of Tanzania's annual fish harvest is consumed locally, accounting for about one-third the country's animal protein supply, more so in the lakeshore and Indian Ocean areas, its Nile perch, sardine, and prawn catch is mostly exported. In general, the fishing sector contributes no more than 2 to 3 percent of Tanzania's annual GDP. The sector's nominal economic contribution is the product of its poor exploitation, investment, marketing, and management as well as the growing problem of fish poaching and pollution of its fisheries. In recent decades, Tanzania has initiated reforms (including the formation of the Tanzania Fisheries Research Institute, TAFIRI) designed to promote maximal and sustainable use of its fisheries. These reforms also include greater inclusion of the private sector, local communities, and nongovernmental and community organizations in the development, management, and sustainable use of its fisheries.

Forests

Nearly 40 percent of Tanzania's land area (131,275 square miles) consists of forests and woodlands—mostly savannah forests and intermediate woodlands.[16] With only 6,178 square miles in protected water-catchment forest reserves, most of the remainder is open for use for lumber production, especially that of tropical hardwoods such as African rosewood, cedar, podocarpus, and mahogany. Besides localized manual tree cutting for fuel wood (which accounts for 92% of the country's total heating and cooking energy needs) and lumbering, much of the country's commercial lumber comes from mechanized sawmill operations that mostly feed the country's furniture and joinery, construction, and wood-based panel (fiberboard, plywood) industries. Most of Tanzania's annual softwood consumption of 24,720,267 cubic feet comes from about 18 national plantations with plenty of room for higher levels of production.

Beyond their economic uses, Tanzania's forests also have a critical environmental role. They provide a habitat for wildlife that supplies game meat to local communities and supports the tourism and beekeeping industry, help regulate the country's rainfall and general climatic regimes, help preserve soil by controlling erosion, and provide pasture for livestock. In addition, they also help with nitrogen fixation, absorb excessive carbon dioxide from the atmosphere, and serve as critical water catchment areas that help to preserve the country's and globe's biodiversity. There are potentially many other unknown uses for these forests that would serve Tanzania well for many years to come.

The main challenges facing Tanzania's forestry sector include deforestation, insufficient forestry extension services, poor utilization of its wood resources at the domestic and industrial level, poor infrastructure, outdated legislation, fragmented government administration of forests, poor local community and other stakeholders, participation in forest management, incomplete forest resource databases, and lack of up-to-date plans on forest resource use. Because deforestation is probably the biggest threat facing the sector, the government of Tanzania has worked hard to involve local communities, nongovernmental organizations, and the general public in national afforestation activities. For instance, in 1999 nearly 100 million seedlings were planted. Simultaneously, the government promulgated the National Forest Policy (NFP) to promote sustainable economic use of its forests.

Minerals

Tanzania has an active commercial mining sector that is centered on gold, base metals, diamonds, and other minerals. The sector contributes the bulk of Tanzania's foreign-exchange earnings and is a growing source of employment and industrial development. The government's 1997 mineral policy is designed to maximize the sector's potential by virtually eliminating import duty and value-added tax (VAT) on mining equipment and supporting materials, allowing for 100 percent depreciation on equipment and essential materials, easing rules on the repatriation of mining capital and profits, and allowing for private development of mines without mandatory government participation. Moreover, Tanzania's 1998 Mining Act makes the country's mining sector even more attractive to investors by, among other things, simplifying and consolidating past mining and mineral trading statutes, guaranteeing the right to trade in mineral rights, and simplifying the country's mining licensing system.[17]

Wildlife and Scenic Tourism

Tanzania has a vibrant domestic and international tourism sector that accounts for 14 percent of the country's GDP, employs over 30,000 people, and fuels the growth of other sectors, including agriculture.[18] Some of the many tourism activities that Tanzania is known for include game viewing and hunting, safaris or expeditions, beach holidays, mountain climbing, sightseeing, and photo shoots. In 2005, for instance, Tanzania received 624,000 tourists and had gross receipts of US$1 billion. Both figures represent substantial increases over 2001.

The country's tourist assets include scenic landscapes like Mount Kilimanjaro, the Great Rift Valley, and Olduvai Gorge; spectacular wildlife (fauna and flora); near-virgin environments; the imposing fourteenth- through sixteenth-century ruins of Kilwa Kisiwani (Island) and Zanzibar's historic stone town; clean white sand beaches; the Laitoli hominid (an evolutionary term that is derived from *Hominidae*, which means all of the great apes, including humans) footprints of prehistoric humans south of Olduvai Gorge; the Mafia Island marine park; and its welcoming people. Together, these resources have helped make Tanzania one of the premier tourist destinations in Africa.

Tanzania's wildlife includes a variety of primates, antelopes, fish, over 380 species of birds like ostriches and Kori bustards, large and small mammals (e.g., elephants and lions), reptiles such as crocodiles, amphibians, invertebrates, and nearly 11,000 plant species. The country also has a growing beekeeping subsector that has a potential production capacity of hundreds of tons of honey and beeswax per year.

There are 15 national parks, 17 game reserves, and 38 game-controlled areas in the country. The Serengeti, which contains some of the largest concentrations of large mammals in the world, is Tanzania's most renowned game park. The park's annual wild beast migration is considered one of the wonders of the modern world. Tanzania's other major parks and game reserves are shown in Table 1.5.

As in many other sectors of the economy, Tanzania has in recent decades worked hard to create a regulatory framework through the Wildlife Conservation Act of 2009 that seeks to spur the development of its natural-resource-based tourism sector.

Agriculture

Agriculture is one of the key mainstays of Tanzania's economy. It accounts for about 27 percent of the country's GDP, produces 37 percent of its foreign exchange earnings, and employs 78 percent of its population.

Table 1.5 Tanzania's National Parks and Game Reserves

	National Parks	Area			Game Reserve	Area	
		km^2	mi^2			km^2	mi^2
1.	Serengeti	14,750	5,695	1.	Selous	50,000	19,305
2.	Ruaha	13,000	5,019	2.	Ruangwa	9,000	3,475
3.	Ngorongoro	8,320	3,212	3.	Kigosi	8,000	3,089
4.	Mikumi	3,230	1,247	4.	Moyowosi	6,000	2,317
5.	Tarangire	2,600	1,004	5.	Ugalla	5,000	1,931
6.	Katavi	2,252	870	6.	Uwanda	5,000	1,931
7.	Saadani	1,100	425	7.	Burigi	2,200	849
8.	Udzungwa	1,000	386	8.	Maswa	2,200	849
9.	Kilimanjaro	750	290	9.	Kizigo	2,000	772
10.	Rubondo	460	178	10.	Umba	1,500	579
11.	Kitulo	442	171	11.	Biharamulo	1,300	502
12.	Mahale	410	158	12.	Mkomazi	1,000	386
13.	Lake Manyara	325	125	13.	Kilimanjaro	900	347
14.	Arusha	117	45	14.	Rumanyika	800	309
15.	Gombe Stream	52	20	15.	Mount Meru	300	116
				16.	Ibanda	200	77
				17.	Saa Nane Island	50	19

Sources: National Bureau of Statistics, Ministry of Finance and Economic Affairs, United Republic of Tanzania (June 2009), *Tanzania in Figures 2008*, p. 9, http://www.nbs.go.tz/; author's calculations.

Besides feeding the nation, the sector further contributes to the country's economy by indirectly employing many people in agro-processing enterprises and by providing industries with raw materials and a market for their products.

Despite its large size, only 11 percent (or nearly 9,500,000 hectares, 23,475,011 acres, or 36,680 square miles) of Tanzania's dry land area is arable or suitable for crop production. An additional 28 percent supports animal husbandry. About 1.5 percent of Tanzania's arable land is under permanent crops such as coffee, tea, coconuts, oil palms and cloves while the rest is either uncultivated or used for the production of annual food and cash crops such as maize, sorghum, millet, rice, wheat, pulses (mainly beans and peas), cassava, Irish and sweet potatoes, bananas, plantains, sunflower, soy beans, simsim, pyrethrum, and barley. While Tanzania has 3,196 square miles (827,760 hectares or 2,045,440 acres) of total irrigable land, only 1,471 square miles (or 381,000 hectares or 941,471 acres) are currently under irrigated agriculture.

Tanzania's export crops are coffee, cotton, cashew nuts, oil seeds, tobacco, sisal, pyrethrum, tea, cloves, and various horticultural produce, such as fruits (pears, apples, plums, passion fruit, grapes, and avocado), vegetables (cabbages, tomatoes, sweet pepper, cauliflower, lettuce, and indigenous vegetables), flowers, and other ornamental plants. While a sizable portion of Tanzania's cash crops are produced on large plantations, smallholder cash crop production is also widespread in the country. Overall, much of Tanzania's agriculture takes place on smallholder farms that average 1 to 3 hectares in size and which are cultivated by women using simple hand implements such as hoes. Because of economic limitations, few Tanzanian farmers have access to ox- and tractor-drawn ploughs.

Economic hardships in many of Tanzania's urban areas have also given rise to a strong urban agricultural sector that helps many urban households meet their basic food needs as well as diversifying their income. Besides supporting many households, urban agriculture is also important in meeting the nation's food security goals as some of the produce is also sold to other urban households as well as to schools, hotels, hospitals, bars, cafeterias, and restaurants. Much of the country's urban agriculture takes place in the front and back yards of residences and on larger farms on the urban fringe that are dedicated to the production of vegetables, milk, broiler chickens, eggs, and other ready-for-market items. As in many African countries, Tanzanian urban managers were not so welcoming of urban agriculture in the 1960s and 1970s. But since the economic hardships of the 1980s, the urban agricultural sector has come to be seen as a welcome and integral part of the urban economy.

Tanzanian agriculture is faced with many challenges, including erratic yields due to overreliance on unpredictable rainfall, falling labor and land productivity as a result of poor utilization of modern farming techniques and technology, soil exhaustion due to overuse, decreasing farm size in some areas in the face of rapid population growth, poor agricultural support systems, a decreasing agricultural labor force due to the HIV/AIDS epidemic, unpredictable commodity prices, and poverty. Poor agricultural marketing has also been a major obstacle in the country's agricultural development. Additionally, overreliance on a few export markets and agricultural products, coupled with the global price volatility of many of Tanzania's agricultural products, has led to a general deterioration of the terms of trade for its agricultural sector. To boost the sector, the country has in recent decades enacted legislation to streamline its agricultural regulatory, investment, research, marketing, and land management and administration framework and has invested significantly in agricultural extension services, in irrigation, and in measures designed to minimize postharvest losses as well as attract more private-sector investment in its agricultural sector.

A key component of Tanzania's agricultural sector is its livestock subsector, which accounts for nearly 30 percent of the country's agricultural GDP; with roughly equal contributions from beef, milk, and poultry and small livestock production.[19] While much of the subsector's production is for domestic use, there is an important export market for live animals, hides, and skins. Currently, the country's potential for beef, milk, and poultry-product exports is highly underutilized as, for instance, Tanzania's cattle population is the third largest in Africa, next to Ethiopia (31 million) and Sudan (30 million).

Apart from food, many of the country's overwhelmingly small-scale livestock producers depend on their livestock for manure, hides and skins, cultivation and transport, income, and a fairly inflation-free store of economic value. Aside from being a way of creating value from the country's vast rangelands, livestock are a preferred form of dowry (bride price) in much of the country as well as being a key source of livelihood, prestige, and respect among the country's pastoral communities such as the Maasai. Agropastoralism, the combined production of crops and animals, is common in Mwanza, Shinyanga, Arusha, Kilimanjaro, Tabora, Mara, and Morogoro, where production methods vary from systematic grazing among the Sukuma of Mwanza to the intensive stall-feeding of the Chagga in the highly populated Kilimanjaro region.

Commercial ranching in Tanzania has since the late 1960s been dominated by the government-owned National Ranching Company (NARCO), which currently owns nine ranches that cover nearly 230,000 hectares (568,342 acres) and hold thousands of head of cattle. Though impressive, these holdings have decreased as NARCO has been downsizing and privatizing some of its assets in line with the Tanzanian government's economic liberation since the mid-1980s.

Many of the challenges facing Tanzanian agriculture also affect its livestock subsector. Nevertheless, the subsector has its own unique challenges including diseases such as Nagana or bovine trypanosomiasis, east coast fever, and foot-and-mouth disease; low reproduction due to poor nutrition and overgrazing, disease, and the poor quality of the traditional breeds; lack of sufficient quantities of abattoirs or meat-processing plants; and poverty, which limits many small livestock herders' ability to afford modern animal-husbandry inputs such as high-calorie feed. As with the challenges of the general agricultural sector, the government is trying to address the livestock subsector's problems to varying degrees of success.

Industry

Although Tanzania's industrial sector is young, it accounts for 8 percent of its GDP. It is the country's largest urban employer with about 140,000 workers who earn about 48 percent of the country's monthly wages. It also earns the country substantial amounts of foreign exchange, is a key source of government revenue, and is a valuable platform for the country's technological development through invention, innovation, nurture, and adoption of modern technologies.

While the sector is focused on the production of basic consumer products such as food, beverages, salt, shoes, tobacco, apparel and textiles, footwear, paper and paper products, and furniture and related wooden merchandise, it has other important aspects including fertilizer, cement, oil refining and allied petrochemicals, plastics, rubber, ceramics, steel rolling and foundries, metal fabrication, electrical control equipment, cosmetics, and mineral processing (mostly of gold, diamonds, iron, and soda ash).

Most of the foreign investors in the country's industrial sector are from United Kingdom, United States, South Africa, Kenya, China, Canada, Germany, Netherlands, Italy, and India. With the exception of South Africa, all of the other countries have been Tanzania's traditional economic partners.[20]

From independence to the mid-1980s, Tanzania had a state-led import-substitution industrialization (ISI) policy that was designed to promote self-sufficiency by locally producing as many imported products as possible to preserve the country's meager foreign-exchange earnings. ISI also sought to promote domestic control of industry. However, the ISI policy culminated in uncompetitive and loss-making industries with poor-quality, low-value products that were unattractive to local and export markets. By the start of the liberalization of the country's economy in the mid-1980s, installed industrial capacity was all but idle. Since the start of liberation and privatization, Tanzania's industrial output has recovered. The country's 1996 Sustainable Industrial Development Policy (SIDP) sought to build on this momentum and to transform Tanzania into a vibrant semi-industrialized country by 2020, a goal that essentially requires the country to switch its economic base from agriculture and mining to industry.

In the meantime, Tanzanian industry has to contend with many challenges including unreliable and costly power supplies, inadequate infrastructure, loss of market to imports, and limited exports, value-addedness, and global market share.

Services

The Tanzanian service sector accounts for 52 percent of the country's economy. Service-sector employment, which mainly involves the provision of public, consumer, and business services, is concentrated in the health care, tourism, government, finance, retailing, and education subsectors. Service-sector jobs are generally characterized by a wide range of income and educational and skill requirements, for instance those of domestic maids versus the directors of multinational corporations; significant involvement of women in some sectors such as health care and education; intense labor use in some subsectors such as education; and low levels of unionization in many low-ranking service jobs.[21]

Because the productivity of any country's labor force is partly dependent on its level of education and training, Tanzania has since independence sought to improve the quality of its human resources. In the socialist era (1967–1985), the country sought to improve the quality of its human resources through villagization (to ensure adequate access to basic services such as health care and education), the provision of universal primary education, mass literacy programs for the adult population, and promotion of Swahili as the national language. However, many of these top-down programs proved to be unsustainable even though they united Tanzania to an extent that is the envy of many other African countries.

Since the advent of its economic liberalization in the mid-1980s, Tanzania has sought to develop its human resources through the joint action of public, private, and nongovernmental actors; the creation of an education system that seeks to meet the country's labor needs; and development of the basic primary education sector and the vocational training system to ensure that all eligible children and citizens have access to self-employment skills.[22]

Economic Challenges

Two of the main challenges of the Tanzanian economy are inadequate power supplies and limited communications and transport. Much of Tanzania's commercial energy is derived from petroleum, hydropower, and coal while fuel-wood and charcoal supply 92 percent of domestic heating energy needs. Being a nonproducer, Tanzania imports all of its oil from the United Arab Emirates—which in 2005 amounted to nearly 25,000 barrels per day. Much of the petroleum is used in the transportation sector. In the future, Tanzania could use its 22 billion cubic meters (776 billion cubic feet) of proven natural gas reserves and nearly 1,200 million metric tons (2,645 billion pounds) of coal to reduce its petroleum importation while simultaneously increasing its electricity production. Such a development would transform Tanzania into a net power exporter and would especially benefit neighboring energy-starved countries such as Malawi.

Much of Tanzania's electricity comes from hydropower sources that are subject to the country's often unpredictable rainfall regimes. As a result, some of the country's estimated electric power consumption of 1.199 billion kilowatt hours is imported. Planned interconnection of the national grid to the Uganda and Zambia networks will most likely stabilize Tanzania's electric power supplies even as demand continues to grow at an estimated 13 percent a year. While there is significant potential for thermal, wind, and solar power generation, these power sources are vastly underutilized. A majority of Tanzanians live in rural areas and are not connected to the national grid. This is one reason for the country's high dependence on biomass heating energy, which contributes to deforestation.

Transport and Communications

The integration of a country the size of Tanzania requires a good transport and communications system.[23] But despite the country's growing investment in its transport and communication infrastructure, the networks are far from optimal. Tanzania's main mode of transport is walking and animal transport followed by road, rail, water, and air transport. Overall, all of the country's mechanized forms of transport are poorly integrated, inconvenient, costly, and unreliable.

In the communications sector, the country mainly relies on oral, face-to-face communication as well as radio, mobile telephony, and, to a smaller extent, newspapers, television, and the Internet. Mobile telephony is by far the most noteworthy change in the country's communication in recent decades. This is because, as in other African countries, Tanzania has witnessed mind-boggling growth rates in mobile telephony adoption. This is largely because of pent-up demand for telephone services and the prohibitive cost of providing fixed-line telephony to widely dispersed populations like Tanzania's.

GOVERNMENT, DEFENSE, AND FOREIGN RELATIONS

Officially, Tanzania is known as the United Republic of Tanzania because it is a union of Tanganyika and Zanzibar, a unitary republic with a multiparty parliamentary democracy. The country has three branches of government: the executive, the judiciary, and the legislative. Headed by the president, who is also the head of state, the head of government, and the commander-in-chief of the armed forces, the country's executive branch also includes the vice-president, the president of Zanzibar, the prime minister, and the cabinet ministers.[24]

While the vice-president largely serves as the president's deputy, the prime minister mainly serves as the leader of government business in the National Assembly and supervises the day-to-day operations of the government. Conversely, the president of Zanzibar heads that island's Revolutionary Council and government.

The Cabinet, including the prime minister, is appointed by the president from members of the National Assembly. The government executes its functions through sectorial ministries (e.g., the Ministry of Finance) that are led by cabinet ministers. Currently, the government consists of 29 ministers and 21 deputy-ministers.[25]

The judiciary consists of three branches: the Court of Appeal of Tanzania, the High Courts of Mainland Tanzania and Zanzibar, and the Judicial Service Commission of Tanzania Mainland, which consists of the chief justice of the Court of Appeal of Tanzania (chairman), the justice of the Court of Appeal of Tanzania, the principal judge of the High Court, and two members appointed by the president. Below the national judicial organs are the nationwide primary court, district courts, and resident magistrate courts. Cases generally flow from the primary courts to the district courts, resident magistrate courts, high court, and then to the Court of Appeals. While the Tanzanian legal system is primarily based on English common law, it also has Islamic and indigenous African elements. Review of the country's laws is managed by the Tanzania Law Reform Commission.

The country's constitution was officially promulgated on April 25, 1977, underwent major revisions in October 1984, and is slated for a major overhaul in the October 2010 to 2015 period.

The legislature consists of the presidency and the National Assembly, whose occupants are concurrently elected by popular vote for five-year terms. Lawmaking in Tanzania is a two-stage process that involves passage by the National Assembly followed by the president's assent. The National Assembly is the principal organ of the United Republic of Tanzania. It creates laws and oversees the other government branches' discharge of their respective responsibilities on behalf of the Tanzanian people.

The current unicameral National Assembly consists of 357 members including the attorney general, 239 elected constituency representatives (members of Parliament, or MPs), 102 special-seat women members, 10 presidential appointees, and 5 members elected by the Zanzibar House of Representatives. The current distribution of MPs by party is as follows: Revolutionary Party (Chama Cha Mapinduzi, CCM) with close to 90 percent of the seats; Civic United Front (CUF) with 8 percent; and other parties with 2 percent. Parliament is headed by the speaker, the deputy speaker, and the clerk of the National Assembly.

Because of its union structure of government and the substantial autonomy that Zanzibar enjoys within the United Republic, Zanzibar is proportionally overrepresented in the National Assembly. Moreover, while Zanzibari parliamentarians have a vote on nonunion matters affecting the mainland, their mainland colleagues do not vote on nonunion matters affecting Zanzibar. This is increasingly a contentious issue in the country.

The country has 26 administrative regions, below which are various levels of local governments including district councils (also known as local government authorities), city councils (Dar es Salaam and Mwanza), municipal councils, and various town councils.

While officially Tanzania gained independence from Britain on April 26, 1964, its constituent parts gained independence earlier at various times— Tanganyika on December 9, 1961, and Zanzibar on December 19, 1963. The two then united on April 26, 1964, to form the United Republic of Tanganyika and Zanzibar, which was later renamed Tanzania on October 29, 1964. The country's main national holiday, Union Day, is celebrated annually on April 26.

Since its birth in 1964, Tanzania has had four presidents: Julius Nyerere (1964–1985), Ali Hassan Mwinyi (1985–1995), Benjamin Mkapa (1995–2005) and the incumbent Jakaya Mrisho Kikwete, who was first elected in 2005 and reelected in 2010. As president for the first 21 years of the country's history, Nyerere's ghost still looms large in the country and over its present leaders. A key aspect of his enduring legacy is his significant success in creating a nation characterized by relative social and racial equality, individual liberty, and a civil service attuned to public welfare rather than self-aggrandizement. All this started in 1967 when Nyerere launched the Arusha Declaration to create a more just society and to promote economic self-sufficiency. But by the mid-1980s, several internal and external factors had made it difficult for the country to be self-sufficient or economically robust. Nevertheless, the nationalization of land, promotion of Swahili as a national language, and attempts to minimize negative ethnicity and create a just society had succeeded in creating one of Africa's most united countries.

Sensing that Tanzania needed a change of direction, Nyerere resigned in 1985 to pave the way for Mwinyi, who initiated key economic and political reforms, including the liberalization of the economy and setting the stage for the country's adoption of multiparty politics in 1992. Mwinyi's rule has come to be seen as characterized by high levels of corruption.

Tanzania's third president, Mkapa, continued with Mwinyi's economic reforms and privatized many state corporations. He attracted significant foreign investment into the country and succeeded in getting some of Tanzania's foreign debts cancelled.

Current president Kikwete was first elected in December 2005 and reelected again in October 2010 for a second and final term. One of his key objectives is to reform the constitution to meet the country's twenty-first-century challenges. Because the current and previous presidents have all been members of the ruling CCM and its predecessors, opposition parties have

Jakaya Mrisho Kikwete, president of Tanzania. (AP Photo/Ed Betz)

frequently accused the current constitution of favoring CCM candidates; hence the pressure on Kikwete to reform it.

An integral part of the country is its Tanzanian People's Defense Force (TPDF) which consists of the Army, Navy, Air Defense Command (which includes the Air Wing), and the National Service. Formed in 1964, the TPDF is under the control of the country's civilian authorities and is also well integrated and representative of Tanzania. Except for the short-lived mainland army mutiny and the 1964 revolution in Zanzibar, the country's civil-military relations have long been some of Africa's most cordial. Tanzanians can volunteer for military service from the age of 18, and currently the total annual number of people (both males and females) reaching the militarily significant age (16–49 years of age) is nearly 1 million. While the size of the TPDF is classified, it is estimated that the country's military expenditure is about 0.2 percent of its GDP—one of the lowest military expenditures in the world.

Tanzania is party to many international organizations, including the African Union (AU), and has strong diplomatic relations with many countries, 85 of which have diplomatic missions in the country. The major transnational issues facing Tanzania include the large number of refugees from Burundi and the DRC and minor boundary disputes with Malawi. The country also has a growing role in illegal international drug transshipment and money laundering.

HISTORY

Early History

The area that consists of present-day Tanzania, Kenya, and Ethiopia, especially the area around Oldupai (formerly Olduvai) Gorge in northern Tanzania, is thought to be the "cradle of humanity" because archeologists have unearthed what they believe to be the oldest remains of human ancestors there. Yet the history of humans in Tanzania goes back 5,000 to 10,000 years, with most of the ancestors of modern Tanzanians moving to the area from about the first millennium AD to the 1700s.[26]

The earliest settlers in what is now Tanzania were hunter-gatherers from southern Africa who took advantage of the area's warm tropical climate, Rift Valley caves, and abundant wildlife and wild fruits to flourish before the Iron Age. They fashioned various stone and wooden tools and weapons and used them for hunting and self-defense. Remnants of these early settlers in contemporary Tanzania are the Sandawe and Hadzapi of north-central Tanzania. Other than the shelters, stone tools and weapons, skeletal remains, and rock paintings, there are few material remains, oral histories, or written records from the region's early history. As a result, much remains to be known about the area's early peopling. A lot more of the country's history is lost forever.

Starting in the early first millennium BC, Cushitic cattle herders, believed to be from the Horn of Africa, moved into contemporary northern Tanzania and spread out among the hunter-gatherers who were already in the area. Around the first millennium AD, some of these early pastoralists, whose remnants include the modern Iraqw, became agriculturalists and invented iron tools.

In the first millennium AD or early Iron Age, another set of peoples reached northern Tanzania after centuries of migration from western Africa. They were the ancestors of modern agricultural Bantu groups whose Iron Age settlement sites are known to exist around Lake Victoria; the foothills of the Pare and Usambara mountains; the Digo hills along the coastal area between Tanga, Tanzania, and Mombasa, Kenya; and the Uvinza saltwater springs on the eastern shores of Lake Tanganyika. These early Iron Age Bantu groups settled on the moist areas of northern Tanzania, where they subsisted on grown vegetable diets that were supplemented with gathered edibles and, for those around local lakes, fish. Because of the very sparse populations of the time, there is no evidence of any interaction between the area's earlier agricultural and herder inhabitants, a situation that must have limited both groups' food supplies.

All this changed in the late Iron Age when more non-Bantus moved in from the north and introduced cattle and cereals to northern Tanzania, helping to spur greater food security and the associated higher population densities. With population growth and increased contact between the various people groups of northern Tanzania of the time, a need arose for higher forms of political organization.

The second millennium to the 1700s witnessed the in-migration of central Sudanic, Nilotic, and Paranilotic peoples. But because of their small numbers, they were absorbed by the area's preexisting Bantu groups, though they left linguistic, agricultural, and animal-herding influences on the Bantu groups. However, later infiltrations of Paranilotics such as the Tatog/Datog (ancestors of the contemporary Tatoga) made it to contemporary central Tanzania and brought with them cereal farming and cattle herding. In the 1600s and 1700s, the Paranilotic ancestors of the present-day Maasai made it to northern Tanzania. But neither the in-migrating animal herders nor the agriculturalists managed to inhabit the modern central region of Tanzania because of its limited rainfall and tsetse-fly infestation. For this reason, the area was barely settled until the start of twentieth century. As shown in

Tables 1.1 and 1.2, central Tanzanian regions like Manyara and Singida are still characterized by low population levels.

For much of this early period, political organization was largely small scale, not least because of the area's widely dispersed population. Thus, large-scale political systems did not emerge in the interior of Tanzania until well into the 1700s and 1800s and were concentrated in the interlacustrine region (that is, between Lakes Kivu, Tanganyika, and Victoria) and the Pare area in northeast Tanzania, where ecological conditions allowed for dense settlements that facilitated and justified the existence of such systems. However, some form of chieftainship may have emerged by the 1300s in the ecologically favorable interlacustrine region and the wet highlands in the south and southeast parts of the country.

Kingdoms and City-States

Although Tanzania has been settled for millennia, conditions for the formation of monarchical political systems like kingdoms materialized mainly in the Kagera and coastal regions. In the Kagera region, various kingdoms arose among the Haya people to counteract the power of the traditional Kingdom of Buganda in contemporary Uganda. The Haya, being part of the earliest Bantu groups to reach modern Tanzania during the Bantu migrations from Central Africa, settled in the well-watered Kagera region west of Lake Victoria which had close historical and cultural ties with the Baganda people and other communities in modern southern Uganda.

Some of the Haya kingdoms included Kiziba, Karagwe, Ihangiro, and Kyamutwara. Of these, Kiziba is, perhaps, the most famous and the one with the best-documented history. Founded in about 1400 AD, it lasted until 1962 when Tanzania abolished traditional kingdoms with the creation of the modern state. Nestled between Lake Victoria and the Kagera River, Kiziba rose to prominence partly because its founders were descended from the royal line of the Kitara-Bunyoro kingdom in modern-day Uganda, and, for a while, its kings were born and buried there while its princes were also brought up there until the end of the 1700s. For much of its existence, it was in constant conflict with the neighboring kingdoms of Karagwe and Kyamutwara and, later on, with Buganda to the north.[27]

The political structure of Kiziba and most of these other kingdoms included the king (*Omukama*), his prime minister (the *Katikiro*) and portfolio ministers (*Abatongole Bemurika*), the chiefs of counties (*Abami*), and the village headmen (*Abakungu*). From the 1870s to 1962, the kings (*Bakama*) of Kiziba were Mutatembwa (1870–1903), Mutahangarwa (1903–1916), Mboneko (1916–1927), Mutakubwa (1927–1937), and Lutinwa (1937–1962).[28]

Besides their kingdoms, the Haya were sophisticated in other ways, including their over 2,000-year-old history of advanced metallurgical technology, which enabled them to make carbon steel 19 centuries before Europeans did. This technology was successfully reenacted by Haya elders in 1978, thereby helping to "change scholarly and popular ideas that technological sophistication developed in Europe but not in Africa."[29] The Haya were also skilled in pottery, bark-cloth making, and woodwork. Some of the iron products that they made include sickles, hoes, spears, knives, bill-hooks, hippopotamus traps, anvils, and hammers. Some of their pottery products included cooking, water, and milk storage pots; coffee pots; cups; jugs; and smoking-pipe bowls. Prior to the arrival of cotton clothes in Haya country, bark clothes were the normal dress. Subsequently, bark cloth was used in funeral and burial rituals and the preparation of bedsheets and royal regalia. In the area of woodwork, local craftsmen made milk jars, mallets and hammers, ladles, and boats for fishing and beer making. Basket and rope production were also widespread.[30]

In addition to the Haya kingdoms, city-states arose in coastal Tanzania due to trade links between locals and foreigners. Although there is evidence that contact between the present-day Tanzanian coast and the outside world dates to before 500 AD, the best records of such contacts from Persian Gulf Arab traders date to the period from 800 to 1000 AD. By the 1100s, trading posts had emerged on the coast as well as the islands of Zanzibar and Pemba. As this trade between coastal Bantus and Arabs flourished, these settlements developed into small city-states that thrived well into the 1500s and 1700s. Largely Islamic and mercantile, by the 1200s the most important of these city-states was Kilwa Kisiwani (i.e., Kilwa Island), which controlled sea trade routes that stretched as far south as modern-day Mozambique. By the 1400s, Zanzibar (derived from "Land of Zenj"—a dark and tall people with legendary oratory skill and fighting spirit), which eventually became the capital of the Oman Arab Empire, had overtaken Kilwa.

From 1498 to 1698, the Portuguese dominated these city-states, though their 200-year rule left little lasting impact. From 1698 until the advent of formal European colonialism, the East African coast, including present-day coastal Tanzania, was ruled by Omani Arabs.

German and British Rule

Although German and British explorers and missionaries had been active in modern Tanzania since the first part of the 1800s, much of the country did not come under German colonial rule until after the larger European scramble for Africa in the mid- to late 1880s.[31] While Britain had greater influence over the modern Tanzania region at the time, the Anglo-German agreement of 1886 formally carved up present-day Kenya and Tanzania into British and German colonial spheres of influence while allotting the islands of Zanzibar, Pemba, Mafia, and Lamu, a ten mile (sixteen-kilometer) wide strip along the coast from Tungi Bay (in Mozambique) to the Tana River (in Kenya), and some towns in Somalia to the Sultan of Zanzibar. In 1887, the Germans granted an imperial charter to the German East Africa Company, whose ruthless exploitation of the "German territory" and opposition from coastal traders led to rebellion and the eventual establishment of a formal German government administration over its East Africa territory in April 1891. Subsequent conflicts between German and British interests in contemporary Uganda necessitated the signing of the Anglo-German Agreement of East Africa in 1890 that established British rights in Uganda and a British protectorate in Zanzibar and Pemba. Soon the Sultan of Zanzibar surrendered control of the island of Mafia and the coastal strip to the Germans in exchange for protection.

With the completion of the Anglo-German boundary-demarcation exercise, German colonial control started expanding inland but was fiercely opposed by groups like the Hehe. Thus, the Germans spent the 1890s trying to consolidate their rule. With the restoration of peace, the Germans started to reengineer the economy of their colonial territory with the development of transportation systems such as railways and the introduction of cash crops such as coffee, cotton, sisal, and rubber. While some of these crops, especially coffee, had been cultivated by African peasants prior to the arrival of the Germans, the Germans introduced plantations to expand production. This necessitated the appropriation of African land and labor through coercion, cash taxation, and other means, mostly for the benefit of European plantation owners. Nevertheless, peasant production managed to dominate in some areas with the Haya of Bukoba district (now Kagera) and the Sukuma of Mwanza being respectively responsible for three-quarters of the colony's coffee and peanut output before World War I.

Besides these isolated cases of African cash-crop production, colonial German agricultural development brutalized Africans, and, in the region south of the Ruvuma River, this was to foment the Maji Maji rebellion of 1905 to 1907 under the leadership of Kinjikitile, a charismatic local witch doctor. Although the rebellion was eventually suppressed, it forced changes in German colonial administration, including the replacement of military administrators with civilian ones. Moreover, the reforms ended the practice of forced African labor, increased the protection of their land rights, and encouraged their cash crop production and access to education. The emphasis on education gradually made missionaries the core purveyors of European culture in the country relative to colonial administrators, soldiers, and settlers. Christian missionary influence in the country continues to be substantial.

With the advent of World War I, Anglo-German hostilities erupted in East Africa, and Tanganyika became a battleground. Thus, British soldiers from Kenya attacked German soldiers in Tanzania and succeeded in expelling them in 1917. On July 22, 1922, the League of Nations (the precursor to the current United Nations) mandated Britain to administer Tanganyika on its behalf, a situation that morphed into a UN trusteeship in 1946. While the League of Nations' mandate had many provisions on the governance of Tanganyika, Africans mostly felt them in slight improvements in their labor conditions. Moreover, because British victory came with the expulsion of all Germans from the country, including missionaries, the economic role of Asians in the territory increased as they took over some of the farms and assets that were abandoned by the Germans. It was not until 1925 that the Germans were allowed to return to Tanganyika. Eventually they and the Greeks became the largest European groups in the country.

While British colonial rule of Tanganyika retained many of the preexisting German administrative structures, it nevertheless introduced its time-tested system of indirect rule that made use of preexisting or created chieftaincies. Because the chiefs were the colonial authorities' law enforcers and tax collectors, they in time became quite unpopular. The British also introduced a Legislative Council consisting of British subjects and Asians (and no Africans), strengthened African land rights, and encouraged African peasant cash-crop production among the Chagga and the Haya in northern and northwestern Tanganyika, respectively. In so doing, they, like their German predecessors, set these two groups up for domination of independent Tanzania's economy. While the British initiated the provision of social services such as health care and education in the territory, finances and other factors limited the scale of these services. In the 1930s, the African Association and the African Commercial and Welfare Association emerged. While both of them focused on social and educational activities, the African Association occasionally delved into politics and eventually formed the heart of the post–World War II African independence movement.

In Zanzibar, socioeconomic developments generally paralleled those on the mainland with the main differences being greater political autonomy, higher social status of the Arab population, economic reliance on clove and coconut production, Asian control of economic activity, and Arab control of the civil service except for the highest posts, which were held by the British. Africans and Afro-Arabs did not fare as well.

Independence Movements

The road to independence started after World War II when Britain reluctantly agreed to place Tanganyika under UN trusteeship in 1946. This change of status meant, among other things, that (1) Africans would be represented on the Trusteeship Council, (2) Africans had a right to directly submit grievances to the Trusteeship Council, (3) the UN had some oversight over political and constitutional matters in the territory, and (4) that the UN would visit the territory every three years to ensure the colonial government's compliance with the terms of the trusteeship. In hindsight, these changes may have served to diminish the British colonial government's investment in the territory.

Despite these changes, the British colonial administration in Tanganyika did not anticipate that independence for the region would be reality in about 15 years. As a result, it had no sense of urgency in preparing Tanganyikans for self-government in the 1940s and 1950s. Thus, investments in education, infrastructure, and industry and attempts to incorporate Africans into the higher echelons of government were limited. Only a few communities, such as the Chagga and Haya, had reasonable access to education, and this at their own expense. Consequently, by the 1960s, Tanganyika was one of the least-developed African countries.

Colonial underinvestment in African development and other failures caused the African Association and its successor the Tanganyika African Association (TAA) to become overtly political and to start agitating for better conditions in the mid-1940s. For instance, at this time, TAA started (1) criticizing government agricultural and educational policies, (2) opposing the loss of African land, (3) resisting greater government policy coordination with colonial Kenya's white minority government with its harsher treatment of Africans, and (4) agitating for the abolition of race-based pay scales and the lifting of de facto racial discrimination despite its ban in 1947. TAA also challenged the composition of the then Legislative Council (considering its two African chiefs to be unrepresentative) and expressed its concerns to visiting UN delegations—all to the chagrin of the British colonial government. Feeling threatened, the government banned the participation of civil servants in TAA and any other overtly political organizations in 1953. This was a major blow to TAA and, later, the Tanganyika African National Union (TANU). Equally debilitating is that at the time, TAA had neither a strong mass base nor an effective national leadership or association until the rise of Nyerere.

Nyerere, the son of a Zanaki community minor chief from northwestern Tanzania who had been educated at Makerere and Edinburgh universities and had in 1952 become a teacher at a Roman Catholic secondary school, was forced to resign for his political activities. Subsequently, he became the leader of TANU, which succeeded TAA in July 1954. While initially TANU's support came from frustrated educated Africans who were unable to progress in the European- and Asian-dominated socioeconomic system, it eventually started attracting the masses even with government opposition, including the proscription of some of its branches. However, government opposition to TANU and sluggishness in changing the unpopular system of indirect rule played into the hands of TANU which eventually boiled its grievances and mission down to these issues:

> that Tanganyika be prepared for self-government; that tribalism be rejected in favor of nationalism; that a democratic government be established; that all governmental bodies have African majorities; that all forms of racialism be eliminated; and that TANU encourage and cooperate with unions, cooperatives, and other groups, such as trade unions, if they were sympathetic.[32]

Eventually, a reconstituted Legislative Council with 31 official and 30 unofficial seats was created in 1954. In the elections of 1958 and 1959, TANU or TANU-affiliated candidates won all of the unofficial seats and forced then governor Turnbull to grant the creation of purely African councils (as opposed to the previous government policy of multiracial councils) that pointed to the eventual dominance of Africans of both the Executive and Legislative Councils, thereby reversing decades of colonial government refusal to admit that Tanzania was an African country. Nevertheless, the colonial government did not set a timetable toward eventual self-rule. In the elections of August 30, 1960, TANU won most of the seats, paving the way for the appointment of Nyerere as prime minister. Full internal self-government commenced on May 15, 1961, and Tanganyika gained its full independence on December 9, 1961. Meanwhile, Zanzibar achieved independence on December 10, 1963, paving the way for the creation of the United Republic of Tanganyika and Zanzibar (Tanzania) on April 26, 1964.

Since independence, the key milestones in Tanzania's history are the 1967 Arusha Declaration that launched the country's socialist era; the 1970–1977 implementation of the country's villagization policy that resettled up to 80 percent of the country's population; the 1975 declaration of Tanzania as a single-party state; Tanzania's 1979 counterattack on Uganda and eventual overthrow of Idi Amin for invading northwest Tanzania; Nyerere's reelection as president in 1980; Nyerere's resignation from the presidency in 1985, which officially ended the socialist era and was followed by Mwinyi's rise to power later in the same year and his launch of liberal political and economic reforms; the country's adoption of multiparty politics in 1992; Mkapa's election as Tanzania's third president in November 1995 and his reelection in 2000; Kikwete's election as president in December 2005 and his reelection in October 2010; and the country's celebration of the 50th anniversary of independence in 2011.

NOTES

1. Tanzania National Website, "2002 Population and Housing Census: General Report," 2003, http://www.tanzania.go.tz/censusf.html; National Bureau of Statistics, "Tanzania in Figures 2008," June 2009, http://www.nbs.go.tz/, accessed November 5, 2010.

2. Ervin Dyer, "The Battle against Malaria Builds Strength in Tanzania," *Pittsburgh Post-Gazette*, June 7, 2006, http://www.post-gazette.com/pg/06158/696104-114.stm, accessed November 5, 2010.

3. United Republic of Tanzania, "Education," http://www.tanzania.go.tz/profile1f.html, accessed January 19, 2011.

4. Ministry of Education and Vocational Training, "Vision," "Mission," and "About MoEVT," 2010, http://www.moe.go.tz/index.php, accessed January 19, 2011.

5. Ministry of Communications, Science and Technology, "About the Ministry," 2008, http://www.mst.go.tz/, accessed January 19, 2011.

6. Tanzania Commission for Universities, "Welcome to Tanzania Commission for Universities (TCU) website," http://www.tcu.go.tz/, accessed January 19, 2011.

7. Tanzania Commission for Universities, "Universities Corner," http://www.tcu.go.tz/, accessed January 19, 2011.

8. Wachira Kigotho, "PhD: Rare Qualification in African Universities," *The Standard*, July 10, 2008, http://www.eastandard.net/, accessed January 19, 2011.

9. MekaTroniks, "Tanzania City & Town Population," 2008, http://www.tageo.com/index-e-tz-cities-TZ-step-4.htm, accessed January 19, 2011.

10. John Briggs and Davis Mwamfupe, "Peri-urban Development in an Era of Structural Adjustment in Africa: The City of Dar es Salaam, Tanzania," *Urban Studies* 37, no. 4 (2000): 797–809; Camillus J. Sawio, "Perception and Conceptualisation of Urban Environmental Change: Dar es Salaam City," *Geographical Journal* 174, no. 2 (2008): 164–68; J. M. Lusugga Kironde, "Received Concepts and Theories in African Urbanization and Management Strategies: The Struggle Continues," *Urban Studies* 29, no. 8 (1992): 1277–91.

11. James Brennan, Andrew Burton, and Yusuf Lawi (eds.), *Dar es Salaam: Histories from an Emerging African Metropolis* (Dar es Salaam/Nairobi: Mkuki na Nyota, 2007), 13–75; Utalii Travel & Safari Ltd., "The City of Dar es Salaam," 2000–2008, http://www.utalii.com/Dar-es-salaam/Dar-es-Salaam_the_city.htm; Andrew Burton, *African Underclass: Urbanization, Crime & Colonial Order in Dar es Salaam* (Dar es Salaam: Mkuki wa Nyota, 2005); Adolfo Mascarenhas, "The

Growth and Function of Dar es Salaam," in L. Berry (ed.), *Tanzania in Maps* (London: University of London Press, 1975), 134–35; Adolfo Mascarenhas, "Land Use in Dar es Salaam," in L. Berry (ed.), *Tanzania in Maps* (London: University of London Press, 1975), 136–37; Adolfo Mascarenhas, "The Port of Dar es Salaam," in L. Berry (ed.), *Tanzania in Maps* (London: University of London Press, 1975), 138–39; Mohamed Amin, Duncan Willetts, and Peter Marshall, *Journey through Tanzania* (Nairobi: Camerapix Publishers International, 1984), 60–66; Kirsten Strandgaard, *Introducing Tanzania through the National Museum*, Dar es Salaam: The Museum, 1974.

12. "Zanzibar, City, Tanzania," *Columbia Electronic Encyclopedia*, 6th ed., 2007, http://www.infoplease.com/ce6/world/A0853281.html, accessed September 5, 2008; MekaTroniks, "Tanzania City & Town Population," 2008, http://www.tageo.com/index-e-tz-cities-TZ-step-4.htm, accessed September 5, 2008; SADC, "United Republic of Tanzania: Agriculture," *The Official SADC Trade, Industry and Investment Review 2007/2008*, Harare: SARDC.

13. Dean Sinclair, " 'Memorials More Enduring than Bronze': J. H. Sinclair and the Making of Zanzibar Stone Town," *African Geographical Review* 28 (2009): 71–97.

14. Central Intelligence Agency, "The World Factbook: Tanzania," January 25, 2011, https://www.cia.gov/library/publications/the-world-factbook/geos/tz.html, accessed January 25, 2011.

15. Mohamed Amin, Duncan Willetts, and Peter Marshall, *Journey through Tanzania*, 25, 29, 40, 44, 48–49, 61–62, 99, 119, 124.

16. Government of Tanzania, "Mining," 2001–2008, http://www.tanzania.go.tz/miningf.html/, accessed September 11, 2008; SADC "United Republic of Tanzania: Forestry. . . ."

17. Ibid.

18. Government of Tanzania, "Wildlife Resources," 2001–2008, http://www.tanzania.go.tz/miningf.html/, accessed September 11, 2008; John McKay, "Tourist Industry," in L. Berry (ed.), *Tanzania in Maps* (London: University of London Press, 1971), 94–95.

19. Government of Tanzania, "Livestock," 2001–2008, http://www.tanzania.go.tz/economyf.html/, accessed September 11, 2008; Donald P. Whitaker, "The Economy," in Irving Kaplan (ed.), *Tanzania: A Country Study* (Washington, D.C.: American University, 1978), 210; SADC, "United Republic of Tanzania: Agriculture . . .".

20. Robert Schroeder, "South African Capital in the Land of *Ujamaa* [Socialism]: Contested Terrain in Tanzania," *At Issue Ezine* 8, no. 5 (September 2008), http://www.africafiles.org/atissueezine.asp, accessed October 1, 2008; United Republic of Tanzania, Ministry of Industries and Trade, "Sustainable Industries Development Policy—SIDP 1996–2020," October 1996, http://www.tzonline.org/pdf/sustainableindustrial.pdf, accessed October 3, 2012.

21. Frederick P. Stutz and Barney Warf, *The World Economy: Resources, Location, Trade and Development* (Upper Saddle River, NJ: Prentice Hall, 2007).

22. Government of Tanzania, "Human Resource," 2001–2008, http://www.tanzania.go.tz/human.html/, accessed November 20, 2010.

23. Government of Tanzania, "Public Administration," 2001–2008, http://www.tanzania.go.tz/administration.html; Central Intelligence Agency, "The World Factbook: Tanzania"; National Bureau of Statistics, *Tanzania in Figures 2008*, June 2009, http://www.nbs.go.tz/.

24. Government of Tanzania, "Public Administration," 2001–2008, http://www.tanzania.go.tz/administration.html, accessed July 5, 2012; Herman Lupogo, "Tanzania: Civil-Military Relations and Political Stability," *African Security Review* 10, no. 1 (2001).

25. Tanzania Parliament, "About Us," 2003–2010, http://www.parliament.go.tz/, accessed January 28, 2011.

26. Amin et al., *Journey through Tanzania*, 7–24; Kaplan, *Tanzania: A Country Study*, 1–85.

27. J. B. Webster, B. A. Ogot, and J. P. Chretien. "The Great Lakes Region, 1500–1800," in B. A. Ogot (ed.), *General History of Africa V: Africa from the Sixteenth to the Eighteenth Century* (Berkeley, CA: University of California Press, 1992), 816–20.

28. Abel G. M. Ishumi, '*Kiziba: The Cultural Heritage of an Old African Kingdom* (Syracuse, NY: Maxwell School of Citizenship and Public Affairs, Syracuse University, 1980).

29. Ishumi, *Kiziba*; "Africa's Ancient Steelmakers," *TIME*, September 25, 1978, http://www.time.com/time/magazine/article/0,9171,912179,00.html, accessed January 28, 2011; J. D. Fage and Roland Oliver (eds.), *The Cambridge History of Africa: From c. 1600 to c. 1700* (London and New York: Cambridge University Press, 1979).

30. Ishumi, *Kiziba*, 15–18.

31. Irving Kaplan, "Historical Setting," in Irving Kaplan (ed.), *Tanzania: A Country Study* (Washington, D.C.: American University, 1978), 1–83.

32. Kaplan, "Historical Setting," 57.

2

Religion and Worldview

THE TANZANIAN WORLDVIEW is predominantly shaped by religion. Tanzanians, like many other Africans, are among the most religious people in the world.[1] To many Tanzanians, the physical (material) and spiritual worlds are inseparable and are a seamless continuation of reality in which the spiritual realm supersedes and controls the physical one. Thus, everyday Tanzanian life is filled with various acts of veneration of good spiritual forces (e.g., God/gods and the ancestors) and attempts to appease and cope with the evil ones (e.g., Satan, demons, and witchcraft). Thus, religion defines many Tanzanians' sense of identity and community and plays a central role in their daily life. Popular participation in religious ceremonies, events, and holidays is thus very high.[2]

The high religiosity of Tanzanians is evident in a recent nationally representative religious survey that showed that

- 93 percent consider religion to be very important in their lives;
- 80 percent attend weekly religious services;
- 94 percent believe in God and are absolutely certain of the belief, and, of these, 66 percent believe in a personal God while 27 percent believe in an impersonal God;
- 97 percent of those who believe in God believe in one God;
- 95 percent believe in angels and miracles;

- 96 percent believe in evil spirits, 93 percent in witchcraft, and 80 percent in the "evil eye," that is, that certain people can cast curses or spells that cause bad things to happen to others;

- 60 percent believe that sacrifices to spirits or ancestors can protect one from bad things;

- 70 percent believe that certain spiritual people can protect a person from bad things, and 49 percent believe that *juju*, shrines, or other sacred objects can protect one from bad things, though the proportion of those who believe in this is 44 percent for Christians and 55 percent for Muslims;

- 89 percent believe in heaven (where good people are eternally rewarded) and hell (where bad or unrepentant people are eternally punished);

- 55 percent pray daily while another 35 percent pray weekly or monthly;

- 48 percent have experienced divine healing, and 51 percent have experienced or witnessed the devil being driven out of a person; and

- 62 percent of Christians believe that Jesus will return in their lifetime while 43 percent of Muslims believe that the caliphate will be reestablished to rule in their lifetime.[3]

Because religion plays a central role in Tanzanian life, key life events such as funerals, weddings, graduations, and many public celebrations incorporate religious invocations, readings, songs, and dances. Spiritual leaders are usually widely respected and held in higher esteem than many political leaders. In particular, the national leaders of Christianity and Islam are very influential in the country.

The main religious traditions of Tanzania are African traditional religions (ATRs), Christianity and Islam. There are also many minor ones like Hinduism, Sikhism, Buddhism, the Baha'i faith, and Ismailia. In terms of religious practice, many Tanzanians are syncretists who adhere to select tenets from the above religions. There are hardly any atheists in the country.

Since Tanzania removed religious surveys from its official censuses after 1967, there are now no official data on the country's religious breakdown. Thus, estimates of this breakdown vary widely, though recent surveys suggest that the country is predominantly Christian (Table 2.1).[4] While nearly

Table 2.1 Estimates of Tanzania's Religious Composition over Time

	Census 1967 (%)	Demographic and Health Survey (DHS) 2004 (%)	Afro-barometer 2008 (%)	Pew Global Attitudes Project 2008 (%)	Pew Forum 2009 (%)
Christian	34	57	63	64	60
Muslim	31	30	29	35	36
Other/None	35	13	8	—	4

Source: Pew Research Center, *Tolerance and Tension: Islam and Christianity in Sub-Saharan Africa,* April 2010, p. 64, http://features.pewforum.org/africa/country.php?c=216.

everyone (99%) in the Zanzibar archipelago is Muslim, some sources continue to insist that nationally Christianity, Islam, and ATRs still retain their relative 1967 proportions.[5] On the basis of the more recent surveys that suggest that Christianity is now dominant, it is evident that much of Christianity's growth has come at the expense of ATRs—refer to the decreasing percentages for the "Other/None" row in Table 2.1.

Most of the practitioners of ATRs and Christianity live on the more populated Tanzanian mainland while most of the Muslims are in Zanzibar, coastal Tanzania, and in mainland urban areas, especially those along the caravan trade routes. While most Tanzanian Muslims are Sunnis, there is also a substantial Shia Muslim population.

Although ATRs are native and widespread on the mainland, Christianity has also made significant gains there because of concerted Christian missionary activity since the late precolonial era. Expectedly, the mainland has the vast majority of the country's Christian missionary stations and schools. Let us now examine the country's religious make-up in greater detail.

AFRICAN TRADITIONAL RELIGIONS (ATRs) AND CHANGE

Prior to the coming of Islam and Christianity to Tanzania, ATRs were dominant, and they still form the religious backdrop of most native (i.e., African) Tanzanians, including those who are now Christians and Muslims. While ATRs are strongest among communities like the Maasai, Sukuma, and Waha, their tenets are widespread because native Tanzanians are religious syncretists who adhere to select elements of ATRs and either Christianity or Islam. While both Christianity and Islam abhor syncretism, the practice is still widespread among native Tanzanians because

> followers of African religion make no distinction between religion and other aspects of their lives. Their beliefs are so closely bound to their culture that religion and culture are one. Religion is therefore not something people do at certain times and in certain places, but it is part of the fabric of living. . . . People and gods are constantly interacting through ritual, prayer, and sacrifice, but mostly through the business of living.[6]

Thus, certain aspects of ATRs, for instance belief in the evil eye, participation in ceremonies to honor ancestors, and the use of traditional religious healers, are common and are practiced by a significant number of Tanzanians (Table 2.2).[7] *Juju* protection from the harmful effects of witchcraft and sorcery is widespread even among the urban Tanzanian elites, and it often involves specially prepared trinkets, necklaces, wristbands, waistbands, and other charms.

Table 2.2 Prevalence of African Religious Traditions in Tanzania

	Total Population (%)	Among Christians (%)	Among Muslims (%)
Do you believe in the evil eye—that certain people can cast spells and curses?	80	78	83
Do you believe that *juju*, shrines, or other sacred objects can protect you from harm?	49	44	55
Do you ever participate in traditional African ceremonies to honor ancestors?	34	31	35
Do you or your family ever use traditional religious healers?	43	35	53

Source: Pew Research Center, *Tolerance and Tension: Islam and Christianity in Sub-Saharan Africa: African Traditions,* April 15, 2010, http://features.pewforum.org/africa/question.php?q=12.

One of the key points from Table 2.2 is that a lower proportion of Christians than Muslims adhere to the various ATR practices. This is because Christianity has from its introduction had a frontal assault on ATR practices even as it has absorbed and continues to absorb those that are compatible with its teachings. Christianity's ability to maintain its core teachings and communicate them in ways that are compatible with local cultures has been a major aid to its growth in the country, often at the expense of ATRs (Table 2.1).

Because Tanzanian ATRs vary widely by geography and culture, they defy easy generalization. In fact, the country's ATRs are as diverse as its nearly 120 indigenous ethnic groups. Because ATRs are usually anchored in their local human and natural environments, the two often change in tandem. Thus, the main threat to Tanzania's ATRs is the country's growing cultural diversity due to the in-migration of people from other parts of the world—people who often have religions, cultures, and worldviews that are diametrically opposed to those of the country's ATRs.

Moreover, the growing modernization of the country is increasingly making it difficult to pass on knowledge of ATRs to younger generations because of the growing scarcity of the multigenerational living arrangements that characterized traditional societies. Moreover, the advent of more effective modern solutions to certain diseases and problems that ATRs traditionally dealt with has significantly undermined the attraction and power of many ATR practices.

Gender plays an important role in many ATRs. For instance, women serve as priestesses, spirit mediums, and shamans who offer community prayers to the ancestors and the gods. While traditional healers can be either male or female, it is usually women who provide the bulk of traditional medical services to women and children.[8] On the downside, it is women who also most often tend to be accused of being witches.

Yet the persistence of certain existential problems, incurable diseases, and misfortunes that are seen to be beyond the realm of the foreign religions and technologies continue to drive people to seek more effective solutions to these problems in the supernatural realms of ATRs. Thus, ATRs persist even with the intense onslaught of Christianity because the latter is sometimes seen as impractical and more relevant for addressing issues of the afterlife while ATRs are seen as being more effective in dealing with present material and spiritual challenges. Moreover, ATRs endure because African communal life often makes it difficult for individuals to risk being ostracized for avoiding certain family and community ATR rituals. In any event, because ATRs accept syncretism, many Tanzanians seldom see any inconsistency in being simultaneous practitioners of an ATR and Christianity.[9]

Another key reason for the failure of Christianity to dislodge ATRs in Tanzania is that early Christian missionaries, ignorant of the depth, intensity, and influence of ATR beliefs on local people's daily lives, discounted such beliefs as mere superstitions based on ignorance or lack of scientific knowledge. In so doing, they unwittingly presented to Africans a Christianity that seemed incapable of responding to their daily supernatural challenges. In the process, many Africans came to see Christianity as a religion that is confined to the church building and one that is unable to offer them the kind of protection that ATRs offer outside the church walls against magic, sorcery, witchcraft, and malevolent spiritual beings.[10] Many of these same arguments also explain why many other Tanzanians syncretically practice ATR and Islam.

Unsurprisingly, many aspects of ATRs, such as belief in the evil eye and witchcraft, are still prevalent in modern Tanzania (Table 2.2). This said, it is important to distinguish between traditional religious healers and herbalists. While the former use healing techniques like divination and the removal of spells, the latter use local medicinal plants to cure certain diseases and are the equivalent of modern doctors in traditional societies. Moreover, herbalists (e.g., Lutheran herbalist Babu Ambikile Mwasapile) are an integral part of the Tanzanian health care system and are often patronized by people from all social and religious backgrounds.[11]

Despite the plethora of ATRs, they are primarily characterized by "belief in the Supreme Being, the spirit world (spirits subordinate to the Supreme Being) and mystical powers."[12] This Supreme Being is believed to be a remote, everlasting, and all-powerful creator that is approached through intermediaries such as fetish priests. This Supreme Being is thought to be evident in prominent or unusual natural things such as the sun, rock formations, or trees, which often serve as ATR places of worship and sacrifice. Thus, ATRs are animistic in that they see souls and spirits in all elements of the natural environment as well as a direct connection between the material and spiritual worlds.

ATRs have no sacred writings but are orally passed down from generation to generation because traditional Tanzanian societies had no written tradition prior to the advent of Arabs and Europeans. Instead, the religious knowledge of ATRs was (and is) resident in seasoned priests or shamans who passed (pass) it on to their blood relatives (usually children) through apprenticeship. While the oral transmission of ATR knowledge meant that it evolved with the times, a lot of it has died with its possessors for lack of written records. This realization has led to efforts to preserve this knowledge before it is lost forever.

ATRs have no central organization or hierarchy. As such, their priesthoods, though often hereditary, tend to be responsive to and reflective of local conditions and needs. ATR adherents approach the spirit world and the Supreme Being through a line of command that begins with the fetish priests, diviners, or fortune tellers and then continues to dead ancestors (spirits) and culminates in the gods and the Supreme Being. ATR practitioners maintain links with their ancestors through the pouring of libations, invocations, chants, and offerings of animal sacrifices to appease any angry ancestors. ATR followers also believe in the exorcism of evil spirits, and when faced with major decisions, they often consult diviners and fortune tellers to find out the will of the ancestors, gods, or the Supreme Being. There is a fair amount of fatalism in ATRs.

ATR believers have a firm sense of good and evil and believe that either behavior draws a reward or punishment in this life. Because, in the worldview of ATRs, the spiritual and material worlds are intimately connected and the spiritual world is intimately involved in everyday people's lives, it is not hard to see why the notion of immediate recompense for one's conduct is widespread in these religions.

As one's behavior in this life is believed to determine one's place in the spirit world, there is an emphasis on moral living not only to please the ancestors and the gods but also to ensure success in the material and spiritual world. While upright living ensures that one becomes an ancestral spirit that mediates between the living and the gods at death, immoral living not only brings curses and failure in the material world but also causes one to become an evil spirit at death. Besides, ill conduct like murder, disrespect of the elders and the ancestors, or breaking taboos can cause one to be haunted by the ghosts of the people wronged. Unless such ghosts are appeased through sacrifices and other forms of atonement, they can wreak havoc on the living offenders and their families.

Death, while feared, is considered in ATRs to be the beginning of a person's full communion with the material and spiritual world, the end of the physical life and the start of the spiritual one where one can operate in the visible and invisible worlds. Thus, the ultimate purpose of life is to become an ancestor or a good spirit worthy of veneration after death. To ensure the realization of this goal, dead people are given proper funeral services, with strict observance of appropriate rites, lest the dead become wandering ghosts that are neither benevolent to the living nor able to thrive in the next world.

Nevertheless, ATRs have no clear conception of what life after death is like even though they believe in the persistence of life after death. Consequently, many ATR practitioners also adhere to Christianity because of its promise of eternal life in heaven.[13] In short, ATRs have a decidedly materialistic worldview that even conceives of the afterlife in physical terms.[14] ATRs also lack an explanation for the origin of evil, though many local communities have fables that try to account for this in mostly humanistic terms.

While Christianity and Islam are seen as the dominant religions of Tanzania, neither has quite managed to infuse itself into every aspect of society as have the ATRs. As a result, there has been a resurgence of ATRs in many parts of the country (e.g., in Sukumaland) since independence. Moreover, the country's indigenous cultural revivalism is also a boon to ATRs. Much of this revivalism is due to the realization that some of what was taught to Tanzanians as Christianity or Islam is actually the cultures of the areas that originated these religions. Besides the push by many Tanzanian communities to practice cultures that make sense to them, many Christian missionary groups are increasingly realizing that their long-term success lies in embracing aspects of ATR that are consistent with the teachings of Christianity.

Although each of Tanzania's indigenous groups has its own ATR, these religions have many similarities because to a large extent they draw on similar or near-similar environmental conditions. Moreover, neighboring communities often have many sociocultural exchanges including religious beliefs and practices. For instance, the clients of famous traditional herbal healers have long included people from nearby ethnic communities.

ISLAM AND ITS IMPACT

Islam is the religion of between 30 and 36 percent of Tanzania's population, and this proportion has been constant since the 1960s (Table 2.1). Nevertheless, this proportion translates to about 13 to 15 million Muslims who significantly influence the country's affairs. Islam's major holidays are Idd-El-Hadji (January 9), Maulid (April 11), and Idd-El Fitr (November 24 and 25), and these often fall on different dates because they are based on the lunar calendar. Idd-El Fitr is one of Tanzania's national holidays.

Islam was the first nonindigenous religion to reach Tanzania. It came through the trading activities of Persian Gulf Arab traders who first reached coastal Tanzania before 500 AD and later introduced Islam between 800 to 1000 AD, or 200 to 400 years after the founding of Islam by Mohammed in 600 AD. By the 1100s, African–Arab trading posts had emerged on the Tanzania coast as well as the islands of Zanzibar and Pemba. Eventually, this African–Arab trade became so valuable that Sultan Majid of Oman transferred his capital to Zanzibar in 1841. But by then Islam had been present in contemporary Tanzania for about 1,000 years.

Unlike Christianity, which got to Tanzania through missionary work, Islam mainly spread through trade between Arabs and Africans. For this reason, Islam first spread along the inland ivory- and slave-trade caravan routes, which later became some of the country's major roads. While nearly all of the people on Zanzibar are Muslims, on the mainland, the number of Muslims generally decreases with distance from the Indian Ocean coast and from the main transportation arteries. Moreover, African ethnic groups that directly participated in the precolonial ivory and slave trades, such as the Nyamwezi, have higher proportions of Muslims among them because they came into direct contact with the Arabs who brought Islam to Tanzania.

Tanzania's Muslim population is one of the most diverse of any African country (Table 2.3). While most Muslims in Tanzania are Sunnis, there are also Shias, Ahmadiyya Muslims, and other uncategorized Muslims ("Just a Muslim" in Table 2.3), who are mostly African converts to Islam who practice "folk Islam," which mixes Islamic and ATR beliefs.[15]

There are many differences among Sunni, Shia, and Ahmadiyya Muslims. The Sunni branch of Islam accounts for the majority (85%) of the world's Muslim population while the Shia and other minority branches account for the rest. The Sunni and Shia branches of Islam arose in 632 AD due to political differences among the early followers of the Prophet Mohammed as to who should succeed him. Sunnis are descended from those who wanted Mohammed's

Table 2.3 Affiliation of Tanzanian Muslims

Sunni (%)	Shia (%)	Ahmadiyya (%)	Some-thing Else (%)	"Just a Muslim" (%)	None/Don't know/Refused to Answer (%)	Total (%)
41	20	15	1	20	4	100

Source: Pew Research Center, *Tolerance and Tension: Islam and Christianity in Sub-Saharan Africa,* April 2010, p. 21, http://features.pewforum.org/africa/country.php?c=216.

successor, or caliph, to be popularly elected from one of his companions and tribesmen, the *Qurayah*, while Shias wanted a successor from Mohammed's household, especially Shi'a Ali. Over time, these two main branches of Islam have diverged significantly in their theological and religious practices.

Sunni Muslims hold in high regard the religious conduct, sayings, and practices (or *Sunna*) of the initial four caliphs (i.e., Abu Bakr, 632–634 AD; Umar, 634–644 AD; Uthman 644–656 AD, and Ali, 656–661 AD) because they believe that their lifestyle closely mirrors that of the Prophet Mohammed and is thus binding to Muslims. Sunni Muslims derive their name from *Ahl al-Sunna*, or "people of Sunna," because they model their life on the sayings and actions of Mohammed as passed to them by the first four caliphs noted above.

Shia Muslims derive their name from *Shia-t-Ali*, or "party of Ali." They highly esteem members of Mohammed's family and have elaborate rituals and shrines for them. Their religious leaders are known as imams or ayatollahs ("sign of Allah"). They expect the return of the last imam (the Mahdi) to establish the Shi'ite Islamic faith before Judgment Day; consider as sacred the cities of Karbala and Najaf (in Iraq) and Meshed (in Iran); and hold the annual Karbala festival in remembrance of Husayn ibn Ali, who was killed at Karbala in 680 AD while fighting with Yazid for the caliphate. Because the 680 AD internal Islamic war marked the final separation between Sunni and Shia Islam, Husayn ibn Ali is regarded as the founder of Shia Islam.

In Tanzania, most Shia Muslims are members of the Ismaili community, whose worldwide head is His Highness Prince Karim Aga Khan, who is the 49th hereditary imam of the Shia Imami Ismaili Muslims. Ismailis in Tanzania are prominent businesspeople and their community institutions, some of which are operated by the Aga Khan Development Network, which has vast business and charitable interests, works to promote private-sector enterprise, and is engaged in the revitalization of historic cities around the world. In Tanzania and Kenya, the Ismailis operate braches of the Agha Khan University, and their Aga Khan Trust for Culture (AKTC) is actively involved in the restoration of Zanzibar's Stone Town.[16]

The Ahmadiyya Muslim community was founded by Mirza Ghulam Ahmad (1835–1908) in India in 1889. Ahmadi Muslims (or Ahmadis) believe that their founder is the long-awaited Christian Messiah (or Jesus Christ) and Muslim Mahdi (the Guided One). Because Ahmadis renounce violence and view "jihad by the sword" to be un-Islamic, they promote the "jihad of the pen" as the best defense of Islam. Consequently, they are some of the most educated, law-abiding, and community-engaged Muslims in the world. Being a more proselytizing branch of Islam, they account for a large share of new converts to Islam in countries where they are active.

However, they have been bitterly opposed by mainstream Islam because they, among other things, do not hold Mohammed to be the last prophet.[17]

Table 2.4 summarizes key aspects of the worldviews, beliefs, and practices of Tanzanian Muslims and Christians, many of whom have strong ATR influences. While Table 2.4 shows substantial agreement among many Christians and Muslims in Tanzania on (1) the nature of God; (2) frequency of prayer and participation in weekly religious services; (3) importance of religion in life; (4) the existence of heaven, hell, angels, miracles, evil spirits, and witchcraft; and (5) the undesirability of abortion, homosexuality, and sex outside marriage, the two groups differ on which is the ultimate holy book (the Bible versus the Koran), the frequency of fasting, the uniformity of interpretation of their scriptures, the experience of divine healing and the exorcism of demons or evil spirits, the acceptance of polygamy, the ordination of women clergy or clerics, end-times theology, and government treatment of Muslims.

Table 2.4 Tanzanian Christian and Muslim Worldviews, Beliefs, and Practices

	% Christians	% Muslims
(a) Core Beliefs and Practices		
Percent who believe in God	99	99
Percent who believe in one God	97	99
Percent certain about their belief in God	94	94
Percent saying their holy book is the literal word of God	78 (Bible)	86 (Koran)
Percent saying they attend weekly or more frequent religious services	83	82
Percent saying they pray at least once a day	56	55
Percent who fast	70	93
Percent who say religion is very important in their life	95	95
Percent who say heaven is where people who have led good lives are eternally rewarded	93	86
Percent who say hell is where people who have led bad lives and die without being sorry are eternally punished	91	87
Percent who believe in angels	96	97
Percent who believe in miracles	96	93
Percent who believe in the existence of evil spirits	97	93
Percent who agree that there is only one true way to interpret the teachings of their religion	61	63
Percent who have ever experienced divine healing of an illness or injury	63	26
Percent who ever give tithe or *zakat*, that is give a set percentage of their wealth to a church, charity, or mosque	85	65
Percent who have experienced or witnessed the devil or evil spirits being driven out of a person	62	33
Percent who believe in reincarnation—that people are reborn in this world again and again	32	32

Table 2.4   (Continued)

	% Christians	% Muslims
(b) Influence of African Traditional Religions		
Percent who believe in witchcraft	94	92
Percent who believe in the evil eye	78	83
Percent who believe that *juju*, shrines, or other sacred objects can protect a person from harm	44	55
Percent who participate in traditional African ceremonies to honor ancestors	31	35
Percent who believe that sacrifices to spirits or ancestors can protect them from bad things happening?	56	66
Percent who individually or whose family ever use traditional religious healers	35	53
Percent who believe that certain spiritual people can protect one from harm	72	68
Percent who have traditional African sacred objects in their home, such as shrines to ancestors, feathers, skins, skulls, skeletons, powder, carved figures or branches, spears, cutlasses, or animal horns	17	20
Percent who ever participate in traditional African puberty rituals or manhood/womanhood initiation rituals for friends, relatives, or neighbors in their area, such as endurance or challenge tests, or initiation to a traditional dance	39	57
(c) Eschatology and Apocalypticism (End-Times Theology)		
Percent who believe Jesus will return during their lifetime (Christians only)	62	0
Percent who believe caliphate will be reestablished to rule in their lifetime (Muslims only)	0	43
(d) Views on Gender and Social Issues		
Percent who agree that women should be allowed to serve in religious leadership roles, such as pastor, priest, or imam	61	30
Percent who agree that only men should be allowed to serve in religious leadership roles	37	68
Percent who favor punishments like whippings and cutting off of hands for crimes like theft and robbery	26	50
Percent who favor stoning people who commit adultery	19	45
Percent who think there is a natural conflict between being a devout religious person and living in a modern society	48	47
Percent who completely agree that AIDS is God's punishment for immoral sexual behavior	70	78
Percent who believe it is morally wrong to have an abortion	91	94
Percent who believe homosexual behavior is morally wrong	91	91
Percent who believe it is morally wrong to be polygamous (have more than one wife)	75	29
Percent who believe sex between people who are not married to each other is morally wrong	87	87

(*continued*)

Table 2.4   (Continued)

	% Christians	% Muslims
(e) Views on Interreligious Relations		
Percent who ever participate in interfaith religious groups, classes, or meetings with Muslims/Christians	27 (Muslim)	43 (Christian)
Percent who have any other immediate family members, such as children, siblings, or parents, who are Muslim/Christian	27 (Muslim)	39 (Christian)
Percent saying most/many/all Muslims/Christians are hostile towards Christians/Muslims	43 (Muslim)	27 (Christian)
Percent who have any other immediate family members, such as children, siblings, or parents, who are part of an ancestral, tribal, animist, or other traditional African religion	19	20
Percent who see Muslims/Christians as violent	43 (Muslim)	12 (Christian)
Percent who completely agree that members of their religion have a duty to try and convert others to their religious faith	69	75
Percent who consider their religion as the one true faith leading to eternal life	53	70
(f) Views of Religion and State Relations		
Percent who think that Christians/Muslims are "very often" treated unfairly by the government in their country	5 (Christian)	20 (Muslim)
Percent who favor making the Bible/Sharia the official law of the land	39	37
Percent very concerned about extremist religious groups in their country these days	30	29
Percent who are "mostly concerned about Muslim extremist groups"	34	16

Source: Pew Research Center, *Tolerance and Tension: Islam and Christianity in Sub-Saharan Africa,* April 2010, http://features.pewforum.org/africa/country.php?c=216.

CHRISTIANITY AND ITS IMPACT

The basic tenet of Christianity is that Jesus Christ is God and the savior of mankind through his crucifixion, death, and resurrection; and that those who believe in him have eternal life. Thus the main Christian holidays of Christmas (December 25) and Easter focus on the birth, death, and resurrection of Jesus Christ and are now major national holidays in Tanzania. Christianity is the religion of between 34 and 64 percent of Tanzania's population (Table 2.1). Thus anywhere from 14 to 27 million Tanzanians are Christians, which confers significant Christian influence on many aspects of the country's affairs. Tanzanian Christian views on core Christian beliefs and practices,

ATR influences, end times, gender and social issues, interreligious relations, and state-religion relations are shown in Table 2.4.

The breakdown of Tanzanian Christians is as follows: Protestants (44%), Catholics (51%), and others (5%). The country's major Christian denominations are Roman Catholic, Orthodox, Protestant, and Pentecostal. There are also groups like Seventh-Day Adventists, Mormons (or the Church of Jesus Christ of Latter Day Saints), and Jehovah's Witnesses that many mainstream denominations consider cultic. There is very little denominational switching in the country, though Protestants have a minor advantage in this regard over Catholics (Table 2.5).

While Tanzanian Christians and Muslims are heavily influenced by ATR beliefs and practices, this influence is slightly lower among Christians (Table 2.4b). Additionally, the influence of ATRs varies widely among the country's various Christian denominations and is generally highest among members of African independent churches (AICs) and Roman Catholics and lowest among members of mainstream Protestant churches. In some Tanzanian AICs, the influence of ATRs is so great as to render these churches cultic in the eyes of mainstream Christian churches.

In recent decades, Tanzanian Lutherans and Anglicans have been caught up in their churches' global controversies on same-sex marriages and gay or homosexual clergy. As Tanzanian and other African churches abhor these practices, they have often found themselves in the unfamiliar position of having to provide refuge for their similarly minded counterparts in the Global North.[18]

This role reversal is also part of the larger shift of Christianity's demographic center to Tanzania and other Southern Hemisphere countries where believers exhibit greater (1) enthusiasm for the faith; (2) submission to the authority of scripture and Biblical morality; (3) belief in the supernatural aspects of scripture, hence their more common experience of miracles, visions and healings; and (4) belief in the continuing power of prophecy and regard for the Old Testament. The fervency of Tanzanian and Southern Hemisphere Christianity is also because (1) Christianity's exorcism and spiritual warfare

Table 2.5 Switching within Christianity in Tanzania

Raised Catholic (%)	Currently Catholic (%)	Net Change (%)	Raised Protestant (%)	Currently Protestant (%)	Net Change (%)
32	31	−1	23	27	+4

Source: Pew Research Center *Tolerance and Tension: Islam and Christianity in Sub-Saharan Africa,* April 2010, p. 24, http://features.pewforum.org/africa/country.php?c=216.

provides a powerful counterforce to the region's belief in the devil and the fearful practices of paganism, witchcraft, omens, and alleged human sacrifices; (2) the high harmony between the hemisphere's and the Bible's mostly rural culture of herding, farming, and fishing (in contrast to the industrial and postindustrial livelihoods of the global North that often hinder its people's appreciation for the Bible); and (3) the widespread appeal of the biblical promise of a better present and future life in exchange for the global South's commonly short and harsh life due to widespread pestilence and poverty. Moreover, while Christians in the global North have to contend with secularism and doubt, Tanzanian and other global South Christians live in a spiritual environment that is not only suspicious of secularism but is also highly charged by competition among Christianity, Islam, and other religions.[19]

The following is a brief overview of Tanzania's major Christian branches of Roman Catholicism, Protestantism, and AICs.

Roman Catholicism

There are nearly 9 million Catholics in Tanzania. Catholicism was first introduced in the country by Portuguese Augustinian missionaries who came to Zanzibar with the explorer Vasco Da Gama in 1499. But they soon faced opposition from Muslims, and their mission ended in 1698 when Zanzibar was conquered by Omani Arabs. From the mid-1800s, a lasting Roman Catholic missionary foundation was laid by the Holy Ghost Fathers, the White Fathers, and the Benedictine Monks. The Holy Ghost Fathers arrived in Zanzibar in 1863 and crossed over to Bagamoyo on the mainland in 1868. There they opened freed slaves' villages, converted the slaves to Catholicism, and trained them as catechists who helped the Holy Ghost Fathers to evangelize the Bagamoyo-to-Mount Kilimanjaro region. While many European priests continue to serve in Tanzania, it is the African catechists who have long been pivotal in the local acceptance and spread of Roman Catholicism and Christianity in general in the country and elsewhere in Africa.[20]

At the same time, the White Fathers (or missionaries of Africa) arrived on the shores of Lakes Tanganyika and Victoria in 1878 and introduced Catholicism all over western Tanzania and the nearby countries. Similarly, the Benedictine missionary monks of St. Ottilien arrived in Dar es Salaam in 1887 and expanded their missionary work southwards to the Ruvuma River on the Tanzania-Mozambique border. Their monasteries at Ndanda and Peramiho soon became the centers of their work and of the development and modernization of southern Tanzania. After the first and second world wars, other Roman Catholic missionaries came to Tanzania and greatly aided their church's missionary effort. The country's 29 Catholic dioceses are all led by

St. Joseph's Cathedral, Dar es Salaam, Tanzania. (De Agostini/Getty Images)

African priests and are scattered across the country, with particular concentrations in Mbinga, Sumbawanga, Bukoba, Mahenge, and Moshi. These areas have long been epicenters of Catholic evangelism in the country.

Through its Tanzania Episcopal Conference (TEC), the Catholic Church works closely with the protestant Christian Council of Tanzania (CCT) on issues like Swahili and other local-language Bible translations, development of the country's common secondary school religious curriculum, and delivery of social services like education and health. Together, the two groups operate more than 50 percent of the country's medical institutions and secondary schools and run many kindergartens, seminaries, technical and vocational schools, teacher-training colleges, and some universities.

Protestantism

The distribution of Christians in Tanzania is shown in Table 2.6, with Lutherans, Anglicans, and Pentecostals being the largest Protestant groups. While the British introduced Anglicanism, the Germans introduced

Table 2.6 Affiliation of Tanzanian Christians

Pentecostal (%)	AICs (%)	Anglican (%)	Baptist (%)	Seventh-Day Adventist (%)	Lutheran (%)	Non-Protestant Christian (Catholic) %	Total (%)
10	5	10	1	3	13	56	≈100

Source: Pew Research Center *Tolerance and Tension: Islam and Christianity in Sub-Saharan Africa,* April 2010, p. 23, http://features.pewforum.org/africa/country.php?c=216.

Moravianism during their colonial control of the country between 1885 and World War I. From the initial creation of the Moravian mission station at Rungwe in southern Tanzania in 1891, the Moravian Church in Tanzania (MCT) has grown to 404 congregations, 494 pastors, and an estimated membership of 500,000 in four Moravian provinces. MCT is especially strong in Tukuyu, Mbeya, Sumbawanga, and Tabora and is the proprietor of Bishop Kisanji University and Theological Seminary.[21]

Tanzanian Protestant churches have since 1934 operated under the umbrella of the CCT. Membership in the CCT grants churches the right to operate nationally.

African Independent Churches (AICs)

AICs were started by Africans in the 1870s as a protest against the rigidity and racism of mainstream Christian churches that were under the control of European and American missionaries until independence. AICs go by many other names, including African indigenous churches, African initiated churches, or African instituted churches. A distinguishing feature of AICs is that from the start they sought to incorporate local languages and other cultural practices (e.g., dancing and drumming) into their theology and worship services, though the extent to which this was done has long varied widely. Initially, and to some extent now, some AICs also permitted their members to engage in polygyny and to participate in certain traditional initiation ceremonies. This sensitivity to local cultures has helped make AICs key players in the growth of Christianity in Tanzania and elsewhere in Africa.[22] There are an estimated 110 million AIC members in Africa.

The growth of AICs in colonial and postcolonial Tanzania has long been unwelcomed by mainstream denominations, which often see many of them as cults. Although the cult label applies to some, many AICs maintain the theological traditions of the mainstream churches that converted their founders to Christianity. For this reason, AICs can be categorized as

Anglican, Roman Catholic, Orthodox, Pentecostal, Methodist, Apostolic, Zionist, or Messianic. Also, many AICs, despite being independent, tend to maintain strategic affiliations with their founders' original denominations. Since the 1980s, some AICs have taken advantage of increased African migration to Europe and North America to launch missionary outreaches to these regions.

In terms of core beliefs, AICs

- believe in the Christian God and use the Bible as their main source of inspiration;
- are characterized by intense spiritual experiences that they attribute to spiritual beings, with God and the Holy Spirit being the source of good experiences and Satan the source of the negative ones;
- promote individual spiritual and material well-being within the context of communal well-being;
- believe in the Christian notion of the afterlife but differ on whether personal salvation is attained upon death, is collective, is millenarian, or is earthly and through individual behavioral change;
- follow the Christian religious calendar, though they often add religious holidays that memorialize the lives of their founders;
- usually consider the birthplaces of their founders to be sacred, with many religious festivals, ceremonies, and pilgrimages occurring there;
- have ceremonies and rituals that commemorate people's life stages, especially birth, initiation, marriage, and death;
- often use drumming to induce possession by the Holy Spirit;
- often follow the worship structure of their alleged mainstream Christian denomination, though they usually conduct services in local African languages;
- encourage regular prayer and fasting by members and often abstain from certain foods and intoxicants, for instance pork, alcohol, and tobacco;
- variously use Western Christian and African symbols and objects like water, fire, crucifixes, and staffs;
- strive to have leaders who have genuine calls or visions from the Holy Spirit;
- treasure and form mutually supportive spiritual and socioeconomic communities that are modeled on African notions of community and social structure even as they promote individual social and moral development;
- are usually led by men, though most congregations are predominantly female, something that has often led to the formation of some women-led AICs; and
- because they yearn for healthy, productive, and modern African people and societies, they are usually politically active and fairly involved in uniting and empowering their people against threats of foreign domination.[23]

INTERRELIGIOUS RELATIONS AND DIALOGUE

By definition, interreligious relations and dialogue only make sense in the context of two or more religions that are competing in the same space or geography. As Tanzania's major religions are ATRs, Christianity, and Islam, this section looks at their interactions in the precolonial, colonial, and postcolonial periods.

As ATRs ruled supreme over the spiritual affairs of modern-day Tanzania for much of the precolonial era, there was no need for interreligious relations and dialogue. However, things began to change when Islam reached the Tanzanian and larger East African coast in around 800 AD. Between 1000 AD and the late 1880s, ATRs and Islam generally coexisted peacefully in coastal Tanzania and along inland caravan routes as Africans and Arabs traded and intermarried and eventually gave rise to the Swahili people and language. This long period of gradual change, coupled with limited overt proselytization by Islam, minimized any potential conflicts between the two religions, though by the late 1800s Islam had become dominant at the coast. While Arab Muslims had control of the Tanzanian coast for much of this time, the control came more by trade than by conquest, thereby minimizing conflicts between Africans and Arabs and their religions.

There are only two notable interruptions to the peaceful religious environment of precolonial Tanzania. The first is that between 1499 and 1698, when the Portuguese conquered the Arab domains of coastal East Africa (including Tanzania), introduced Roman Catholic Christianity with modest Muslim opposition, and technically put Christianity in a superior position through military means. But because Christianity hardly gained any converts, Islam's dominance remained intact, thereby obviating any need for interreligious dialogue, which became even more moot when the local Muslim Omani Arab rulers overthrew the Portuguese in 1698 and effectively ended the presence of Christianity in the region for the next 150 years.[24]

It was not until the 1850s that Islam's coastal dominance and ATRs' supremacy elsewhere in Tanzania began to be increasingly challenged with the start of a new wave of concerted Christian missionary work in the region. This wave coincided with the arrival of the superior military might of the Christian British naval force that was out to end the barbaric Arab Muslim East African slave trade. But unlike in 1698 when Omani Arab Muslims managed to thwart the encroachment of Christianity, this time around luck was not on their side. Thus by the start of the colonial era, the stage was set for an intense three-way competition between ATRs, Islam, and Christianity, a competition that was to eventually culminate in the need for religious dialogue and coexistence.

In the colonial era, a full-fledged contest for supremacy among Islam, Christianity, and ATRs developed. But with the enabling environment provided by the colonial state, Christianity grew rapidly in the country to the distinct disadvantage of Islam and ATRs. As education in colonial Tanzania was dominated by Christian missionary schools, Muslims were not as free to enroll in them. Eventually, this caused Muslims to lag behind Christians in access to education and formal-sector employment. Soon, Muslims began to agitate against the colonial state. But in

> any uprising against the colonial state Muslims took that opportunity to attack missionaries and Christian establishments. Muslims perceived both missionaries and the colonial state as fellow collaborators and therefore enemies to Islam . . . Christianity meanwhile became a reactionary force siding with the colonial state. [Even in] . . . the Maji Maji War of 1905 some Christians fought alongside the German army against the people to safeguard Christianity . . . [and] some Muslims were hanged particularly for killing missionaries and for waging a war against German rule.[25]

In response to Muslim opposition, the colonial state further marginalized Muslims even as it increased the privileges of educated Africans, many of whom were products of Christian missionary schools. Simultaneously, this class of educated Africans increasingly grew distant from their African roots, thereby further weakening the social influence of ATRs. All this worked against cordial interreligious interaction.

By the early 1960s, the wide Christian-Muslim educational gap was such a sore point that some Muslims were willing to delay the mainland's independence in order to buy time to educationally prepare their people for the opportunities of the postindependence state. When these efforts failed, the country gained independence with an enduring Christian advantage over Islam and ATRs.[26] Correctly sensing that this religious inequality was a threat to the future of the country, Tanzania's first president, Julius Nyerere, sought to address it by (1) asking Christians to open up their educational institutions to Muslims; (2) validating the Muslim quest for equal socioeconomic opportunities, in the process managing to forestall the rise of radical Islam for a few decades; (3) ensuring that important state addresses, the national anthem, and opening parliamentary prayers used language that was acceptable to Christians, Muslims, and traditionalists; (4) ensuring that his *Ujamaa* policy generally promoted values agreeable to most Christians, Muslims, and traditionalists; and (5) ensuring that Tanzania is a secular state whose constitution guarantees everyone freedom of worship and religion. Moreover, after 1967, the government stopped collecting religious affiliation data, thereby depriving religious extremists of some ammunition. By the end of Nyerere's reign, the country had created enough religious harmony to even allow many Christians and Muslims to intermarry.[27]

Tanzania's founding president, Julius Nyerere. (Keystone/Getty Images)

Nevertheless, there have in recent decades been increasing Muslim-Christian conflicts even though moderate Christians and Muslims have managed to cool tempers and minimize outbreaks of open religious conflict. The causes of these conflicts include both groups' extremism, ignorance of each other's religion, limited participation in interreligious activities, and pursuit of converts in the hope of saving them from eternal damnation (Table 2.4).

Besides interreligious conflicts, there are also tensions within the major religions and denominations of the country. Thus, within Islam, the Sunni-Shia fault lines persist as well as those between liberals and conservatives over issues such as the consumption of alcohol and the taking of non-Muslim wives. These intra-Muslim differences are partly reflected in the rivalry between Tanzania's major Muslim organizations, including the Muslim Council of Tanzania (BAKWATA) and the Supreme Council of Islamic Organizations (*Baraza Kuu*).[28] There are also many differences among and within Tanzania's Catholics, Protestants, and AICs.

Growing tensions between the country's Christians and Muslims have long undermined dialogue and cooperation between them. But there has been more cooperative success within each of these religions. For instance, since the 1970s the country's Christians have cooperated and managed their internal conflicts under the auspices of their umbrella Catholic and Protestant organizations, that is, the TEC and the CCT, respectively. Moreover, TEC and CCT have formed various ecumenical bodies to advance issues of common interest. These include (1) the Christian Social Services Commission (CSSC), which facilitates TEC and CCT's cooperation in the provision of social services like health and education; (2) the Tanzania Ecumenical Dialogue Group (TEDG) that enables TEC and CCT to lobby government and other nonstate actors on behalf of its members, advocate for human rights and socioeconomic and political justice in the country, shape the country's policy environment, and monitor the country's elections and provide civic education to citizens; and (3) the Bible Society of Tanzania that enables CCT and TEC to make common Swahili and other local-language Bible translations.[29]

RELIGION AND POLITICS

Tanzania's politico-religious environment is good but complicated given the country's many religions and competitive political landscape. While Tanzania is a secular state, its political system has long been significantly influenced by religion. The country's relatively poor government has also long relied on various religious groups to meet many socioeconomic needs.[30]

While there was no unified state in Tanzania in the precolonial era, ATRs and Islam played an important role in the politics and governance of the country's mainland and Zanzibar, respectively. Because both ATRs and Islam are lifestyles, it has long been difficult to separate them from their respective societies' everyday life. Thus, Islam's rise to prominence in Zanzibar in the precolonial era eventually led to Islamic jurisprudence, including the Kadhis courts. While these courts were abolished shortly after independence, Islam's legal influence on the island is inescapable. On the mainland, many traditional governance and dispute-resolution systems that are often informed by ATRs have also been in use since the precolonial times.

When Europeans colonized Tanzania, their new political systems had to contend with preexisting politico-religious traditions. Thus, in 1895, the secular British colonial authorities in Zanzibar accommodated Muslim interests by signing a treaty with the sultan that barred the British from interfering with the island's and coastal Tanzania and Kenya's Islamic jurisprudence. While the colonial authorities were generally respectful of ATRs on the mainland, the close and mutually beneficial relationships between European missionaries and administrators eventually led to close ties between the state and Christianity, ties that have since politically benefited Christians and disadvantaged Muslims and ATR practitioners.

At the start of European colonialism, the Muslims, who at the time were far more educated than Africans, largely manned the colonial civil service. In the early colonial period, then, state-religion politics were generally good all around as control of the state had not become an issue. But as European colonial rule got entrenched and as Africans got more Christianized and educated, they gradually took over the civil service, to the chagrin of the Muslims, who soon started opposing the colonial state and agitating for independence. As expected, colonial Christian missionaries threw their weight behind the colonial state and even discouraged African Christians from joining Muslim-led freedom movements. Moreover, many of the African civil servants were slow to join the freedom struggle because of their conflicted allegiance to Christianity and their European employers. Even though Tanzanians eventually united around Nyerere (a Christian) and won their country's independence, the freedom struggle had obvious religious undercurrents because Muslims and Christians favored different leaders. Moreover, in the run-up to independence, some Muslims sought to delay independence until there were enough educated Muslims in the country who would compete better with the Christians in the postindependence era.

While by independence Tanzania had near-equal proportions of Christians, Muslims, and ATR practitioners, Christians dominated government. Muslims were proportionally less represented in government even as the traditionalists, or ATR practitioners, who were in the majority, were largely absent from it because they were generally uneducated and politically disorganized. Muslim underrepresentation in government, despite their dominant role in the country's freedom struggle, has long soured Tanzanian Muslim-state relations. Religion remains central in the country's politics because the Christian elite that belatedly joined the freedom struggle not only reaped most of its fruits but also strengthened its control of the state after independence.[31]

In 1967, Nyerere launched his *Ujamaa* policy to, among other things, redress Tanzania's religious, racial, and ethnic cleavages. Thus, his government stopped collecting religious adherence data, nationalized most religious schools and hospitals to ensure their access to all Tanzanians, and eventually made the country a single-party state in 1975. The latter move, nevertheless, not only banned ethnic and religious parties, it also benefited African Muslim political interests and severely undermined the power of the country's nonnative Arab, Asian, and Ismaili Muslims. The Jehovah Witnesses were also banned with the tacit approval of mainstream churches.

The various religious communities' responses to these measures were varied. Because by independence Muslims substantially lagged behind Christians in education, they never quite caught up with them even under

Ujamaa and never fully trusted Nyerere given his Christian background. Arab, Asian, and Ismaili Muslims opposed *Ujamaa* because it undermined their business interests. Conversely, African Muslims supported *Ujamaa* because they saw it as a vehicle for their advancement as well as a way of redressing the injustices they had suffered at the hands of non-Africans, including Arab, Asian, and Ismaili Muslims. Soon, African Muslims formed the Muslim Council of Tanzania (BAKWATA) in 1968 to replace the non-African Muslim-dominated East African Muslim Welfare Society (EAMWS) that was banned in the same year. It was not until 1992, after the fall of *Ujamaa*, that a more inclusive Tanzanian Muslim body, the Supreme Council of Islamic Organizations (*Baraza Kuu*), was formed.

Among Christians, acceptance of *Ujamaa* was also not uniform because Catholics resisted it (because it nationalized many of their institutions) while Protestants embraced it more quickly, in part because many of them occupied senior political positions. Smaller Protestant churches with few institutions also prospered under *Ujamaa*'s villagization policy because they were able to respond more quickly to it relative to the more established Catholic Church. The Chagga, Haya, and Pare people of northern and northwestern Tanzania, who by the time of proclamation of *Ujamaa* in 1968 were more Christianized and capitalist in their outlook, also resisted *Ujamaa* and were demoralized by it. But on the whole, the Christian church largely supported the policy.

When Mwinyi (a Muslim) succeded Nyerere (a Roman Catholic Christian), he continued Nyerere's policy of promoting peaceful racial, ethnic, and religious coexistence. Nevertheless, he also introduced multiparty politics and replaced *Ujamaa* with a neoliberal political and economic environment. Mwinyi's presidency also raised Muslim expectations that culminated in calls for the creation of Kadhis courts, which led to intra-Muslim and Muslim-Christian conflicts as both sides became somewhat radicalized. Any Muslim expectations of better things were soon dashed when Mwinyi's administration was forced to take tough action against domestic radical Islamic elements following the 1998 U.S. Embassy bombings in Kenya and Tanzania. Since then, the country's politico-religious situation has changed drastically for the worse due to heightened Christian suspicion of Muslims, the growing presence of radical Islam in the country, and increased Muslim complaints of unfair treatment by the country's government. Equally worrisome is that the future of the unity government may be in jeopardy given Muslim Zanzibar's growing calls for economic independence and possible secession.[32] Hopefully, the country's religious and political leaders will rise to the occasion and help to keep Tanzania united.

Notes

1. John S. Mbiti, *Introduction to African Religion* (London: Heinemann Educational, 1991); Pew Research Center, *Tolerance and Tension: Islam and Christianity in Sub-Saharan Africa*, April 2010, p. 3, http://features.pewforum.org/africa/country.php?c=216.

2. Tanzania Tourist Board. "Religion," 2010, http://www.tanzaniatouristboard.com/about-tanzania/religion/, accessed September 29, 2012.

3. Pew Research Center, *Tolerance and Tension*.

4. Ibid., 20.

5. Central Intelligence Agency, *The World Fact Book: Tanzania*, 2010, https://www.cia.gov/library/publications/the-world-factbook/geos/tz.html, accessed November 5, 2010.

6. Aloysius M. Lugira, *African Traditional Religion* (New York: Chelsea House, 2009), 17

7. Pew Research Center, *Tolerance and Tension*.

8. John Mbiti, "The Role of Women in African Traditional Religion," *Cahiers des Religions Africaines* 22 (1988), 69–82.

9. Richard Cox, "Why Rangi Christians Continue to Practice African Traditional Religion," *GIALens* (2008): 3, http://www.gial.edu/GIALens/issues.htm.

10. Ibid.

11. Tom Mosoba, "Thousands Scramble for 'Miracle' Drink," *Daily Nation*, March 22, 2011, http://www.nation.co.ke/, Accessed March 31, 2011.

12. Richard J. Gehman, *African Traditional Religion in Biblical Perspective* (Nairobi: East African Educational Publishers, 2005), xi.

13. Allan Anderson, "African Religions," *Encyclopedia of Death and Dying*, 2011, http://www.deathreference.com/A-Bi/African-Religions.html, accessed February 24, 2011; Richard Cox, "Why Rangi Christians . . . ," 7.

14. John S. Mbiti, *African Religions and Philosophy* (London: Heinemann, 1969), 4–5.

15. Richard Cox, "Why Rangi Christians . . . ," 3–4.

16. The Agha Khan Development Network, "AKDN in Tanzania and Zanzibar" and "Revitalising Zanzibar's Stone Town," 2007, http://www.akdn.org/, accessed March 31, 2011.

17. Ahmadiyya Muslim Community, "Ahmadiyya Muslim Community: An Overview," 1995–2011, http://www.alislam.org/introduction/index.html, accessed March 6, 2011; Humanity First International, "Humanity First: Serving Mankind," 2009, http://humanityfirst.org/.

18. Miranda K. Hassett, *Anglican Communion in Crisis: How Episcopal Dissidents and Their African Allies Are Reshaping Anglicanism* (Princeton, NJ: Princeton University Press, 2007); Evangelical Lutheran Church in Tanzania, "The Dodoma Statement [on Same Sex Marriage]," January 7, 2010, http://www.elct.org/news/2010.04.004.html, accessed April 1, 2011.

19. Philip Jenkins, *The New Faces of Christianity: Believing the Bible in the Global South* (New York: OUP, 2006).

20. Method M. P. Kilaini, "The Tanzania Catholic Church," 1998, http://www.rc.net/tanzania/tec/tzchurch.htm, accessed March 18, 2011.

21. World Council of Churches, "Moravian Church in Tanzania," 2011, http://www.oikoumene.org/en/member-churches/regions/africa/tanzania/moravian-church-in-tanzania.html, accessed March 17, 2011; Michael Westall, "Anglican–Lutheran Relations in Tanzania," presented at the Anglican–Lutheran Society Annual General Meeting, March 7, 2009, http://www.anglican-lutheran-society.org/Westall%20paper.htm, accessed March 17, 2011.

22. Patheos, "African Independent Churches," 2008–2011, http://www.patheos.com/Library/African-Independent-Churches.html, accessed March 17, 2011.

23. Ibid.

24. Method M. P. Kilaini, "The Tanzania Catholic Church."

25. Mohammed Saeed, "Islam and Politics in Tanzania," Muslim Writer's Organization, Dar es Salaam, http://www.islamtanzania.org/nyaraka/islam_and_politics_in_tz.html, accessed September 29, 2012.

26. Frieder Ludwig, *Church and State in Tanzania: Aspects of Changing Relationships, 1961–1994* (Boston: Brill, 1999), 53; Amos Mhina, "State-Religion Relationships and Religious Views on Development Policies," in Amos Mhina (ed.), *Religions and Development in Tanzania: A Preliminary Literature Review*, Religions and Development Research Program, Philosophy Unit, University of Dar es Salaam, RaD Working Paper 11-2007 (2007).

27. Bruce E. Heilman and Paul J. Kaiser, "Religion, Identity and Politics in Tanzania," *Third World Quarterly* 23, no. 4 (August 2002): 691–709; Frieder Ludwig, *Church and State in Tanzania*, 53.

28. Robert Leurs, Peter Tumaini-Mungu, and Abu Mvungi, *Mapping the Development Activities of Faith-based Organizations in Tanzania*, Religions and Development Research Programme, Working Paper 58-2011 (Birmingham, UK: International Development Department, University of Birmingham, 2011).

29. Tanzania Ecumenical Dialogue Group, "Report of Faith Based Organizations (FBOs) on National Strategy for Growth and Reduction of Poverty [NSGRP] Implementation Gaps—Submitted to the Vice President's Office," http://www.policyforum-tz.org/files/FBO.pdf, accessed March 26, 2011; Method M. P. Kilaini, "The Tanzania Catholic Church"; Method Kilaini, "An Overview of the TEC Secretariat's Activities 1997–2000," http://www.rc.net/tanzania/tec/secgenrep.htm, accessed March 26, 2011.

30. Frieder Ludwig, *Church and State in Tanzania*, 53; H. Majamba, "Possibility and Rationale of Establishing Kadhi Courts in Tanzania Mainland," paper prepared for presentation at the 20th REDET RMC Workshop, Council Chamber, University of Dar es Salaam, November 10, 2007.

31. Frieder Ludwig, *Church and State in Tanzania*, 12, 53, 230–35.

32. Constantine Sebastian, "Experts Support Zanzibar's Quest for Economic Independence," *The Citizen*, November 13, 2010, http://www.thecitizen.co.tz/, accessed April 4, 2011.

3

Literature, Media, and Film

TANZANIA HAS YOUNG literary, media, and film sectors. Though growing by the day, these sectors' development is constrained by factors such as the paucity of accomplished writers, poor media distribution networks, and small markets for literary, media, and film products. In turn, this situation is due to factors like the country's low reading culture and small personal incomes, which limit the market for literary, media, and film products. In this chapter, we review the state of the country's literature, media, and film sectors and explore opportunities for their future growth.

ORAL LITERATURE

Much of Tanzania's literature is oral and is primarily spread orally rather than in written form. Because the producers and consumers of oral literature need little or no formal training, oral literature is far more widespread than its written counterpart, which began to blossom in the country in the colonial era. Tanzania's oral literature exists in all of its nearly 135 living indigenous languages, though many of them are in decline and some are in danger of being extinct.

It is impossible to know the exact extent of oral literature in Tanzania because this literature exists in the minds of people rather than in depositories like libraries. Any quantification of this literature is also complicated by the fact that many of its elements, for instance riddles, are dynamic and are always changing in response to changing sociocultural circumstances. Moreover, the purveyors of this literature, such as storytellers, have a broad ability to dynamically tailor and contextualize it to their diverse audiences.

While the country's oral literature can be recorded and preserved, this process is costly and is complicated by the plethora of the country's indigenous ethnic groups and languages. Thus, much of the country's recorded oral literature is in Swahili—one of the country's national languages. Despite the many challenges of preserving Tanzania's traditional oral literature, it is important for the exercise to commence before most of the country's true living "libraries" of this literature die off. Currently, the Tanzanian government is attempting to preserve the country's oral literature, though the scope of this project is unclear.[1]

Tanzania's oral literature is also in decline for other reasons, including the government's promotion of Swahili proficiency for political reasons, the breakdown of the country's traditional multigenerational social setup that previously facilitated the efficient transmission of knowledge from older to younger generations, and the increasing modernization of the country and the attendant devaluation of traditional oral literature.

The main types of Tanzania's oral literature are folktales, songs, poems, proverbs, and riddles. In Tanzania, these literary devices often use symbolic language and fictional animal and human characters to communicate. In some cases, inanimate objects like trees and rocks are anthropomorphized (or given human forms and attributes, such as mouths that can speak) by communicators and used to extol or denounce certain human behaviors.

Poems and Songs

Whereas there were many traditional bards (i.e., people who composed and recited epic or heroic poems, often while playing the harp or lyre) in Tanzania up to the 1950s, their number has declined drastically in recent decades due to changing socioeconomic circumstances, lack of individual or public support, insufficient replenishment of the bard or performer ranks, lack of recordings that could be used to train emerging bards, and insufficient exposure of the younger generations to this aspect of traditional Tanzanian culture.[2]

Yet there are such artists in the country, though most of them are aged and unknown beyond their localities. For instance, among the Haya of northwestern Tanzania, some traditional bards still live in the former traditional kingdoms of Kiyanja (Kihanja), Ihangiro, and Karagwe in the Kagera region near Lake Victoria. Moreover, many of the younger contemporary songsters, such as Saida Karoli, perform love songs that are popular with younger audiences.

One of Tanzania's greatest oral literary artists was the late Habibu Selemani, or Habibu Rajani Gwakubabenda (c. 1929–1993), whose life work is highlighted here.[3] He was born in Haya country in around 1929 in the village of Lukurungo in the traditional kingdom of Kiziba, nearly 16 kilometers (about 10 miles) from the present-day town of Bukoba, near the Bukoba-Kampala Road. He grew up Muslim because his father was probably an itinerant trader who was one of the first converts to Islam in Haya country. As a member of the Abakyaija clan, he was considered a commoner in the traditional Haya hierarchy. He, however, had royal heritage on his mother's side because she was a Muzibakazi, or a member of the Luo Bito clan that ruled Kiziba. She was also a spirit medium who died a few years before him.

Despite being a Muslim, Selemani was a virtual illiterate who never attended even the local *madrasa* or Koranic school, where he might at least have become literate in Arabic. Growing up in Lukurungo helped him hone his music performance skills because the village was then the epicenter of the *enanga* tradition in Kiziba, named after the local eight-stringed trough zither (*enanga*) used in epic and song performances. At the time, Kiziba had some of the most eminent epic or heroic poets of the early 1900s, including Rutahindurwa Nyabushaija (Lukuuka). These bards' benefactor was a wealthy nobleman known as Lukuuka olwa Kagasha, the father of Rutahindurwa, who both performed and maintained the family tradition of hosting *enanga* performances after his father's death. By age 13, Selemani was an accomplished *enanga* performer who was later to surpass his masters. After training at Lukurungo, he left the village and settled permanently in his nearby maternal village of Bugandika. Because Haya culture is patriarchal and does not allow a child to own or inherit land in his maternal clan, Selemani lived on his mother's plot of land in Bugandika. In the end, this custom and his move were to consign his family to poverty because the land reverted to his mother's brothers upon his death in 1993.

In the 1940s, Selemani moved and became a court poet for Omukama (chief) Gabriel Rugabandana at Kabale, where the late South African musicologist Hugh Tracey found him in 1950 and created the first existing record of his work. Prior to his royal service in Kabale, Selemani had primarily performed the commoners' *enanga* poetry that he grew up with in Lukurungo. But on joining Omukama Gabriel Rugabandana's court, he became an accomplished royal epic performer under the tutelage of various eminent royal bards such as Kabyoma Mashulano and Abdallah Feza Ibrahim, who had themselves been schooled by Magangala ga Bwile (c. 1870–1939)—perhaps the region's most famed royal bard of the twentieth century. At Kabale, Habibu especially excelled at playing the *enanga*.

Although he traveled to Nairobi in the mid-1950s and recorded some of his works, he remained at the royal court until Tanzania abolished traditional chiefdoms in the early 1960s. This change cost him and his fellow bards their royal patronage, forcing them to start earning a living through commercial performances in emerging colonial urban centers such as Bukoba. In 1961, he was among the traditional performers who helped usher in independence with shows in the then capital city of Dar es Salaam. Subsequently, Radio Tanzania recorded some of his performances in 1967. His traditional Haya panegyric song "Lukuuka," which he modified to praise then president Nyerere and vice president Kawawa, went on to become a fixture on Radio Tanzania. Afterwards, he was included in an artistic troupe that represented Tanzania at the Expo 70 festival in Japan in 1970. By the 1980s, his performances had been recorded by many researchers, traditional music enthusiasts, admirers, and music producers. He had two children with his first and estranged wife, Asina, and four children with his second wife, Janati Kokulamuka. As Selemani hardly received any royalties from his recordings, he died destitute on January 12, 1993.

Selemani's artistic success was due to his acute sensitivity to context (or awareness of his audience, time, and place of performance), his willingness to work hard to interest and retain the attention of the audience, and his constant expansion of his legendary repertoire that transcended epics from his own ethnic community.

Yet Selemani remained relatively unknown outside Tanzania because his music tradition was relatively obscure and, moreover, in the 1950s there were few Western or local scholars who had the linguistic, cultural, literary, or ethnomusicological background and training to analyze his work. Although scholars now have the facility to study his work and that of other *enanga* artists, this expertise has, unfortunately, become available when the *enanga* tradition is in decline and Selemani himself is gone. The *enanga* epics that Selemani and his fellow Kagera bards performed can be timeless, semihistorical, or fully historical, narrative or nonnarrative, and can be delivered in speech, recitative, or song mode. Most bards use the song presentation style.

Folklore

Tanzania has an immense wealth of varied and sophisticated folklore as each of its many ethnic communities has its own myths, music, oral history, jokes, legends, folk tales, riddles, proverbs, and sayings.[4] In this section, we mainly focus on stories, riddles, and proverbs as other aspects of the country's folklore are covered in Chapters 2 and 8.

Stories

In Tanzania, as in other African countries, storytelling plays an important role in educating, informing, and entertaining society, and more so children. Aside from imparting religious, moral, environmental, and historical lessons, stories also offer children and other members of society lessons in social roles and codes of conduct and help to build the intergenerational bonds that enable members of society to share experiences and ideas. Stories can also be used to teach desirable social straits such as intelligence, courage, and generosity as well as helping members of society to pick the community heroes that they would like to emulate.

The natural landscape is also well represented in Tanzanian stories. For instance, Mount Kilimanjaro features prominently in the folklore of the communities that inhabit its slopes. For example, the Chagga have a story that explains why the mountain's twin peaks, Kibo and Mawenzi, have a different appearance. As the story goes, Kibo and Mawenzi were once two equally beautiful women who had different predispositions in life. Kibo had a careful manner and used her food wisely while Mawenzi had a wasteful streak that kept her from saving food for lean times and was thus forced to depend on Kibo during times of famine. In one particular famine, Mawenzi came to Kibo for food for three days in a row. At first, Kibo obliged, but on the third day, with her generosity exhausted, she hit Mawenzi on the back with a cooking spoon. This led to Mawenzi's current rugged appearance. Moreover, this fight seems to have permanently severed relations between Kibo and Mawenzi, hence their current physical separation. The moral of the story is that community members should be hardworking, wise, and self-reliant.

In Tanzanian storytelling, local animals like elephants, hyenas, rabbits, and tortoises are often given various human qualities and used to foster or discourage certain social behaviors. Therefore, in many such tales, elephants, hyenas, rabbits, and tortoises are generally understood to represent strong, greedy, quick or shrewd, and slow people, respectively. As these imputations are scalable, they can be used to refer to individuals, families, clans, and even entire communities. Moreover, these and other animals can be used to metaphorically refer to individuals in everyday conversations. In other cases, they can be used as metaphors to warn, rebuke, describe, or praise individuals. For example, instead of telling a friend to be careful of a certain shrewd, greedy, or sneaky individual, you can tell him or her to be careful of that "rabbit," "hyena," or "snake."

Riddles

Riddles are a common language-art form in virtually all ethnic groups in Tanzania and elsewhere in Africa. A riddle is an ambiguous, puzzling, or uncertain statement with a hidden meaning that the audience is expected to uncover.[5] Riddles are used to educate, train, entertain, amuse, or socialize members of society, and more so children. Specifically, riddles transmit language and knowledge to children and help to develop their memory and other mental faculties, including their critical thinking, wit, observation, and deep reasoning skills. Moreover, they help to teach, explain, and interpret inexplicable social and natural phenomena. Among many Tanzanian groups such as the Chagga, riddles provide a socially acceptable way for dealing with social taboos and other sensitive subjects, and skillful riddling is highly respected.[6] Riddles can also be used to obscure conversations in certain social situations, such as in the presence of underage children.

Because the riddles of many Tanzanian communities usually deal with local natural, social, biological, cultural, and domestic phenomena, they can be quite puzzling to people from different sociocultural or environmental contexts. As riddles are often quite responsive to changing social and material conditions, the repertoire of many Tanzanian communities' riddles is constantly changing. Thus, there are now riddles that deal with modern items like cars. Conversely, there are riddles that have been discarded because they have become obsolete.

Tanzanian riddling is a participatory activity that uses the call-and-response style to keep both the riddler and the respondent on their toes. For example, in the Swahili language, a typical riddle unfolds as follows:

Riddler: *Kitendawili!* (Riddle! Or here comes a riddle!)

Respondent: *Tega!* (Go ahead and riddle!)

The riddler then riddles something like: *Nyumba yangu kuu ina mlango mdogo!* (My house is large but its door is small!)—*Jibu* (Answer): *Chupa* (bottle).

Then the respondent starts throwing back answers until he or she either solves the riddle or gives up and the riddler provides the answer. In many cases, riddling is a back-and-forth process in which the riddler seeks to stump the respondent while the respondent seeks to embarrass the riddler by solving his or her riddle in record time. Once a riddle is solved, the players trade places and the game goes on until one or both players gets tired and stop it.

Among the Haya people, riddling can involve opposing teams of children with a mother or grandmother serving as a referee. In other cases, the mother or grandmother can duel with individual children or teams of children and award symbolic trophies to the winning child or team. As is the case in many Tanzanian communities, to successfully solve Haya riddles, one needs good knowledge of, among other things, Haya domestic and social life, the human body and its attributes, and local animals, insects, plants, foods, and geography.

In most Tanzanian communities, riddling is age and gender specific. Thus, riddles such as those that refer to sex and other potentially embarrassing subjects are avoided when the riddling session involves a mixed audience of, say, children, respectable adults, or members of the opposite sex. As a rule, sexually explicit riddles are only told to one's friends or age mates of the same sex.

Proverbs

Like riddles, proverbs are widely used in Tanzania, and they have the same general purpose as riddles but at a higher level. So while riddles are mostly used to instruct young children, proverbs work better when dealing with older children and adults. In Tanzania and many other African countries, one's mastery of language, intellectual aptitude, and breadth of knowledge is best shown by skillful use of language including riddles, proverbs, and other complex sentence structures. As the Nigerian novelist Chinua Achebe has observed, in Nigeria and much of Africa, ". . . proverbs are the palm-oil with which words are eaten."[7]

Unlike riddles that mostly develop the human intellect, proverbs seek to evaluate and change human behavior. Although proverbs are simple and concrete expressions of truth based on local common sense or experience, they are often figurative as opposed to literal. Because their meaning is often hidden, one must exercise high-level thinking to understand them. Although some proverbs are universal, many are culture specific. They thus embody, teach, and help to preserve certain elements of the host culture, such as its age and gender roles, morality, appropriate behaviors, and the relative value of work and things. In transmitting desirable social traits, proverbs also play an important role in cultural preservation and in the promotion of social cohesion.

Proverbs also transmit knowledge, build language skills, and encourage critical thinking among members of society. Like riddles, proverbs can also be used to communicate sensitive information in certain social situations, such as when underage children are present. Although Tanzanian proverbs are usually disseminated orally, they are also beginning to be spread in print form in books and newspapers and are often printed on *khangas*, or the large aprons or shawls that are popular with Tanzanian women.

The most popular proverbs in Tanzania and much of East Africa are those of the Swahili language that serves as the national language of Tanzania and Kenya besides being the *lingua franca* (language of business) of Eastern Africa. Swahili proverbs are also widespread because they have long been written and translated into other languages, including English. In contrast, the proverbs of Tanzania's many other indigenous languages are disappearing rapidly with these languages' decreasing use. Hopefully, they will be preserved in print before they are completely lost.[8]

WRITTEN LITERATURE

Tanzania's literary scene is fairly poor because the country has a predominantly oral culture. Thus, the country lacks the lifelong reading culture that would support a thriving literary environment. Moreover, access to books is low because of their limited quantities, relatively high cost, and limited library and bookshop facilities. The prohibitive cost of books is in turn the result of high book-publishing costs and small markets that limit investment and innovation in the industry. Additionally, neighboring Kenya's larger publishing industry has long stifled the growth of its smaller Tanzanian counterpart. Therefore, to stay alive, many Tanzanian publishers focus on the production of books with a sure domestic market, such as textbooks.

Tanzania's bad literary situation is also exacerbated by the lack of writers and their low pay and social status. To make ends meet, many of the country's writers often leave the country, go into more lucrative careers, focus on writing textbooks, or target their books at more affluent readers, such as tourists, even though this often limits the readership of the books. The task of alleviating the country's current literary situation is likely to get more complicated with the advent of more dynamic and entertaining information media like the Internet.[9]

Yet the country's government, book publishers, and writers are working to turn things around by promoting lifelong reading and learning as key avenues to people's ability to eradicate personal poverty and to maintain high standards of living. To this end, industry players created the Book Development Council of Tanzania (BAMVITA) in 1999 to help coordinate their various reading initiatives including the annual National Book Week Festival. Moreover, BAMVITA seeks to provide adequate quantities of quality books to readers of all ages across the country—a goal that requires an exponential increase in the country's number of authors, bookshops, libraries and quantity and quality of published materials. In the long term, BAMVITA hopes to transform Tanzania into a knowledge society that can thrive in the current global information society.[10]

Indigenous-Language Literature: Swahili Literature

Indigenous-language literature is published in any of the native Tanzanian languages and not in colonial languages like English. Except for Swahili literature, the country has very little other indigenous-language literary works because the market for such books is quite small.[11] In most cases, the non-Swahili-language books that are in existence are those that are published by government presses for use in elementary school reading classes. Outside of these, the Christian Bible is about the only book that is widely published in many local languages, including Kimaasai, Kihaya, Kichagga, Kisukuma, and Kihehe.

The paucity of Tanzania's indigenous-language literature is due largely to Tanzania's 1966 decision to primarily promote Swahili as the main national language and medium of instruction in all primary schools at the expense of the country's many other indigenous languages.[12] This policy, together with the country's rapid urbanization, means that most of the country's indigenous languages have a bleak future given the rapid decline of young people who speak them. The following is a review of Tanzania's Swahili literature.

Unlike other indigenous languages in Tanzania, Swahili has a long history of published works that dates to the thirteenth century, though the oldest Swahili manuscript is Mwengo wa Athumani's 1728 *Utenzi wa Herekali* (The Epic of Herakleios) a chronicle of the seventh-century war between Emperor Herakleios and the Muslim Prophet Mohammad. Because of its long history as a spoken and written language, it has an extensive literature throughout the East African region. This literature has grown significantly since Swahili became one of Tanzania's national languages and medium of instruction for the lower school system as well as the main language of worship for the country's major religions.

Prior to the eighteenth century, Swahili writings used the Swahili-Arabic script. But from the eighteenth century to the 1930s, Swahili writings in East Africa were in three dialects: Kimvita (the dialect of Mombasa, Kenya), Kiamu (the dialect of Lamu, Kenya), and Kiunguja (the dialect of the island of Unguja or Zanzibar, Tanzania). Since the 1930s, the Kiunjuga dialect has become dominant because of its use in colonial and postcolonial Swahili standardization efforts. Thus, many of the Swahili books in the East African region now use this dialect.

Whereas much of the classical Swahili literature (1750s–1820s) came from the Kenya coast, most of the modern Swahili literature has been from Tanzania, more so since the adoption of its Kiunguja dialect as the basis of standard Swahili. Unlike the historical chronicles that dominated classical Swahili literature, modern Swahili literature has grown to include new genres and subgenres such as prose, fiction, and written drama/theatrical pieces. Initially, especially in the 1920s–1940s period, modern Swahili literature consisted mainly of Swahili renderings of indigenous and Arabic folklore as well as various European literary works such as Rider Haggard's *Allan Quatermain* and *King Solomon's Mines*. In the 1960s, such translations were to include Julius Nyerere's translation of Shakespeare's *Julius Caesar* and *Merchants of Venice* into Swahili.[13]

The first bona fide Swahili literary works from Tanzania are those of Sheikh Shaaban bin Robert, or Shaaban Robert (1909–1962), who wrote in the new Standard Swahili and is widely considered to be the father of modern

Swahili literature because he wrote many poems, novels, and essays in the 1940s, 1950s, and 1960s that are still popular today. Among his 20 books are the short fictional tale *Adili na nduguze* (Adili and His Brothers); his biographical works *Maisha Yangu* (My Life) and *Baada ya Miaka Hamsini* (After 50 Years); the social satirical tales of *Kufikirika* (The Imaginable), *Kusadikika* (The Believable), *Siku ya Watenzi Wote* (The Day of Reckoning), and *Utenzi wa Vita vya Uhuru* (The War of Freedom); and the posthumous volume of his first complete works, *Diwani ya Shaaban*. In his earlier works, especially in the social satirical works *Kufikirika* and *Kusadikika*, he uses highly symbolic language, visions of utopia, Western literary styles, and African traditions to address issues like the social changes that European colonialism brought to Tanzania. Whereas his biographical works, *Maisha Yangu* (My Life) and *Baada ya Miaka Hamsini* (After 50 Years), provide a window into the social changes that took place in his lifetime, *Utenzi wa Vita vya Uhuru* (The War of Freedom) documents Tanzania's struggle for independence.[14]

His writings are noted not only for their humanistic themes but also for their stylistic refinement and political activism, the latter being his intellectual contribution to Tanzania's liberation from German and British colonial rule. Although he worked alongside Nyerere in Tanzania's struggle for independence, his highly metaphorical writing helped him avoid arousing the anger of the colonial authorities. His superb Swahili language skills also enabled him to address enduring human injustices in Tanzania and elsewhere. His life philosophy is best shown in his autobiographical works *Maisha Yangu* (My Life) and *Baada ya Miaka Hamsini* (After 50 Years). The former covers themes from his early life and experiences under German colonial rule while the latter deals with his life under British colonial rule and the struggle for freedom and independence.[15]

Two other Swahili writers from the 1940–1960 period are Muhammed Saleh Farsy, who wrote the minor classic novel *Kurwa na Doto* (Kurwa and Doto), and Muhammed Said Abdulla of Zanzibar, the author of many detective stories, including *Mzimu wa Watu wa Kale* (Shrine of the Ancestors). Farsy and Abdulla's works were the precursor of contemporary Swahili fiction, and they focused on the social, economic, and political challenges of 1960s Tanzania and much of East Africa. The maturation of authentic Tanzanian Swahili fiction came with the publication of Faraji Katalambulla's crime detective story *Simu ya Kifo* (Phone Call of Death). Subsequently, Swahili publishing grew considerably.

While romance, detective fiction, and traditional tales continue to be the mainstay of Swahili literature, there are several novels and plays that deftly and elegantly examine East Africa's historical and contemporary social and political problems. Adam Shafi Adam's romance work, *Vuta N'kuvute* (Let's

Tangle), is based in Zanzibar and Tanga and is the love story of an Indian bride and a Swahili groom during the country's struggle for independence.

Swahili-language translations now also include works by African as well as Western writers. For instance, *Barua Ndefu Kama Hii* is Professor C. Maganga's translation of Mariama Ba's *So Long a Letter*, which details women's struggles in Senegal and many other African countries, including Tanzania. Other notable translations include Gabriel Ruhumbika's *Viumbe Waliolaaniwa* (a Swahili cotranslation of Frantz Fanon's *The Wretched of the Earth*) and *Afrika Inakwenda Kombo* (a Swahili translation of René Dumont's *False Start in Africa*).[16]

Besides Shabaan Robert, other acclaimed Swahili writers include the novelists Mohammed Said Abdalla, Said Ahmed Mohammed Khamis, Mohamed Suleiman Mohamed, Euphrase Kezilahabi, and Gabriel Ruhumbika, and the dramatists Ebrahim Hussein, May Materru Balisidya, and Penina O. Mlama Mhando. Before briefly reviewing these authors' works, it should be noted that few of Tanzania's authors are women because the society has traditionally valued and invested more in boys' education.

Muhammed Said Abdalla was born in Makunduchi, Zanzibar, on April 25, 1918, and he spent the rest of his life there. His Islamic cultural heritage features prominently in his work alongside Western traditions that he acquired from his formal missionary schooling, which lasted until 1938. After completing his studies, he worked as a colonial health inspector for 10 years before becoming a journalist and editor of a newspaper in Zanzibar in 1948. Between 1948 and 1958, he also worked as an assistant editor of other newspapers in Zanzibar including *Al Falaq*, *Al Mahda*, and *Afrika Kwetu* (Africa Our Home).

In 1958, he became editor of *Mkulima* (Farmer), the national agricultural magazine, from which he retired in 1968. His writing career started in 1957 when his story *Mzimu wa Watu wa Kale* (Shrine of the Ancestors; Kenya Literature Bureau, 1966) won first prize in the Swahili story-writing competition sponsored by the East African Literary Bureau in 1957–1958 and was subsequently published as a novel in 1966. This detective story was to be first in a series featuring detective Bwana (i.e., Mr.) Msa, a character loosely patterned on Sir Arthur Conan Doyle's Sherlock Holmes.

Although Abdalla's books generally pit the clever hero, Bwana Msa, against his superstitious and less informed adversaries, the plot becomes increasingly complex and sophisticated with time, and his legendary Swahili language skills more refined. As a result, many of his books are school texts that have been reprinted many times. Abdalla's books draw heavily on the cosmopolitan Zanzibari culture that consists of Arab, Indian, African, and European influences. His stories revolve around incest, illegitimacy, greed, revenge, and land conflicts. Aspects of his own family's experiences before and after the Zanzibar Revolution also feature in his books.[17]

Said Ahmed Mohammed Khamis was born in Zanzibar and studied linguistics, literature, education, art history, and development studies at the University of Dar es Salaam. After his masters degree in linguistics, he obtained a doctorate at the University of Leipzig, Germany, where he wrote a dissertation on Swahili dialects in Pemba. Upon his return to Zanzibar, he worked as a teacher, school director, teacher-training-college instructor, and as director of the Institute of Kiswahili and Foreign Languages. He is currently the head of the Department of African Language Literature at the University of Bayreuth, Germany. Although Mohamed is an accomplished novelist, playwright, and poet, he is better known for his novels.

A reputed socialist and skilled Swahili novelist, many of Mohamed's works focus on class exploitation and struggle. For instance, in *Kiza Katika Nuru* (Darkness in Light) he focuses on Tanzania's contemporary social and political realities, especially the ignorance, poverty, and misfortune of the masses and how these unfavorable conditions predispose the masses to exploitation by the political elite. Although he juxtaposes the opposite extremes of darkness (*kiza*) and light (*nuru*) in the novel and seems to suggest that the ignorance, poverty, and misfortune of the masses are overwhelming, he is nevertheless hopeful that one day light will triumph and that the masses will shake off their oppressive social condition or darkness. The novel also deals with the ideological split between the young and older generations of Tanzania. Similarly, *Utengano* deals with social exploitation in postrevolutionary Zanzibar and is a harsh evaluation of postrevolutionary politicians whose rhetoric of social idealism is corrupted by their urban and Western lifestyles that make them obstacles to the emergence of a society with more just class, generational, and gender relations.

Conversely, *Babu Alipofufuka* (When Grandfather Came Back to Life) is the story of "K," a degenerate public official who is haunted by the spirit of his grandfather on account of his indifferent and corrupt lifestyle. In the end, his lifestyle sets off a vicious cycle of poverty that eventually ensnares his children. "K" is common in the modern Tanzanian civil service, and in showing him the consequences of his lifestyle, Mohamed hoped that he and his ilk would mend their ways and save the future of their posterity.[18]

Mohamed Suleiman Mohamed is one of the most skilled Swahili novelists and is the author of *Kiu* (Thirst) and *Nyota Ya Rehema* (Rehema's Fortune), which won the 1973 Kenyatta Prize for Literature. *Kiu*, which is set in postrevolutionary Zanzibar, deals with the ruinous effects of an insatiable thirst for love and money and the frequently unfavorable place of women in the Islamic coastal Swahili culture of Zanzibar. Mohamed was born in Zanzibar in 1945, and his novels are so appreciated that they are required readings in many East African schools. He has also written a collection of short stories, *Kicheko cha Ushindi* (The Laughter of Victory).

Euphrase Kezilahabi was born on April 13, 1944, in the village of Namagando on Lake Victoria's Ukerewe Islands in northwest Tanzania and is a novelist, poet, and scholar. He completed primary and secondary education at a mission school near Lake Victoria before commencing his undergraduate studies at University College, Dar es Salaam, in 1970. In the mid-1970s he obtained a masters degree from the same university and a doctorate from the University of Wisconsin, USA, in the 1980s. He has worked as a high school teacher and a professor of African oral and written literature and creative writing at the University of Dar es Salaam, and is presently associate professor of African languages and literature at the University of Botswana.

While an undergraduate student at the University College, Dar es Salaam, Kezilahabi started writing his first novel, *Rosa Mistika* (Mysterious Rose), which deals primarily with gender issues. Since the 1970s, he has been one of the major contributors to contemporary Swahili literature and is in fact the founder of the new Swahili free-verse poetry that eschews the traditional rules of Swahili Arabic poetry. This style, which he pioneered with his publication of the poem *Vipanya* (Mouses), was birthed in controversy, with some traditional Swahili poets considering it to be unacceptable. The style is now widespread.

Kezilahabi's works deal with contemporary Tanzanian social issues such as gender relations (*Rosa Mistika*), postcolonial political developments and the betrayal of the Tanzanian citizenry by a greedy political elite (*Kaptula la Marx* [Marx's Shorts]; *Gamba la Nyoka* [The Skin of a Snake]), the effects of colonialism on individuals and society in general (*Kichwamaji* [Fool]), the role of the individual in society (*Dunia Uwanja wa Fujo* [The World Is a Field of Chaos]), the unsatisfactory implementation and outcomes of Nyerere's *Ujamaa* or African socialism policy (*Dunia Uwanja wa Fujo, Kaptula la Marx, Gamba la Nyoka*), and psychological issues such as alienation. Although much of the inspiration for Kezilahabi's works comes from his native Kikerewe language and the folklore of the Ukerewe Islands, he also draws on Western works, especially those of German existentialist philosophers like Friedrich Nietzsche (1844–1900) and Martin Heidegger (1899–1976). Existentialism considers individuals to be self-determining agents that are fully responsible for their choices.[19]

Gabriel Ruhumbika (1938–) was born in the Ukerewe Islands of Tanzania and got his bachelors' degree at Makerere University, Uganda (1964), and a doctorate in African literature from the University of Paris—Sorbonne in 1969. He has since taught literature at various universities and is currently a professor of comparative literature at the University of Georgia—Athens, USA. He initially started writing in English but switched to Swahili in order to reach as many Swahili speakers as possible. He has written a collection of stories. *Uwike Usiwike Kutakucha* (Whether the Cock Crows or Not It Dawns) is an illuminating portrayal of the failures of the *Uhuru* (independence) elite to deliver on their promises while the novel *Miradi Bubu ya Wazalendo* (Invisible Enterprises of the Patriots) is a social-economic history of Tanzania. His novel *Janga Sugu la Wazawa* (Everlasting Doom for the Children of the Land) deals with witchcraft in contemporary Tanzanian and African society. His only English novel is *Village in Uhuru* (independence). Written in the immediate postcolonial period, it examines the danger that ethnic royalty poses to national unity. Recognizing this challenge, Tanzania's founding president, Julius Nyerere, implemented a socialist system of government that largely succeeded in creating a national identity while avoiding the ethnic divisions that would have imperiled postcolonial Tanzania in ways witnessed in other African countries.[20]

Playwright Ebrahim Hussein was born in 1943 in Lindi in coastal southern Tanzania. His father was a businessman and Koran instructor. Hussein started writing plays while he was a theater arts student at University College, Dar es Salaam, in the 1966–1970 period. While there, he was exposed to and influenced by the works of various twentieth-century drama and theater practitioners, especially those of Bertolt Brecht, the German poet, playwright, and theater director who is famous for his combined theory and practice of epic or grand theater. After his undergraduate studies, he obtained a doctoral degree in theater from Humboldt University of Berlin in 1975, and in 1978 he became a professor of Theater and Arts at the University of Dar es Salaam.

Hussein is noted for adapting twentieth-century epic theater/drama narrative and performative techniques to his native Tanzanian/Swahili context, thereby creating authentic Tanzanian theater/drama; expanding the linguistic, stylistic, and intellectual caliber of Swahili drama and poetry; and being socially and historically relevant as well as transformative. Besides being highly philosophical, many of his works use sophisticated symbolic and metaphoric devices to depict historical and contemporary Tanzanian issues and events—an instructional technique that has enabled him to reach a broad national and international audience. His published plays include *Kinjeketile*, *Michezo Ya Kuigiza* (Theatrical Plays), *Alikiona* (He Got His Just Deserts), *Wakati Ukuta* (Time Is a Wall), *Mashetani* (Demons), *Jogoo Kijijini* (The Village Cock)*; Ngao ya Jadi* (The Shield of Tradition), *Arusi* (Wedding), *Jambo La Maana* (An Important Matter), and *Kwenye Ukingo Wa Thim* (At the Edge of Thim).

Although his works are significantly inspired by his rich Swahili culture, they deal with many Tanzanian issues, including the country's significant historical events such as the Maji Maji rebellion of 1905–1907 (*Kinjeketile*) and the Zanzibar Revolution of 1964 (*Mashetani*); the challenges of national integration (*Kinjeketile, Ngao ya Jadi*); rapid socioeconomic and cultural change and intergenerational conflict (*Wakati Ukuta*); social and class schisms (*Mashetani*); ethnic chauvinism, greed, and corruption (*Kwenye Ukingo Wa Thim*); the dashed dream of a better Tanzanian society (*Arusi*); and the role of oral literature in cultural and linguistic rejuvenation (*Jogoo Kijijini, Ngao ya Jadi*).[21]

The late May Materru Balisidya (?–1987) is one of the few women Swahili writers and playwrights to emerge from Tanzania. Her published works include the novel *Shida* (Hardships), the children's book *Tujifunze Kusoma* (Let's Learn to Read), and *Ayubu* (Job). Her works are renowned for their contribution to Swahili structure and content, social activism, and Tanzania's children's literature. In the novel *Shida*, she examines the country's widening social gap between the leaders and the masses following the 1967 Arusha declaration that launched Tanzania on a socialist path that was supposed to lessen the social gaps created by the country's colonial rulers. She pursues this theme further in her coauthored play *Ayubu*, which portrays the tribulations and exploitation of the masses by Tanzania's political elite.[22]

Penina O. Mulama Mhando was born in 1948 and is one of the country's few female Swahili playwrights of the late twentieth century. She studied education and theater at the University of Dar es Salaam, Tanzania, and later became a faculty member in the university's Department of Theatre Arts. Her plays include *Hatia* (Guilt), *Tambueni Haki Zetu* (Recognize Our Rights), *Heshima Yangu* (My Honor), *Pambo* (Decoration), *Talaka Si Mke Wangu* (I Divorce You), *Nguzo Mama* (Mother Is the Main Pillar), *Harakati za Ukombozi* (Liberation Struggles), and *Lina Ubani* (There Is an Antidote for Rot). Using brilliant characterizations and contemporary standard Swahili, Mhando's plays explore a variety of contemporary social problems in Tanzania, such as the effects of divorce (*Talaka Si Mke Wangu*), social and political hypocrisy (*Heshima Yangu, Harakati za Ukombozi*), women's rights and liberation (*Tambueni Haki Zetu, Nguzo Mama*), the country's political liberation and aftermath, (*Harakati za Ukombozi, Lina Ubani, Nguzo Mama*), Nyerere's socialist experiment (*Ujamaa*), and the country's response to modernization and Westernization. Besides wishing to reach the widest possible audience in Tanzania, Mhando's literary works demonstrate that Swahili and other African languages can be mediums of outstanding literary creations and are a response to colonial and postcolonial assertions to the contrary. Mhando's work has won her the Shabaan Robert Writers Award (1999) and the Zeze Award, or Tanzania's National Culture Award (2000).

In addition to her literary accomplishments, Mhando was one of the pioneers of the theater-for-development movement in Tanzania. This theatrical genre allows communities to use art to educate themselves about various aspects of social and economic development. Her works in this genre focus on issues such as women rights and social and economic justice.[23]

Tanzania has also produced many notable Swahili short story writers, including Mohamed Suleiman Mohamed, Saad A. Yahya, and Said Ahmed Mohamed, whose work has been featured in various media outlets and short story collections.[24] Tanzania's other, less well-known ones include Farouk Topan (whose published plays include *Mfalme Juha* [King Juha], *Aliyeonja Pepo* [He Who Tasted the Wind]; and *Siri* [Secret]); the late John Rutayisingwa (*Papa La Mji, Na Hadithi Nyingine* [City Shark and Other Stories]; *Ngumi Ukutani* [Fist on the Wall]), James H. Bwana (*Kama Ningeweza Kupaa* [If I Could Fly], *Mganga Pazi* [The Medicineman]), and Katama Mkangi (*Walenisi* [The Damned], 1995).

Literature in English

Tanzania's English literature is much less developed compared to its Swahili counterpart. This is for many complex reasons. To begin with, Tanzania's colonial and postcolonial governments have for a long time encouraged literacy in local languages such as Swahili, and as a result, much of the country's literature is in Swahili. Moreover, in 1966, the government of Tanzania chose Swahili as its main national language and subsequently promoted it vigorously. At the same time, the government nationalized the economy, thereby choking the advertising base that had before then supported the country's English publications. In addition, in the early 1970s, when the country faced a serious paper shortage, the government put emphasis on the publication of government documents, school textbooks, and Swahili literature. As it was virtually impossible to get published in English in Tanzania by the mid-1970s, the language lost its prestige and market appeal, and many of the authors who had initially published their works in English switched to Swahili.

Around the same time, many scholars in Tanzania and elsewhere in Africa started questioning the place of European languages like English in postcolonial Africa. Many sought to end the dominance of the former colonial languages because they were hindering national development and were unsuitable mediums for the transmission of African culture as most Africans did not speak them. Thus, many leading African authors of the 1960s and 1970s argued for the abandonment of European languages in favor of local languages. Whereas this call was largely ignored in most African countries, Tanzania's founding president, Julius Nyerere, supported and implemented it, thereby further stifling the development of English in the country.[25]

While Tanzania's weak English literary scene is unlikely to change any time soon, a few Tanzanian authors have produced some English works. In the colonial era, Martin Kayamba (1891–1940) posthumously published two books in 1948: *An African in Europe*, on his travels in England in the 1930s, and *African Problems*, on the challenges of developing Africa. In 1968, Peter Palangyo (1939–1993) published *Dying in the Sun*, Tanzania's first postcolonial English novel. In the book, which mainly deals with inter-generational social conflicts, alienation, and love, Ntanya is torn between his past and future and is unsure if he should return to his familiar precolonial traditional cultural way of life or embrace the new reality brought by the white man. Ntanya resolves to regroup and face the new reality. The story is an allegory of where many African countries found themselves in the immediate postcolonial period.

In 1969, Gabriel Ruhumbika, in his novel *Village in Uhuru* [independence], explored the challenges of forging a unified nation out of Tanzania's many ethnic and regional groupings. In 1974, Barnabas Katigula used his novel *Groping in the Dark* to explore individual and social issues within the context of Ujamaa (socialism). In the same year, Ismail Mbise in *Blood on Our Land* used the 1951 colonial expulsion of the Meru people from their ancestral land to allegorize continued disinheritance in postcolonial Tanzania and other African countries.

In 1977, William E. Mkufya explored Dar es Salaam's corrupting urban sex life in his novel *The Wicked Walk*, a theme that it shares with some contemporaneous Swahili works. In his second novel, *The Dilemma*, Mkufya explores the tragic married life of an older man and an adulterous younger woman who is forced to marry the older man for economic reasons, a not-too-uncommon occurrence in modern Tanzania and many other African countries.

In the late 1970s, Prince Kagwema (a pseudonym of Osija Mwambungu, 1931–) also started going against the norm by openly writing about love, sex, and politics in Tanzania. This countercultural move soon led to the temporary ban of *Veneer of Love* (1975), his first novel in this genre. Although this and his other books—*Married Love Is a Plan: A Novel about How To Be Happy though Married*, *Chausiku's Dozen*, and *Society in the Dock*—remain controversial, they reveal a society that is increasingly open. Some see his books as valuable sources of love and sex education to the many Tanzanians who are increasingly unable to access it through the country's declining traditional initiation systems.

The 1970s also witnessed the emergence of instructional children's literature in English, including Martha Mvungi's *Three Solid Stones* (1975), a collection of Hehe and Bena folktales. Her *Yasin in Trouble* (1990) is a story about a truant school boy who gets in trouble because of his bad behavior.

Currently, Abdulrazak Gurnah (1948–) is probably Tanzania's most accomplished English writer. He was born in Zanzibar but has spent much of his life in the United Kingdom. He has written nine books on the themes of identity and displacement in the context of slavery and colonialism: *Memory of Departure* (1987), *Pilgrim's Way* (1988), *Dottie* (1990), *Paradise* (1994), *Admiring Silence* (1996), *By the Sea* (2001), *Desertion* (2005), *The Last Gift* (2011), and a collection of short stories titled *My Mother Lived on a Farm in Africa* (2006). He has also edited *Essays in African Literature: A Re-evaluation* (1993).

Since 1997, Severin N. Ndunguru (1932–) has written a number of Tanzanian English literary works including *A Wreath for Father Mayer*, *Divine Providence*, *Spared*, and *The Lion of Yola*. His works deal with contemporary Tanzanian issues (e.g., disease and religion) as well as being popular fiction readers and crime thrillers that commingle love, money, crime, and international ransom kidnappings. His works, which are all published by a domestic publisher, probably mark the resurgence of English literature in Tanzania as the country comes to grips with the English-dominated global society. A. M. Hokororo's recent work *Salma's Spirit* also belongs in this genre.

Overall, the volume of Tanzania's English literature is low but is likely to grow in the future given that the language has become the global *lingua franca*, the country's mid-1980s abandonment of socialism and embrace of capitalism, the Internet (an English-dominated medium), and media liberalization that has seen the emergence of English-language media in the country. It is also instructive that the country's younger generation is enthusiastically embracing a global youth culture that is primarily transmitted in English.

MEDIA

At the moment, Tanzania has over 400 newspapers and magazines and over 10 radio and TV stations, many of which are concentrated in the major urban areas of Dar es Salaam, Arusha, Mbeya, Mwanza, Morogoro, and Zanzibar. Most of the country's print and broadcast media is in the Swahili language, though there are also many English media outlets.[26] The distribution of media in Tanzania is influenced by many factors, including government regulation, culture, literacy, income levels, transport facilities, and access to televisions and radios.

Media regulation in Tanzania is not uniform because the country is a federation of the mainland (Tanganyika) and the semiautonomous Zanzibar archipelago. The most restrictive media laws are in Zanzibar, where the government keeps a close eye on the press in a bid to preserve the archipelago's Islamic culture. Accordingly, the Zanzibar press is regulated by laws that provide for state monitoring of the private press, the compulsory licensing of journalists, and their responsibility to help promote national policies and maintain social harmony.[27] The Zanzibar government also regulates the island's media and seeks to dominate its airwaves through the publicly owned Television Zanzibar (TVZ) and *Sauti ya* [Voice of] Tanzania Zanzibar radio. However, the island's private broadcasters dominate its radio and television airwaves.[28]

On the Tanzania mainland, the press is regulated by three main pieces of legislation: the National Security Act of 1970 that prohibits the unauthorized release of classified information, the Newspaper Act of 1976, and the Broadcasting Services Act of 1993. While the Newspaper Act of 1976 (along with the Newspaper Regulations of 1977) governs the operation of print media, the Broadcasting Services Act of 1993 regulates the broadcast media on the mainland.[29] The Tanzania Communications Regulatory Authority (TCRA) has since 2003 spearheaded the government's everyday oversight of the broadcast media.

The foregoing laws give the government of Tanzania a lot of discretionary power over the press, power that it has used on occasion to ban publications and harass journalists perceived to be a threat to society and the government. Although such actions often force Tanzanian journalists to censor themselves, they frequently get around these laws by facilitating the publication of sensitive material in the neighboring countries, especially Kenya and Uganda.[30]

Overall, Tanzania has a reasonable degree of press freedom, and although it could be higher, there are many other factors that influence the country's press situation. These include the recent liberalization of the country's media, the overcommercialization of these outlets, high levels of corruption, low morale among journalists due to poor and irregular pay, limited editorial freedom, laws that hinder the growth of broadcast media by limiting many of them to portions of the country, the use of only Swahili and English, and the country's unbalanced antidefamation laws that are unfair to the press.[31]

Another challenge facing the Tanzanian media is the lack of a union to protect and fight for journalists' interests. Although Tanzanian journalists began uniting in the 1960s with the formation of the Tanzania Journalists Association (TAJA) in 1966, they have not been able to form a union because such entities have been outlawed until recently. Moreover, the journalists are scattered across 17 or so parochial interest associations including the Media Council of Tanzania (MCT), an independent, voluntary, and nonstatutory body that seeks to maintain the freedom of the media in the country by creating an environment that enables the development of a free, strong, responsible, effective, and ethical media that can contribute to a more democratic and just society in the country.[32]

Newspapers and Magazines

The country's major English daily newspapers include the *Daily News* (Dar es Salaam), *The Guardian* (Dar es Salaam), *The African* (Dar es Salaam), and *The Democrat* (Dar es Salaam).[33] The *Daily News* is Tanzania's oldest and largest English daily newspaper, having been continuously published since 1930. It has an estimated circulation of 50,000; has full coverage of local news, business and finance, news analysis, varied columnists, editorials, features, and sports; and has a well-developed advertising and reader-response section. All of these papers have separately branded weekend editions.

The weekly papers include the *Arusha Times* (Arusha), *Business Times* (Dar es Salaam), and the *EastAfrican* (Nairobi, Kenya). Both the mainland and Zanzibar governments have publications that they use to disseminate official announcements. The *Arusha Times* is based in the northern Tanzanian city of Arusha. The paper covers local and regional news, crime, sports, and weather and publishes feature stories and letters to the editor. Because Arusha is a major international conference and business center, it is one of the few Tanzanian cities with a reasonable population of English-media consumers. The *EastAfrican* is a business-oriented regional weekly newspaper that is published in Nairobi, Kenya, by the Nation Media group.

Because Tanzanians are more proficient speakers of Swahili than English, there are many more Swahili daily and weekly newspapers in the country. The country's major English newspapers also have their own Swahili editions. In addition to these newspapers, the country has a host of other periodicals like *The African Review* (Dar es Salaam), which is a semiannual journal of African politics, development, and international affairs published by the University of Dar es Salaam's Political Science Department.

Online News

There are a number of online news sources in Tanzania. The vast majority of these are online versions of the major English and Swahili newspapers. Examples include the IPP Media Group's www.ippmedia.com and AllAfrica.com—Tanzania, which features current news on Africa from many global and continental sources.

In December 2011, Tanzania had nearly 5 million Internet users, or 11 percent of its population of close to 42 million people. Despite the country's low proportion of Internet users, it is noteworthy that this population has grown exponentially since 2000, when the country had only 115,000 Internet users.[34] Thus, online news sources are likely to continue growing in tandem with growing computer literacy and access and Internet use.

Radio and Television

In the late 2000s, Tanzania had close to 47 radio stations and 29 TV stations, and most of these were privately owned. Only a few of them had national coverage. One of the unique aspects of Tanzania's broadcast media is that they are required by law to broadcast only in either Swahili or English in order to help foster a united Tanzanian nation. Major international TV and radio broadcasters like CNN and BBC are also available and have a wide following among the local elite and expatriate communities.[35]

Radio

Because Tanzania is an oral society, radio is, perhaps, the most important mass media in the country. There are an estimated 8.8 million radio receivers in the country—that is, 243 radios per 1,000 people.[36]

The government of Tanzania owns the country's oldest radio station, which was established by the British colonial government in 1951. Initially, public radio broadcasting in the country served only the city of Dar es Salaam and was thus known as *Sauti ya Dar es Salaam* (The Voice of Dar es Salaam). Subsequently, the station became national with the installation of more powerful transmitters in 1955 and was renamed *Sauti ya Tanganyika* (The Voice of Tanganyika). Prior to 1956, *Sauti ya Tanganyika* was a low-key operation in the colonial government's Department of Social Development. But in order to make it more effective, the colonial government transformed it into a semiautonomous public broadcasting corporation like the BBC and renamed it Tanganyika Broadcasting Corporation (TBC). In 1965, following Tanganyika's independence in 1961 and federation with Zanzibar in 1964, the newly formed United Republic of Tanzania abolished the TBC and created a civil broadcasting service known as *Radio Tanzania Dar es Salaam* (RTD). As a civil-service operation, RTD was expected to live by the rules and regulations of the civil service, the most notable being the promotion of government policy. To cope with increasing competition following the country's media liberalization in 1993, RTD and the national television broadcaster, TVT, merged to form the public Tanzania Broadcasting Services (*Taasisi ya Utangazaji*) in 2002.[37]

In January 1994, Radio One became Tanzania's first operational private radio station since the liberalization of the country's airwaves in 1993. Since then, the country has witnessed rapid growth in the radio broadcasting sector, with many of the country's nearly 47 radio stations being private. Most of them are required to operate on the FM frequency, which at best gives them a regional audience. A few private radio stations are allowed to operate on the medium wave (MW) frequency, which can more easily cover the entire country. Besides their restriction to the FM bandwidth, many of the stations are concentrated in the country's most lucrative urban markets. A few of the country's radio stations, notably Radio One, Radio Clouds Entertainment, and Radio Free Africa, are on satellite and can be received throughout the country and beyond with the right equipment—which few Tanzanians can afford.

The country's radio stations mainly serve a commercial, entertainment, religious, political, or educational purpose. While most of the private radio stations are commercial, there are a few noncommercial ones that are owned by various religious organizations. The country's main political party, *Chama Cha Mapinduzi* (The Revolutionary Party, or CCM) has significant invest-ment in one radio station while the St. Augustine University's Radio SAUT is a good example of an educational radio station. The Tanzanian state is also a major broadcaster through its RTD, the FM *Parapanda Radio Tanzania* (PRT) that seeks to attract younger listeners, and Zanzibar's *Sauti ya Tanzania Zanzibar* (Voice of Tanzania and Zanzibar). IPP Media is one of Tanzania's largest commercial radio broadcasters while the Catholic Church is a major player in the religious broadcasting category through its Radio Maria Tanzania, which is available in many areas of the country, including Ruvuma/Songea, Kingo, and Mbeya. Some of Tanzania's radio stations, notably Radio One, are also available on the Internet, though these are lim-ited by the country's low Internet bandwidth and access to computers. Most of the country's commercial radio stations serve younger audiences and play a lot of local and foreign music.

Television

Television came to Tanzania (mainland) fairly recently as part of the coun-try's media liberation wave of the early 1990s. Thus, the number of television sets in the country is relatively low and is estimated at 3 TVs per 1,000 peo-ple.[38] Not only is the proportion of Tanzanians with access to television low but most of those who have TVs are concentrated in the cities and the few rural areas that are connected to the electric grid.

The country's late entry into the television age is due to the socialist poli-cies that its government pursued from independence until the mid-1980s. In particular, Tanzania's founding president Nyerere saw television as a waste of money that would add nothing to the country's quest for self-reliance and as a capitalist tool that could corrupt the country's African culture. Never-theless, soon after the country liberalized its airwaves in 1993, Tanzania got its first TV station (a private one) in 1994. Six more private stations were launched before the government launched its TV Tanzania (or *Televisheni ya Taifa* [TVT]) in 2000. In 2002, TVT became part of the government's Tanzania Broadcasting Services agency. It was for a while the only TV station that was allowed to broadcast nationally before the law was amended to allow more stations to have national coverage.

One of the most impressive accomplishments of TVT is that most of its programming is local despite its limited pool of professional producers, equipment, and budget. Similarly, many of the country's private TV stations have significant local programming in addition to their foreign content. Local music videos are some of the country's popular TV programs.

There are slightly over 30 television station operators in Tanzania, the vast majority of which are private and are based in the country's major cities of Dar es Salaam and Arusha. About half of these are major TV stations. Cable television stations have been operational in some 11 major urban areas in mainland Tanzania since the advent of the country's television age in 1994. Some of the country's TV stations are communal and are operated by municipal and district councils that rebroadcast programming from the more established TV stations, though they are also increasingly producing their own programming as they acquire production capacity.

Aside from TVT, some of Tanzania's other influential TV stations include the IPP Media Group's Independent Television (ITV) that operates three TV channels, the Africa Media Group's Dar es Salaam Television (DTV), Star TV, and the state-run Television Zanzibar.

Tanzania also has a growing Internet TV broadcasting presence. Initially, many of the pioneers of this type of broadcasting, like Pastor Faustin Munishi's GospelTV, had their own web portals. While some of these broadcasters continue to operate their own online TV portals, others use content aggregators like African TV 24 (http://www.africantv24.com/), or more commonly have broadcast channels on YouTube (http://www.youtube. com). Aside from its Christian messages, GospelTV has on occasion broadcast stinging political commentaries on the government of Tanzania, the dominant Revolutionary Party, and the country's 1968–1985 socialist past. For this reason, the Tanzanian government has banned some of Munishi's tapes, and he has in the last decade been living in exile in Kenya.[39]

FILM

Feature Film

While film entertainment came to colonial Tanzania in the 1920s, film making did not start until the late 1930s. Specifically, film making started in 1939 when the British colonial government formed the Colonial Film Unit (CFU) and started using it to disseminate colonial propaganda and various instructional materials on realizing that the medium was able to transcend the communication difficulties posed by the country's then low literacy levels.[40]

Some of the films made by the CFU in Tanzania include *Gumu* (Hard; i.e., city life is hard), which was meant to discourage young Tanzanians from migrating to the cities; *Childbirth Today*, a public health documentary; *Cattle Thieves*, a film that was meant to discourage cattle rustling among the Maasai and other cattle-herding communities; and a World War II entertainment film for African soldiers called *Fumanzi*, which depicted an illicit lover who, on being discovered, was chased, caught, and punished by the husband. The movie was meant to comfort African soldiers who had to endure long separations from their wives during war.

When the CFU closed in 1955, it was succeeded in the late 1950s by South Africa's African Film Production Company (AFP), which largely made 16 mm Swahili feature films using local actors on themes similar to those of the CFU. Thus, films like *Chalo Amerudi* (Chalo Has Returned), *Muhogo Mchungu* (Bitter Cassava), and *Meli Inakwenda* (The Ship Is Sailing Away), all of which starred Rashid Mfaume Kawawa, sought to discourage young Africans from moving to the country's colonial cities because of their many hardships (*Muhogo Mchungu*), their ability to corrupt young people and cost them their families (*Chalo Amerudi*), and their ability to cost young girls marriage opportunities (*Meli Inakwenda*). Naturally, none of these movies blamed African rural-urban migration on the economic dislocations of the colonial economy.

Most of the movies imported into the country in the 1920s for the commercial cinema system for urban white, Asian, and African elite audiences came from the United States, Britain, India, and Arabia, and their numbers increased significantly with the addition of sound to movies in the 1930s. By the 1940s, most of the U.S. films screened in Tanzania were mainly sourced in South Africa and later Nairobi, Kenya. Nevertheless, Indian movies were more popular than those from the United States because most of the moviegoers were Indians. In all cases, foreign movies had to be cleared by government censors before being shown in Tanzania. By independence, Tanzania thus had two movie distribution channels: a mobile rural African-oriented cinema-van system that showed 16 mm instructional and entertainment films and the commercial cinema system for urban white, Asian, and African elite audiences.

Soon after Tanzania became independent, first president Nyerere started aligning his country with the socialist block. Before long he sought to rid Tanzania of Western colonial vestiges, including films. Moreover he did not invest much in the industry though he created the Tanzania Film Corporation (TFC) in 1968 to control foreign film importation and distribution. In 1971, TFC acquired film production capacity for the purpose of jumpstarting the local film production industry as well as producing documentaries for the government. In the end, TFC failed to live up to its mandate and was eventually closed in 1990. By then it had only produced a few movies, including the largely pro-government-policy movie *Fimbo ya Mnyonge* (A Poor Man's Salvation). It also coproduced some titles, including *Wimbo wa Mianzi* (Song of Bamboo, 1983, which satirized the failures of foreign development expertise) and *Arusi ya Mariamu* (Mariamu's Wedding, 1983, codirected by American Ron Mulvihill and the late Nangayoma Ng'oge, which depicted the futility of running from certain African traditions and the superiority of traditional African healing systems over their Western counterparts); and *Mama Tumaini* (1986, codirected by Martin Mhando and Sigve Endresen, which depicts the relationship between Norwegian aid workers and their Tanzanian counterparts).

Martin Mhando, who is now one of Tanzania's most accomplished feature-film directors and is the director of the Zanzibar International Film Festival (ZIFF), later helped produce *Maangamizi* (The Ancient One, 2001, codirected by Martin Mhando and Ron Mulvihill), the first full-length Swahili film from Tanzania and one that has won many international awards.[41] *Hatari* (Danger, 1962) and *Out of Africa* (1985) are other feature films that were either partially or entirely shot in Tanzania. Of these two, *Hatari* (1962) is perhaps the more unusual because its script was written after the fact to suit preexisting footage from Africa.

After Tanzania liberalized its economy in 1985, the country's film industry started to grow thanks to the combination of many factors, including regulatory and economic reform, technological change, and media reform, that have increased the domestic market for films. Among the major postliberalization film developments is the 1997 formation of ZIFF, which has since become Tanzania's and much of East Africa's most important venue for film debuts.[42] In recent years, Tanzania has showcased a number of films at ZIFF, including *Fimbo Ya Baba* (A Father's Rod, 2006, directed by Omar Chande), which shows the downside of greedy parents who sacrifice their children's future and well-being for personal gain; *Hali Halisi* (The Real Situation, 2007), which shows how to courageously deal with HIV/AIDS in the family; and *Kolelo* (2007, directed by Hammie Rajab), which is a folkloric village story about the Luguru ethnic community's ancestral spirit world.

Despite its long history in Tanzania, the feature film has failed to take off there because of prohibitive production costs, a shortage of professional filmmakers, and poor film distribution and lack of theater facilities. Most important, however, is that feature film making and viewing have never really caught on in Tanzania because they have been targeted at Western audiences. Thus, they have never been relevant to the majority of Tanzanians. This is a niche that has now been filled by video films.

Video Film

Unlike feature films, video films are produced by amateur video film-makers. The genre arose when Nigeria's Nollywood movies reached Tanzania in the late 1990s and became wildly popular because most Tanzanians identified with the environment, issues, and traditions in the movies as well as with the appearances of the actors, who, like them, are largely black Africans. Moreover, the lifestyles, values, institutions, myths, and physical environment of the Nigerian movies closely matched those of the typical Tanzanian. Unlike the Hollywood movies that were mostly accessible through the country's few theaters, the Nollywood movies were also readily available on cheap CDs and DVDs.

The success of the Nigerian movies soon caught the attention of local entrepreneurs, and when George Otieno's *Girlfriend* (2002) became a huge commercial success, Tanzania's "Nollywood" was born. It has since gone on to be the second most productive (after Nigeria's Nollywood) on the African continent. By 2010, it was reportedly making 100 films a month. Video films can be shot in as little as one day and be released straight to video DVDs or CDs, which are then sold cheaply on the country's city streets for home use. Some of these video films are also accessible through YouTube and other Internet sites, mobile video trucks, and cheap countrywide pay-per-video halls.[43]

Participatory or Grassroots Cinema

The use of film to depict the daily lives of ordinary citizens is one of the most exciting developments in Tanzania's film industry. Many of the films in this genre feature participatory production methods, with the subjects often playing an important role in writing, filming, and producing the films. Such films have been produced in Tanzania since the 1970s and are designed to more accurately represent their subjects; generate ideas and initiate grassroots discussion about various community issues; give a voice to people who are seldom heard; promote communication among communities whose interaction is often limited by diverse linguistic, social, economic, and literacy levels; raise the living standards of marginalized groups, and disseminate film-production skills to communities that lack access to them.[44]

Some examples of participatory film production in Tanzania are the following:

- *Lost Forgiveness* (2007) is a group of four short films on the lives of Tanzania's street children and is an attempt to use film to teach them skills that can help them lead productive lives.[45]

- *Four Stories* (2007) shows the working lives of four deaf young people from the Neema (Grace) Crafts of Iringa, an Anglican Church organization that provides jobs to deaf and disabled people in Iringa.
- *Kiota* (2007) shows the exploitation of Tanzania's domestic workers, or "house girls," and was written and filmed by six such girls at their rehabilitative Kiwohede Centre in Iringa.

Documentaries

As noted earlier, documentaries have been produced in Tanzania since the colonial era. However, this genre has really taken off since the country liberalized its airwaves in the 1990s. With the proliferation of television stations, local entrepreneurs have since the 1990s been making television documentaries on the country's social, political, economic, and educational conditions. As Tanzania's television continues to grow, its documentary industry will also grow in tandem.

One of the most active producers of this genre of film is Abantu Visions, whose recent documentaries include *Mada Moto* (Hot Issues), a 47-part, 40-minute series on the burning issues of Tanzania's 1995 elections.[46] Many foreign media companies are also involved in the production of documentaries in the country. Examples of these include the following:

- *Darwin's Nightmare* (2005) shows how European weapons exports fuel Africa's civil wars and how the continent further loses by trading its natural resources (e.g., fish) for weapons.[47]
- *Diary of a Maasai Village* (1985) is a five-part BBC series on the daily life of the Maasai ethnic community that straddles the Tanzania-Kenya border.[48]
- *Tree of Iron* (1988) explores the over-2,000-year-old iron production history of the Haya people of the western shores of Lake Victoria.[49]
- *Women's Olamal: The Organization of a Maasai Fertility Ceremony* (1985) depicts the traditional Maasai *Olamal* ceremony that is designed to increase women's fertility.[50]
- *Remembering the Cow* (2006) explores the challenges (e.g., drought) of maintaining the traditional nomadic cattle-herding lifestyle of the Maasai community of northern Tanzania.[51]
- *Falling Mangoes* (2004) challenges Tanzanian parents and the nation at large to prioritize and take better care of their children.[52]

Reality TV Shows and Commercials

Tanzania is a growing production site for reality TV shows and commercials. For instance, part of the January 2004 episode of *The Amazing Race* by the United States' CBS Television and World Race Productions was shot in Tanzania.[53] The country's breathtaking scenery has also provided a back-drop for the production of various television commercials including some by international companies such as Renault, Nissan, Qantas Airlines, and Siemens.

NOTES

1. Lonard S. Klein (ed.), *African Literatures in the 20th Century: A Guide* (New York: Ungar, 1986), 218.

2. M. M. Mulokozi, "The Last of the Bards: The Story of Habibu Selemani of Tanzania (c. 1929–93)," *Research in African Literatures* 28, nos. 1 and 2 (1997): 159–72.

3. M. M. Mulokozi, "The Last of the Bards," 159–72.

4. University of Pennsylvania African Studies Department, "An Overview of Tanzanian Folklore," *Indigenous People of Africa and America* (IPOAA) Magazine, http://ipoaa.com/tanzania_folklore.htm, accessed November 20, 2006.

5. Johnson M. Ishengoma, "African Oral Traditions: Riddles among the Haya of Northwestern Tanzania," *International Review of Education* 51 (2005), 139–53.

6. University of Pennsylvania African Studies Department, "An Overview of Tanzanian Folklore."

7. Chinua Achebe, *Things Fall Apart* (London: Heinemann, 1958), 10.

8. Afriprov, "African Proverbs, Sayings and Stories," 1998–2007, http://www.afriprov.org/, accessed November 20, 2006.

9. Lars P. Christensen, Cecilia Magnusson Ljungman, John Robert Ikoja Odongo, Maira Sow, and Bodil Folke Frederiksen, *Strengthening Publishing in Africa: An Evaluation of APNET*, Sida Evaluation 99/2 (Stockholm: Sida, 1998); Michael Haonga, "Lack of Reading Culture put in Spotlight," *Guardian*, September 6, 2006, http://www.ippmedia.com/, accessed September 6, 2006.

10. BAMVITA, "Home," 2006, http://www.bamvita.or.tz/default.asp, accessed July 16, 2012.

11. Personal communication with Ms. Frida Lyaruu, executive secretary, Book Development Council of Tanzania (BAMVITA) on October 10, 2007.

12. Laura Edmondson, *Performance and Politics in Tanzania: The Nation on Stage* (Bloomington and Indianapolis, IN: IUP, 2007), 67; Lonard S. Klein, *African Literatures*, 214.

13. Carol Eastman, "The Emergence of an African Regional Literature: Swahili," *African Studies Review* 20, no. 2 (September 1977), 53–61; Alamin Mazrui, *Swahili beyond the Boundaries: Literature, Language, and Identity* (Athens: Ohio University Press, 2007), 16.

14. Angelica Baschiera, "Shaban Robert Profile," *Africa Database*, 2003, http://people.africadatabase.org/en/profile/13163.html#profile129743; Alamin Mazrui, "*Swahili Beyond . . .*," 26–27.

15. Carol Eastman, "The Emergence of an African . . . ," 53–61.

16. Gabriel Ruhumbika, "Curriculum Vitae: Dr. Gabriel Ruhumbika," http://www.cmlt.uga.edu/sites/default/files/CVs/Ruhumbika,%20Gabriel%20CV.pdf, accessed September 30, 2012.

17. Angelica Baschiera, "Muhammed Said Abdulla: Profiles," *Africa Database*, 2003, http://people.africadatabase.org/en/profile/16529.html#profile129332, accessed November 20, 2006.

18. Alamin Mazrui, *Swahili beyond the Boundaries*, 29–30; Pompea Nocera, "An Interpretation of Said Ahmed Mohamed's Novel Kiza Katika Nuru and Some Aspects of Translation," *Swahili Forum* 12 (2005): 63–80; Flavia Aiello Traore, "Translating a Swahili Novel into 'Kizungu': Separazione, the Italian Edition of Said Ahmed Mohamed's Utengano," *Swahili Forum* 12 (2005): 99–107; UNESCO, "Mohamed, Said Ahmed: Babu alipofufuka ('When Grandfather Came to Life Again') (Tanzania)," *Literature & Translation*, http://www.litprom.de/littrans/detail.php?id=45, accessed July 16, 2012.

19. Angelica Baschiera "Euphrase Kezilahabi: Profiles (Tanzanian writer & Academic)," *Africa Database*, 2003, http://people.africadatabase.org/en/profile/4783.html#profile117374; Martin Banham, Errol Hill, George Woodyard, and Olu Obafemi (eds.), *The Cambridge Guide to African and Caribbean Theatre* (Cambridge, UK: Cambridge University Press, 1994), 114; Katriina Ranne, *Drops That Open Worlds: Image of Water in the Poetry of Euphrase Kezilahabi*, Masters Thesis, African Studies, Institute for Asian and African Studies, Faculty of Arts, University of Helsinki, Helsinki, Finland, 2006, https://oa.doria.fi/bitstream/handle/10024/4092/dropstha.pdf?sequence=1, accessed July 16, 2012.

20. Gabriel Ruhumbika, "Curriculum Vitae: Dr. Gabriel Ruhumbika . . . "; John P. Mbonde, "Gabriel Ruhumbika: Janga Sugu La Wazawa (2002)–Uchambuzi na Uhakika," *Swahili Forum* 12 (2005), 81–93.

21. Martin Banham et al., "The Cambridge Guide," 113–16; Douglas Killam and Ruth Rowe, "Ebrahim Hussein: Profiles (Tanzanian Playwright)," *African Database*, 2003, http://people.africadatabase.org/en/profile/15704.html#profile119349, accessed November 20, 2006; Angelica Baschiera, "Ebrahim Hussein: Profiles (Tanzanian Playwright)," *Africa Database*, 2003, http://people.africadatabase.org/en/profile/15704.html#profile129304, accessed November 20, 2006.

22. African Writers Index, "Contemporary Swahili Literature," 2000–2002, http://www.oocities.org/africanwriters/Contemporaryswahili.html#balisidya, accessed September 30, 2012; Martin Banham et al., "The Cambridge Guide," 114.

23. Angelica Baschiera, "Penina Muhando Mlama: Profiles," *Africa Database*, 2003, http://people.africadatabase.org/en/profile/12693.html#profile117381, accessed November 20, 2006; Juma Adamu Bakari, "Satires in Theatre for Development Practice in Tanzania," in Kamal Salhi (ed.), *African Threatre for Development: Art for Self-determination* (Exeter, UK: Intellect Books, 1998), 115.

24. Alamin Mazrui, *Swahili Beyond the Boundaries*, 31–32.

25. Simon Gikandi, "East African Literature in English," in F. Abiola Irele and Simon Gikandi (eds.), *The Cambridge History of African and Caribbean Literature*, vol. 2 (Cambridge, UK: Cambridge University Press, 2004), 425–44; Oyekan

Owomoyela (ed.), *A History of Twentieth-Century African Literatures* (Lincoln: University of Nebraska Press, 1993), 61–62.

26. Rachel Mkundai, "Journalist Integrity and Press Freedom in Tanzania," Stanhope Centre for Communications Policy Research, April 19, 2005, http://www.stanhopecentre.org/training/EA/mkundai_seminar.shtml, accessed July 16 2012.

27. Kelly Swanston, "Tanzania: The State of the Media," Stanhope Centre for Communications Policy Research, May 16, 2005, http://www.stanhopecentre.org/training/EA/Tanzania.doc, accessed July 16 2012.

28. Ali Uki, "Isles to Boost Public Media," *Daily News*, July 18, 2006, http://www.dailynews-tsn.com/.

29. Gideon Shoo, "The New Press Bills in Tanzania: Implications for National Communication Policy and Press Freedom," *African Media Review*, 11, no. 2, 2002: 1–11, http://archive.lib.msu.edu/DMC/African%20Journals/pdfs/africa%20media%20review/vol11no2/jamr011002002.pdf, accessed September 30, 2012.

30. Aili Mari Tripp, *Changing the Rules: The Politics of Liberalization and the Urban Informal Economy in Tanzania* (Berkeley: University of California Press, 1997), 103–4; Committee to Protect Journalists, "Attacks of the Press in 2002: Tanzania," http://www.cpj.org/attacks02/africa02/tanzania.html, accessed July 16, 2012.

31. Rachel Mkundai, "Journalist Integrity. . . ."

32. Media Council of Tanzania, "About MCT," 2011, http://www.mct.or.tz/.

33. Stanford University, "Africa South of the Sahara: Countries: Tanzania and Zanzibar: News," 2007, http://library.stanford.edu/africa/tanzania/tanzanews.html, accessed July 16, 2012.

34. Miniwatts Marketing Group, "Internet Users, Population and Facebook Statistics for Africa," December 31, 2011, http://www.internetworldstats.com/stats1.htm, accessed July 16, 2012.

35. Advameg, "Tanzania: The Press," 2012, http://www.pressreference.com/Sw-Ur/Tanzania.html, accessed July 16, 2012.

36. Ibid.

37. Mfuko wa Utamaduni Tanzania, "Film, Audio Visuals and Multi-Media," 2009, http://www.mfuko.or.tz/film_audio_multimedia.htm, accessed July 16, 2012.

38. Advameg, "Tanzania Press, Media, TV, Radio, Newspapers," 2007, http://www.pressreference.com/Sw-Ur/Tanzania.html; Mfuko wa Utamaduni Tanzania, "Film. . . ."

39. Nation Correspondent, "Gospel Tape Banned by Dar Officials," *Daily Nation*, September 23, 2000, http://allafrica.com/stories/200009230025.html, accessed July 16, 2012.

40. Martin Mhando, "Participatory Video Production in Tanzania: An Ideal or Wishful Thinking?" *Tanzanet Journal* 5, no. 1 (2005), 9–15.

41. Mfuko wa Utamaduni Tanzania, "Film, Audio . . ."; Rosaleen Smyth, "The Feature Film in Tanzania," *African Affairs* 88, no. 352 (July 1989), 389–96; Gris-Gris Films, "The Marriage of Mariamu," 1999–2005, http://www.grisgrisfilms.com/html/marriage_of_mariamu.html, accessed July 16, 2012.

42. Zanzibar International Film Festival (ZIFF), "Films Accepted into Festival of Dhow Countries 2007," http://www.ziff.or.tz/, accessed May 10, 2007.

43. Rosaleen Smyth, "The Feature Film in Tanzania," Mona Ngusekela Mwaka-linga, *The Political Economy of the Film Industry in Tanzania: From Socialism to an Open Market Economy, 1961–2010*, PhD Dissertation, Film and Media Studies, University of Kansas, Manhattan, KS; ZIFF, "About ZIFF," 2011, http://www.ziff .or.tz/about/ziff, accessed November 24, 2011.

44. Martin Mhando (2005), "Participatory Video Production in Tanzania."

45. ZIFF, "Celebration of Waters . . ."

46. Abantu Visions, "Abantu Profile," February 14, 2006, http://abantuvisions. com/PreviewProfile.php, accessed November 20, 2006.

47. Coop99 Film Production, "Darwin's Nightmare," http://www.coop99.at/ darwins-nightmare/darwin/html/startset.htm, accessed July 16, 2012.

48. Documentary Educational Resources, "Documentary Films: Diary of a Maa-sai Village Series," 2012, http://www.der.org/films/diary-of-maasai-village_series .html, accessed July 16, 2012.

49. Documentary Educational Resources, "Documentary Films: The Tree of Iron," 2012, http://www.der.org/films/tree-of-iron.html, accessed July 16, 2012.

50. Documentary Educational Resources, "Documentary Films: The Women's Olamal: The Organization of a Maasai Fertility Ceremony," 2012, http://www.der .org/films/womens-olamal.html, accessed July 16, 2012.

51. LocalFilms, "Remembering the Cow," http://www.localfilms.org/maasai/, accessed July 16, 2012.

52. LocalFilms, "Falling Mangoes," http://www.localfilms.org/mangoes/, accessed July 16, 2012.

53. Rinaldo, "Timelines: The Amazing Race 5—Timeline," December 21, 2004, http://www.tarflies.com/article.php?_f=detail&id=424&tarfly=166deb6c693bddc37c 65cf0714135f1c, accessed July 16, 2012.

4

Art and Architecture/Housing

AMONG THE DISTINGUISHING aspects of Tanzanian society are its art, architecture, and housing, which have many functional, aesthetic, and entertainment roles. In this chapter we review the nature and role of the country's art, architecture, and housing.

ART

Artistic expression is a universal human trait. As the oldest human remains have been unearthed in Tanzania and the country has, perhaps, the longest history of human occupation, it also has one of the oldest tradition of artifact making in the world.[1] Besides language, art is central to Tanzania's cultural preservation, expression, and transmission. It preserves, expresses, and transmits the country's history, cultural values, and knowledge as well as its social aspirations, goals, and ideals. Because art is appreciated by all in society, irrespective of class, income, or education level, it has the ability to communicate to people across diverse cultural backgrounds and languages. In contrast, the written word is only able to reach the literate segments of society.

As art and culture are often very tightly interwoven, Tanzanian art is a good reflection of the country's culture. Thus, the country's art reflects the country's immense cultural diversity as well as its overriding communal social orientation.

Tanzanian art has many purposes including serving as gifts; as part of the regalia (e.g., seats, staffs, and scepters) of traditional and contemporary political leaders such as chiefs, sultans, and presidents; as walking sticks for the elderly; as artifacts of secret societies (e.g., those of the Makonde); as teaching aids in various initiation ceremonies; as grave markers; as instruments of divination; and as memorials (monuments or cenotaphs) for prominent deceased or lost members of society.

Tanzanian arts, as in other parts of Africa, tend to emphasize the key cycles of human life (i.e., birth, initiation, marriage, ascent to chieftaincies, and death and ancestorhood) and of the environment within which life is lived (e.g., planting and harvest seasons). In terms of the cycles of human life, emphasis is placed on the production of art that is used in the ceremonies, rituals, and festivals that transition people from one stage to the next. There are also artifacts that are used for various fertility, healing, and cleansing rites. Because many Tanzanians see life as a continuum, even those artifacts that symbolize death also often signal the beginning of one's ancestorhood or spiritual life.

Tanzanian art also exhibits concentric circles of scope that start with the individual and proceed to the family, village, lineage (a group of people with proven descent from a known apical ancestor), clan (groups of lineages that are believed to be related through links that go back to mythic times), ethnic group (groups of lineages with cultural and linguistic ties), cities and city-states, countries, and the globe. While the cycles that run from the individual to the ethnic group have existed in Tanzania since the precolonial era, those from the city-state to the global scale have entered the mindset of the Tanzanian artist since the colonial period. Thus, while tattoos, scarifications, and jewelry are long established individual art forms, the artworks of larger entities such as cities and the nation tend to be newer and larger.

The development of art education in Tanzania can be historically broken down into the period before and after colonialism. In the precolonial era, art education was mainly taught through the apprenticeship system. While precolonial art had aesthetic uses, it was also largely utilitarian and was firmly connected to its social setting.

With the advent of colonialism, European languages and education (German and later English) served as powerful tools of suppression, subversion, division, and alienation. As a result, a gap developed between the arts and arts educational practices of traditional Tanzanian culture and those of the increasingly dominant European religious, cultural, and educational systems. While these two systems naturally influenced and competed with each other, European artistic expression gained power at the expense of local equivalents. At the same time, colonial educational policy limited art and humanities subjects to colonial white schools while locals were taught crafts and basic reading and writing in order to produce menial and basic clerical workers for the colonial capitalist economy. Moreover, the colonial authorities feared that training Africans in the arts and humanities would foment their rebellion against colonialism. The arts curriculum in the white schools was also narrow and Eurocentric and largely restricted to the arts and literature of the colonial mother country. Thus, by the attainment of independence, arts education in Tanzania was woefully inadequate.

Another limitation to arts education in Tanzania in the colonial era was that the country had very limited tertiary education facilities. As a result, the first Tanzanians to study the arts at the university level did so at the then Makerere College's Margaret Trowell Fine Art School (now the Margaret Trowell School of Industrial and Fine Arts) in Kampala, Uganda. At the time, the college, which was affiliated with the University of London, was the only university college in East Africa. The school, which was founded by Margaret Trowell (1904–1985), had by the early 1960s become a leading center of art and design education in eastern and southern Africa. However, few Tanzanians had by then joined it because the country lagged behind its neighbors in basic education. All the same, some of the school's early Tanzanian students included painter Sam Ntiro (1923–1993), Elimo Njau, Ali Darwish (Zanzibar), and Jonathan Kingdom.

Of these four pioneers, the most famous is Ntiro, who, on graduating from Makerere, went on to study fine art at the Slade in London before returning to teach at his alma mater, Makerere College. Later he left for Tanzania and taught at the then Kyambogo Technical Institute (now Kyambogo University) and later at the University of Dar es Salaam, where he facilitated the founding of the Department of Music, Arts and Theatre (now known as the Department of Fine and Performing Arts). An accomplished artist, Ntiro was the first Tanzanian and East African to be exhibited abroad. He was born in Ndereny village, Machame area, Hai District, on the slopes of Mount Kilimanjaro. Before going to Makerere, he attended Ndereny Nkuu Primary School and Old Moshi Secondary School in the Marangu area.

Equally notable is Elimo Njau (1932–). Although he was also in Margaret Trowell's first diploma class, he dropped out of his undergraduate program at the school before obtaining his degree because he differed with the new head, Cecil Todd (who succeeded Trowell as head of the school) over his outspokenness and involvement in the African independence movement. After Makerere, he founded the *Paa ya Paa* (rising antelope) Cultural Center in Nairobi, Kenya, in 1963. Perhaps the only African-owned gallery in Kenya (if not in Africa), Paa ya Paa has since become a major artist training center for artists from East Africa and others from as far away as the Caribbean,

United States, Germany, Switzerland, Austria, and Mexico. Along the way, Njau has become an internationally celebrated painter, sculptor, muralist, and poet who is widely regarded as the father of art in East Africa. Like Ntiro, he was one of the first African artists to exhibit in London.

While Tanzania integrated its schools at independence, the colonial foreign underpinnings of its arts and design education as well as its Western bent did not change. Moreover, after independence the former white schools became private schools whose arts curriculum has continued to supersede that of their public-school counterparts. Thus, art and design education in Tanzania continues to exclude most students in the country's school system.

Simultaneously, for much of the independence era, Tanzanian elites have by omission underplayed the role of the arts in the country's development efforts. Although the country sought to use the arts to promote its socialist development agenda in the late 1960s to the mid-1980s, lack of sufficient funding, teachers, materials, and equipment for arts education, as well as its limited inclusion in the school curriculum, have effectively undermined the role of the arts in the country's development since independence. In order for the arts to take their proper place in Tanzanian society and for them to facilitate Tanzania's social, cultural, and economic development, the country's art education must be reengineered and given a local outlook, approach, and design. Such a change would also need to include the traditional system of apprenticeship in producing future generations of Tanzanian artists.[2]

Although Tanzania has in some ways done better than her neighbors in developing an official cultural policy and in creating institutions like the Bagamoyo College of the Arts and other institutions that train arts teachers for the school system, the need for arts education far exceeds the supply. In any event, in Tanzania and in many of her neighbors, there is a tendency to train teachers in music and ethnomusicology to the exclusion of theater, dance, and the visual arts—a reflection, perhaps, of the cheaper cost of training teachers in music than in the other areas. While Tanzania made the arts (music, fine art, sculpture, and the performing arts) examinable subjects in both primary and secondary schools in 1997, it was not until 2008 that this partially became reality in the secondary school curriculum. Besides the need for a similar move at the primary school level, arts education in the country is beset with many problems, including lack of a political will to implement it, insufficient teachers and teaching and learning materials, absence of the arts from the nation's school timetables, negative social perception of the arts, belief that girls who participate in the arts are morally suspect, belief that the arts are disruptive to the socioeconomic status quo, and perception that arts graduates have poor job prospects, hence the low student interest and enrollment in arts subjects.[3]

The development of Tanzanian art is also faced with many other challenges. First is the limited domestic and international market for its products due to poor marketing, low local appreciation for the arts and art products, and weak copyright protection for art products. Thus, outside of the art sold to tourists, little else makes it to lucrative world markets. Domestically, poor appreciation of the arts means that the country's museums mainly attract tourists and elites.

Second is that economic pressures from external art patrons, dealers, promoters, and collectors have become the dominant factor in the production of Tanzanian art. As a result, many artists have been forced to commercialize and to adapt their work to the needs of the international tourist market, thereby disconnecting the art from its traditional roots as well as limiting its ability to meet local needs. While it is impossible to completely insulate Tanzanian art from external influences, excessive exposure can prostitute the craft, besides interfering with the preservation, development, and production of genuine and culturally relevant art. Granted that art must change with society, a lot of the change in the country's art is not in response to its local needs.[4]

Third is the underpreservation of the country's art due to a shortage of funds, curators, art galleries, and museums. Consequently, much of Tanzania's most prized art is being lost to international art syndicates, foreign art museums and galleries, and private collections that are inaccessible to the average Tanzanian. These external forces are at once a blessing and a curse to Tanzanian art to the extent that they help to preserve it by supporting artists and to destroy it by promoting the production of tourist souvenirs, hyperbolic art works, and other artifacts that satisfy naïve Western notions of Tanzanian (African) art that is divorced from the country's cultural roots.

At the moment, the major depositories of art in Tanzania are local and international museums (e.g., Dar es Salaam's National Museum and House of Culture and the Smithsonian Institution); the fine arts departments of the country's universities (e.g., University of Dar es Salaam) and colleges (Bagamoyo College of the Arts); centuries-old coastal towns such as Stone Town (Zanzibar), Bagamoyo, the Kaole ruins (near Bagamoyo) of East Africa's oldest mosque that was built in the 1200s, and the Arabic and Portuguese ruins on the coastal islands of Kilwa Kisiwani and Songo Mnara; Public Art Commissions such as Dar es Salaam's World War I *Askari* (soldier) Monument, the *Uhuru* (independence) Torch, the Old State House, and the Azania Front Lutheran Church; galleries (e.g., Warm Heart Art Tanzania, Treasures of Africa, Mr Africaart—Handcarved Wooden Art, and Makutano Center for Tanzanian Art and Crafts); and hotels (e.g., Hyatt Regency Dar es Salaam— The Kilimanjaro). Around the country, there are other interesting monuments

Tanzania's Independence Monument. (AP/Wide World Photos)

including that which memorializes Burton and Speke's arrival in Ujiji in 1858 and Henry Stanley's and David Livingstone's meeting in Kigoma in 1871.

Traditional Art

Traditional Tanzanian art is generally that which predates Arab and European colonialism and is either extinct or continuing though with varying degrees of change. Because traditional art is produced by native artists and consumed within its native culture, it usually has a lot of local authenticity and meaning and is usually accessible to all members of society. As a result, it has long been a powerful tool for individual and social expression and communication in the country.

Art has also long symbolized the power and prestige of the country's traditional and modern political leaders as well as being a central part of their regalia (symbols of office). Thus, the country's traditional and modern leaders have long created a large array of art (e.g., figurines, staffs, stools, chairs, drums, jewelry, and clothing) for aesthetic, official, and ceremonial purposes. Some of the most elaborate royal Tanzanian art treasures are those of the former Sultanate of Zanzibar (1856–1964) and various former traditional African chiefdoms and the kingdoms of Karagwe and Unyamwezi. Among the best examples of traditional royal art are the Nyamwezi high-backed chief's stool, the Karagwe kingdom's complex iron *Omusinga* plant (*Hibiscus fuscus*) holders, and the intricately carved wood doors and ornate housing architectures of the former Omani Arab rulers of Zanzibar.[5]

Traditional Tanzanian art has also long taken the form of various functional objects like mats, baskets, pots, and wooden utensils that were made by local or neighboring community craftsmen from locally available materials, designs, and tools. Some traditional Tanzanian communities, such as the Haya of northwest Tanzania, had iron foundries that produced functional artistic items such as knives, swords, and spears.[6]

Tanzania also has some of the best ancient rock painting collections in the world. Some of the best examples of these are the 1,600 Kondoa Irangi rock paintings in Kondoa District, Dodoma Region. While declaring them to be a World Cultural Heritage Site in 2006, the UNESCO World Heritage Committee noted that the "rock art sites at Kondoa are an exceptional testimony to the lives of hunter-gathers and agriculturalists who have lived in the area over several millennia, and reflect a unique variation of hunter-gather art from southern and central Africa and a unique form of agro-pastoralist paintings."[7] Scattered in over 200 sites in the Irangi Hills, the paintings show human figures, rivers, and animal profiles. Some of these paintings are believed to be 30,000 years old, though stone arrowheads from some of the caves date from 8000 BC.[8] Moreover, these rock-art sites are unique because they "are still used actively by local communities for a variety of ritual activities such as rainmaking, divining and healing. These strong intangible relationships between the paintings and living practices reinforce the links with those societies that created the paintings, and demonstrate a crucial cultural continuum."[9]

Contemporary Art Forms

Tanzania has many contemporary art forms that have largely arisen in response to the country's evolving sociological, economic, political, and aesthetic realities. Most of these new art forms have come about due to the country's contact with external forces including Arab, Portuguese, German, and British colonial forces. Since independence, the country has also increasingly come into contact with the larger global world that has influenced its art by, for instance, introducing it to external art traditions and techniques.

The advent of contemporary Tanzanian art has naturally come with modern artists who are either formally trained or use art to earn their living. Formally trained artists work in formal settings such as universities, are more inclined to produce art for its own sake or as a means of self-expression, produce limited numbers of signed artworks, and tend to exhibit their work in formal settings such as galleries, museums, and cultural centers. Examples of this kind of artist include the painters Sam Ntiro (d. 1993), Professor Elias E. Jengo, and the late George Lilanga (d. 2005). Conversely, many commercial artists are self-taught art entrepreneurs who mass produce art in informal settings for sale. This group of artists dominates the modern Tanzanian art scene.

Sculpture

Tanzania has a world-famous Makonde sculpture industry that is dominated by the Makonde people of southern Tanzania and northern Mozambique. Since traditional times, Tanzanian sculpture, including the Makonde genre, has generally been functional and has been used to teach, entertain, and provide a livelihood for the artists. In short, sculpture, along with the more recent art forms of painting, drawing, watercolor, graphics, and architecture, is a good example of Tanzanian fine art. Because the Mozambican Makonde people are more homogeneous than their Tanzanian counterparts, given their secure and isolated territory in the Mueda plateau, their sculpture is more culturally relevant and reflective of their traditional beliefs, folklore, rituals, and other cultural practices, including the use of figurines in boy and girl initiation ceremonies. Conversely, because the Tanzanian Makonde people are more heterogeneous, having endured centuries of invasion and intermixing with their neighbors and other outsiders, their sculpture is less socially anchored. Regardless, the Makonde have been carving for centuries, and their sculpture has evolved from the original naturalistic motifs to the more abstract souvenir-type art pieces that mainly target today's tourist market. The key characteristics of Makonde sculpture are the use of a single piece of wood (irrespective of the complexity of the piece being made) and the dominant use of the dark-colored and fine-grained African blackwood tree (*Dalbergia melanoxylon*).[10]

The most popular sculpture material in Tanzania is wood, and to a smaller extent stone, ceramics, and metal. While this art genre has been practiced in Tanzania since precolonial times, it has especially blossomed since the 1900s because of the commodification and commercialization of art.

While precolonial Tanzanian sculpting was for spiritual and cultural purposes (i.e., sacred and secular), much of today's sculpture is produced for secular reasons, that is, for aesthetics and sale. For instance, the famed Makonde carving industry can be traced to the 1930s when the Makonde started producing artifacts for the commercial art market. Initially, the Makonde, who hail mainly from northern Mozambique, moved to Dar es Salaam, Tanzania, in search of work. When commercial interest in their sculpture arose, encouraged by the Indian entrepreneur Peera, early sculptors such as Manguli Istiwawo and Pajume Allale started meeting the demand. Later, the Makonde gained even more

Intricate Makonde wooden sculptures. (Emory Kristof/National Geographic/Getty Images)

commercial success when they adopted and perfected the more marketable Samaki tradition of *shetani* (devil) sculpture. Since the mid-1970s, the government of Mozambique's encouragement of the Makonde wood-carving tradition has inevitably spilled over into Tanzania, whose many leading Makonde sculptors have family on both sides of the border.

While many frown on the commercialization of Tanzania's Makonde sculpture because of its increasing disconnection from its traditional purposes, the reality is that many artists engage in it for income. Thus, the artists are eager to produce souvenirs and other marketable pieces of sculpture. Many of these pieces, especially those in the *shetani* or devil subgenre, can be terrifying. Some of the country's leading Makonde sculptors include Agustino Malaba, Anthony Bruno, Joakim Mpyuka, and Aloyce Chanua.

Although the Makonde dominate Tanzania's wood-sculpture genre, they are by no means the only ones engaged in this artwork as practically every ethnic community in the country has a wood- or stone-carving tradition. Accordingly, some of the country's other renowned sculptors include the Zaramo, Nyamwezi, and Sukuma. Sukuma carvings tend to be large, standing, rough-looking figures with weathered veneers. Their fetish and dance masks have similar weathered and fearful appearances that have embellished eyebrows, beards, and moustaches.[11]

Tanzania's Makonde sculpture has eight major styles: *binadamu, dimoongo, shetani, mawingu, giligia, kimbulumbulu, mandandosa,* and *tumbatumba.* The *binadamu* (human daily life) style was pioneered by Nyekenya Nangundu in the early 1930s in Mozambique. It is naturalistic and often depicts Makonde men and women in various customary roles, for instance elderly men smoking pipes and women fetching water. The *binadamu* style underlies all the other styles.

Dimoongo (power of strength) was pioneered by Roberto Yakobo Sangwani, a Mozambican who moved to Tanzania in the late 1950s. The style originally showed a wrestling-match winner who is carried should high by a group of friends. A later iteration of this style is the Makonde family tree, which has a female figure at the top of the heap of figures.

The *shetani* (devil) style, which was created by Samaki Likankoa in the 1960s, is by far the most popular carving style. It started when Samaki accidentally dropped and damaged one of his *binadamu* carvings, leaving it with one eye, ear, nose opening, leg and arm. When Samaki carved a duplicate piece for art dealer Peera, it sold quickly, thereby encouraging Samaki and those that came after him to make more of the same.

The *mawingu* style is based on the shapes made by the clouds. It was pioneered by Clements Ngala after Peera encouraged him to distinguish his work from Samaki's. Ngala's original *mawingu* piece was a faceless humanlike figure with some sort of headdress, a raised right hand holding the moon and lowered left hand with the earth in it.

The next four styles, *giligia, kimbulumbulu, mandandosa,* and *tumbatumba,* were all invented by master sculptor Chanuo Maundu, and were based on Makonde traditional beliefs. *Giligia* (being startled or a sudden shock of surprise) depicts the fear that people feel when they walk alone in the forest or some other forbidding place. It usually has a statuette with a large bulging eye and exposed, frightening teeth.

Kimbulumbulu is an anthropomorphic or humanlike sculpture technique that emerged in the early 1990s to represent the disorder that accompanies nervous human behavior. It usually abstractly represents the human face with a large eye, nose, and mouth in abnormal positions attached to a head with legs. The *mandandosa* style depicts the evil spirits that were traditionally used secretly by sorcerers to harm those that they were hired to hurt by feuding family members. Such carvings often have one large eye that was traditionally used to spy on one's foes or enemies. The *tumbatumba* style was revealed in the mid-1980s to depict tattoos and other Makonde body art. Carvings in this style often have a gourd-like appearance that the carver decorates as he or she wishes.

Among the Makonde and other Tanzanian ethnic communities, sculpting is definitely a man's world. Nevertheless, the country has some successful female sculptors, including Harieth Kagangule Rwamula of Bagamoyo, Scolastica Sospeter Malecela of Dodoma, Agnes Kijazi of Bagamoyo, and Mwandale Mwanyekwa of Dar es Salaam. Of these, Mwandale Mwanyekwa is, perhaps, the most accomplished. Affectionately known as "Big Mama," she is one of Tanzania's best wood carvers. She was born in February 1978. As her mother is from the Makonde ethnic community that is renowned for its sculpture, she has stated that "she did not choose sculpture but that sculpture chose her."[12] Her journey to the profession started at an early age. Besides growing up around her maternal grandparents (both of whom were artists), she learned pottery and sculpture from her maternal grandmother and grandfather respectively. In a break with tradition and to her maternal grandfather's credit, he allowed her to play with his tools and even taught her to sculpt in his workshop while her grandmother taught her to make pottery.

As a young woman, she bucked tradition when she chose sculpture instead of the traditionally gender-appropriate profession of pottery. Not gifted in school, she ended her formal schooling at the primary school level and went into sculpting. Though she partially blames her limited formal education on Tanzania's weak arts education, she eventually managed to secure advanced training at the Bagamoyo Sculpture School and at the Gotland College of Fine Arts in Sweden. While her success has not been without challenges, she does not regret her decision to pursue professional sculpting as she finds it satisfying. It brings her happiness because it fully engages her brain, spirit, body, and heart.

Some of her best works are the splendid self-portraits and other sculptures that depict her take on people, animals, cultural beliefs, relationships, and the environment. Based in Bagamoyo near Dar es Salaam, she has been sculpting for over a decade and has exhibited her work in Tanzania, South Africa, Sweden, and the United States. Through training and participation in various workshops and exhibits, she has managed to upgrade her skills as well as the quality of her work.

As a woman in a largely male profession, she is often asked how she has managed to succeed in a largely male world. One of her inimitable responses is that "since women give birth to men . . . what a man can do a woman can do." More importantly, by excelling in her work, she has created a clear path for future Tanzanian women sculptors.[13]

Ceramic Art

Next to wooden artifacts, clay artifacts are, perhaps, the next most widespread form of Tanzanian art. In many rural, traditional Tanzanian societies, earthen cooking and eating utensils like cups, plates, and pots (for cooking and storing water and food) are still popular even in the face of growing competition from modern domestic and imported plastic, aluminum, metal, and porcelain (china) utensils. In the urban areas, modern ceramic utensils are more popular, though traditional pottery is also widely used for decoration.

Since precolonial times, Tanzania's pottery makers have often traded their pottery for basic necessities like food and livestock with neighboring communities. Nowadays, much of the trading involves cash, and the business has expanded to include commercial pottery production for a local and international clientele. Some of the country's functional and decorative earthenware and stoneware includes planters, flower vases, lamp stands, bowls, oven pots (casseroles), figurine sculptors, clay masks, ceramic plates, and candle holders.

Tanzanian pottery is an old tradition that is still being unraveled by ongoing archaeological work across the country. For instance, late Stone Age pottery has been unearthed in parts of the country including in the Lindi area of coastal southern Tanzania.[14] As Tanzania is the cradle of humanity, its pottery tradition dates to the earliest history of humans. Like many traditional crafts, the country's ceramic production has deep spiritual and cultural meaning, with distinction being made between secular and sacred items. Among the Pare and Shambaa, for instance, "pottery often serves as a metaphor for the womb, the vessel from which life emerges. . . . [W]ith the help of traditional healers, sacred ceramic vessels . . . can embody ancestor spirits or harness their transformative powers."[15] The metaphorical link between pottery and the conception of human life has made this a women's profession in some Tanzanian communities (including the Pare), where culture and tradition is invoked to keep men out of the business save for its labor-demanding tasks like excavating and transporting the heavy clay raw materials.

One of Tanzania's most renowned traditions of pottery making is that found among the Pare and Kisi ethnic communities of northeast and southwest Tanzania, respectively. One of the Pare ethnic community's most accomplished and innovative ceramic artists is Namsifueli Nyeki, who was born and raised in Kileti in the West Usambara mountains in the early 1960s. A potter in the same area throughout her life, she learned the craft at an early age from her mother as she helped her with various pottery chores like fetching water, tools, clay, and firewood and hardening the products in makeshift kilns. As part of her early formal training by her mother, she learned the form, function, technology, and aesthetics of pottery as well as the importance of quality, craftsmanship, shape, smoothness, pot stability (i.e., its ability to stand without tipping over), and proper firing. Besides making the secular and sacred pottery products valued by her local community, Nyeki also makes European-style pottery including teacups and saucers, large shallow fruit bowls, casseroles, salad bowls, and wine or juice jars.[16]

Although she produces pots that meet traditional structural and aesthetic standards, she has over time become an experienced potter who masterfully marries tradition and innovation in her pot making. Through experimentation and a willingness to reinterpret and challenge tradition and to move beyond time-honored standards of aesthetics, technology, and form, she has created new pot designs that command a premium in the local and international market. Her success also stems from her willingness to stay true to the enduring aspects of her craft even as she innovates to produce products that meet the needs of her evolving local and foreign clients. Among the key cultural and socioeconomic changes that she has had to adapt to are the growing westernization of Tanzania since its European colonial days; the impact of the country's independence on her, her society, and her craft; the decline of many indigenous ritual practices (including the hereditary rites and prayers that potting families formerly performed at various stages of pot making) due to the advent of Christianity and Islam; the introduction of modern economic, health, forestry, and agriculture practices; and the growing influx of foreign tourists to her home area.

Because of her excellent artistry, Nyeki has since the 1990s taught traditional pottery workshops to domestic and foreign tourists. In 2002, she was an artist-in-residence at the prestigious Nyerere Cultural Center *Nyumba ya Sanaa* (House of Arts) in Dar es Salaam. During her one-week residence, she became the first Tanzanian woman to win the Tanzania Culture Trust Fund Zeze Award in Fine Arts and Crafts.

Photography

Photography is a key artistic medium in Tanzania. As in many parts of the world, Tanzanian photographers make use of film and digital cameras. Tanzania has many accomplished photographers. While some are employed by the country's major media houses and corporations, many more are self-employed. Because of economic, training, and equipment-access constraints, most of the country's amateur and professional photographers are males like Javed Jafferji of Zanzibar. In addition to photography, Jafferji is also a film producer. Nevertheless, there are a few professional female photographers like Mefakii Diwani Jumbe of Tanga. She, among other purposes, uses photography to advocate for women's issues.

Drawing

In Tanzania, drawing as art form is most widely used in architecture, portraiture, and the production of cartoons for the newspaper printing industry. While there are thousands of drawers in Tanzania, including the many unknown artists who created the country's centuries-old rock art, examples of famous contemporary artists include George Lilanga, Edward Said Tinga Tinga, Elias Jengo (Professor), Stephen Ndibalema, David Mzuguno, Raza Mohammed, Thobias Minzi, Robino Ntila, John Kilaka, Godfrey Semwaiko, and Evarist Chikawe.

Painting

Tanzanians have a long precolonial tradition of painting that mostly uses natural color materials like plants and clay, limestone, and other colored soils to executive various paint designs on people (mostly on faces, hands, and legs), house walls, animal skins, and various stone surfaces. Tanzania's world-famous rock art partially includes designs made of many naturally occurring and locally available color materials.

However, as traditional Tanzania had no access to paper or canvas, painting on such surfaces did not commence until the substantial arrival of Europeans in the country in the late 1800s. From the initial introduction of more convenient and affordable painting materials like paper, canvas, and paint brushes, this art form quickly spread to the whole country.

Although arts education was fairly limited in colonial Tanzania, a few Tanzanians learned painting from European missionaries. Others taught themselves to paint and eventually became master painters. One of the first Tanzanians to acquire formal training in painting was the late Sam Ntiro (d. 1993), who went on to play a key role in institutionalizing painting in Tanzania. Since the late 1960s, Tanzanian painting has evolved along the abstract and *tingatinga* traditions. The country's major abstract painters

An example of Tanzania's *tingatinga* art. (INSADCO Photography)

include the late George Lilanga, Professor Elias Jengo, the late David Mzuguno, Raza Mohammed, Thobias Minzi, John Kilaka, and Evarist Chikawe. Robino Ntila and Francis Patrick Imanjama are known for their etching technique—the making of designs or pictures on metal plates or glass through the corrosive action of an acid rather than by a burin.

On the *tingatinga* side, there are over 100 artists, including Edward Said Tinga Tinga, Daudi Tingatinga, Saidi Chilamboni, Noel Kapanda, and Maurus Michael. The *tingatinga* genre, which generally rivals Makonde sculpture in fame, generally depicts people, birds, animals, landscapes, and other objects in bright, colorful, and playful paintings. As *tingatinga* painting makes extensive use of dots, the most popular subjects of this genre are the guinea fowl and the leopard. Since its founding in the later 1960s, this genre has become the dominant tourist-oriented painting style in Tanzania and elsewhere in East Africa. Some of its output is also consumed by local elites and global art dealers.[17]

As the founder of *tingatinga* art, Edward Said Tinga Tinga is definitely this genre's most prominent artist. He was born in the mid-1930s to a poor family in Mindu, Tanzania, where he attended the first four years of primary school before moving to Tanga in northeast Tanzania in search of a better life.

His mother was a Christian from the Makua ethnic community while his father was a Ngindo Muslim.

In 1960, he moved to Dar es Salaam and eventually joined a relative in the employ of a British officer in Dar es Salaam. Later he secured a government job in the city but continued to pursue his interest in Makonde music and dance. In 1968, he launched his painting career using low-cost materials and bicycle paint. Though he was a self-taught artist, he learned on the job and soon began to produce simple and bright paintings of African landscapes and animals that became popular with the city's expatriate community. When his business grew, he employed three of his Makua and two of his Makonde relatives to help him meet the demand. These five employees were to become the first generation of *tingatinga* painters upon his early death in 1972.

In 1971, Tinga Tinga signed a contract to provide the National Arts Council of Tanzania (NACT) with a weekly supply of art. At the same time, Tinga Tinga decided to work full-time on his art business. After his death, his five employees continued to honor the NACT contract and eventually brought on more painters, mostly from the Makua community. In the 1990s, his relatives created the Tingatinga Arts Cooperative Society (TACS). One his children, Daudi Tingatinga, is a renowned *tingatinga* painter in TACS.[18]

Textiles and Fashion

Tanzanian textiles and clothing are a lively art scene. Virtually anything that has cloth material on it, including table and seat covers, aprons, and everyday clothing and headgear, is often decorated with colorful artistic patterns of wildlife, flowers, and plants. Many of these decorative patterns are initially made by the country's artists before being adopted by various clothing designers. Some of Tanzania's art designs have also appealed to international fashion designers. For instance, some of Rubuni Rashidi's paintings were recently used by Tokyo, Japan's, Ayumi Sufu (Jazzkatze) to design some clothing fashion items. The clothing designs were shown at the Tokyo Fashion Show in spring 2010. Other clothing and fashion designs that are based on local painting designs are shown in Chapter 5.

Other Functional and Aesthetic Crafts

Many Tanzanian household items (e.g., cups, plates, and teapots) often also have an aesthetic value depending on the level of their beautification. The same is true of other household items such as prayer mats, carpets, baskets, and chairs. While many imported varieties of these items use foreign paint styles, those that are produced locally often use local aesthetic motifs. The decorated traditional pots of Tanzania, such as those made by the Gogo village of Ihumwa as well as the Pare and Kisi communities, are good examples of functional art, as are the murals (wall paintings) on many public and private buildings, churches, schools, and billboards. For instance, the paintings of Elias Jengo adorn many public and private buildings in Tanzania. Throughout Tanzania, many functional decorative items are popular because of their sacred or cultural value, affordability and authenticity, and their role in supporting local economies.

ARCHITECTURE AND HOUSING

Besides providing shelter, Tanzanian architecture is an important avenue for artistic expression. It falls into three main categories: traditional, modern, and syncretic. Traditional architecture dominates in the rural areas where most Tanzanians live. Zanzibar and many coastal areas of the country have had simple to ornate traditional Middle Eastern architecture since the 1200s. While it varies widely across the country, traditional Tanzanian architecture is generally plain and largely dominated by simple round or square wattle-and-daub grass-thatched huts that increasingly have iron sheet roofs.

The simple architectural designs of rural Tanzanian housing are due to many reasons. First is that the country's warm, tropical climate generally supports long hours of outside work and play, which therefore obviate the need for more elaborate housing. Second, Tanzanians (like other Africans) have historically placed more emphasis on spiritual rather than material things. This focus does to some extent limit the amount of effort and investment that is placed on housing and other material pursuits. Third, because housing is one of the most expensive investments that most humans make, the humble dwellings of many Tanzanians are somewhat indicative of their material poverty. Fourth, the structure of many Tanzanian houses is a reflection of locally available building materials. Thus, in the country's arid and semiarid areas, houses can be quite basic because of the difficulty of securing enough building materials. Finally, because housing is often a lifestyle marker, existing Tanzanian housing is indicative of the country's lifestyles. For instance, Maasai housing has traditionally been makeshift because of the nomadic lifestyle of many Maasai people, and as many of them have shifted to more sedentary lifestyles in recent decades, the quality and durability of their dwellings has similarly improved.

Much of the country's modern architecture is in the urban areas and is mostly dominated by European and American designs that first entered the country in the colonial era. One of the enduring consequences of Tanzania's colonialism is the denigration of local precolonial architectural designs and building technologies and their replacement with Western equivalents that were generally designed to create markets for European construction designs, materials, and building technologies. As many of the country's architects are also trained in the Western tradition, they have not been able to domesticate their craft to suit local conditions.

Throughout the country, there are many modern government offices as well as hospital, church, and education buildings. But whereas modern architecture has worked well for institutions, it has proven to be costly if not inappropriate for many ordinary people's dwellings. Moreover, this architecture has been criticized for failing to promote the use of local building forms and materials. In response, the country's National Housing and Building Research Agency (NHBRA) is actively trying to create suitable local building materials as well as domesticating modern architectural designs and constructions.

Between traditional and modern architecture is a syncretic architecture that has elements of both. This largely uncoordinated trend is driven by individual Tanzanians seeking to harmonize their often conflicting pulls of tradition and modernity in nearly all areas of life, including architecture and housing. In rural areas, for instance, the grass-thatch roof is increasingly being replaced by the iron-sheet one, a change that, in many cases, is also a response to the decreasing availability of traditional building materials like grass.

A grass-thatched house in rural Tanzania. Animal transport is also prevalent in the countryside. (Tony Karumba/AFP/Getty Images)

Rural Settlements and Housing Types

Tanzanian rural settlements generally consist of various-sized villages depending on local environmental conditions, ethnicity, and land availability. Most Tanzanians are agricultural Bantus (e.g., the Chagga, Haya, and Nyamwezi) whose villages tend to be larger, more populated, and generally more concentrated in the more fertile parts of the country, including the Mount Kilimanjaro region. The few Nilo-Hamitic groups (e.g., Maasai) have traditionally had smaller and more sparsely populated villages.

One of the major factors influencing the current distribution of villages in the Tanzanian countryside is the country's *Ujamaa* villagization policy (1967–1985) that sought to create communally planned and organized villages throughout the country for the purpose of promoting self-sufficiency and hastening development through better provision of services such as roads, markets, schools, health, power, and water. Although the program did not fully succeed, it managed to resettle lots of people and to provide them with social services. In spite of its failure due to poor implementation and underfunding, it stands as the boldest attempt at rural socioeconomic transformation in Africa.[19]

While most Tanzanian villages consist of closely related individuals from the same ethnic community, those that are close to the former trade routes (which have since become major roads and railway lines) are more diverse. Currently, villages are the lowest units of Tanzania's local government structure, which consists of villages, wards, districts, regions, and the national government. Village governance includes the village assembly (which consists of all people over 18 years old) and an executive village council that consists of an elected chairman and vice chairman.

Most village houses tend to be the round or square wattle-and-daub grass-thatched variety, with a scattering of modern elements like iron-sheet roofs and cement walls and floors. The use of modern durable building materials tends to be highest in the wealthier households and regions of the country. Many of the wealthier regions are those that are agriculturally rich and have benefitted from missionary schools since the colonial era. Typically, household size and income is a major factor in the house size.

Rural living arrangements often involve separate housing units for males and females. Thus, a family dwelling typically consists of two to three houses: a kitchen or cooking house that also serves as a residence for girls and young children, a main house for parents that is often split into a bedroom and a living room, and another house for older boys. In polygynous families, the male head of the family often has his own house that is surrounded by his wives' houses. Because of the large amount of time spent outdoors and other factors like poverty, many rural Tanzanian houses tend to be modest in size and sparsely furnished. In most cases, outhouses are the main means of dealing with human waste, and cooking and drinking water is usually fetched from nearby streams or wells. Traditionally, people bathed in rivers but nowadays they mostly do so at home in outdoor enclosures.

Urban Settlements and Housing Types

There are two kinds of urban settlements in Tanzania: those that predate nineteenth-century European (German and British) colonialism and those that are the product of the same. Prior to the colonization of Tanzania in the late 1800s, urban settlements had formed in the coastal and Zanzibar regions of the country from as early as 1000 AD. Some of these towns include Zanzibar, Tanga, Bagamoyo, and Dar es Salaam. Along the inland slave caravan routes, trading posts emerged that eventually grew into the modern towns of Tabora, Morogoro, Moshi, Kigoma, Ujiji, and Mwanza. These interior urban settlements depended on trade between Africans and Arabs in slaves, ivory, pottery, animal skins, and copper. The vitality of both the coastal and interior urban settlements depended on the maritime trade between East Africa and the Arabian Peninsula and, to some extent, Persia and South, East, and Southeast Asia.[20]

Except for the few coastal and interior towns that predate nineteenth-century European colonialism, all of Tanzania's other urban areas date to the colonial era. Even those that predate this wave of European colonialism were substantially altered by it, often resulting in the creation of European, Arab, Asian, and African sectors that, in Dar es Salaam's case, are still largely intact even though race has long been replaced by income as a key factor in urban settlement in Tanzania. The quality of life in Tanzania's urban upper-income neighborhoods easily compares to that obtainable in many developed countries. Because of Tanzania's low level of development, its urban middle class is fairly small. Hence, most urban Tanzanians are poor people who make a living in the informal sector of the economy and often have to supplement their income with foodstuffs from their rural areas of origin.[21]

Tanzania is an overwhelmingly rural country with only 25 percent of its population living in cities. Much of the country's urban population lives in the top 24 cities, including Dar es Salaam, Mwanza, Zanzibar, and Arusha. Collectively, these cities account for nearly 60 percent of the country's urban population. By itself, Dar es Salaam has nearly one-quarter of the country's urban population.

As noted in Chapter 1, Tanzanian cities have many similar challenges, including rapid population growth; insufficient urban infrastructure, housing, sanitation, jobs, schools, and hospitals; haphazard development due to insufficient land-use control, inadequate numbers of planners and housing inspectors; and continued reliance on colonial urban planning and housing standards that are not only inappropriate for local conditions but are also a key contributor to the country's urban problems.

Architecturally, urban Tanzania is quite complex, especially in the coastal cities that have been the meeting point of Africans, Arabs, Europeans, and Asians for over a millennium. In Zanzibar, for instance, the architectural heritage is so immense that the city's Stone Town was declared a World Heritage Cultural Site in 2000. Nevertheless, most of the buildings in Stone Town are structurally unsound and their upkeep costly and inadequate. Thus, many have collapsed in recent decades, "leaving yawning gaps in the narrow, winding alleys lined with Arab palaces, Persian baths, British colonial offices, Indian shops and onetime slave chambers."[22]

On the mainland, where most of the urban housing dates to the colonial era, modern and postmodern architecture dominates, more so in Dar es Salaam, where residential and commercial buildings that date back to the late 1800s coexist with newer ones. Some of the city's major landmarks include St. Joseph's Cathedral on Sokoine Drive, Azania Front Lutheran Church, and the Kivukoni Front's colonial German architecture.

Tanzanian urban housing also varies by use and ownership. In terms of use, the main categories are residential, commercial, secular, and sacred. As in many other cities around the world, land use in Tanzanian cities is typically dominated by residential uses, followed by commercial, secular, and sacred uses in that order. Each of these land uses tends to concentrate in particular parts of the city, with the residences being on the outskirts and the commercial uses being highest in the central business district. Secular and sacred uses are often broadly scattered throughout the urban areas, though in Dar es Salaam there is a discernible government enclave. Intense competition for land in downtown Dar es Salaam is gradually giving the city a modern skyline. On the ownership side, a distinction can be made between public and private buildings, with the latter being the most common.

Class and demographic diversity drive Tanzania's variety in urban residential housing. Thus, the country's African, Arab, Asian, and European ethnic variety is generally also reflected in the country's urban residences. In Dar es Salaam, there are discernible racial and ethnic enclaves, each with its unique geography and architectural character. But on the whole, European architecture dominates the landscapes of many Tanzanian cities even though their European population is miniscule.

Additionally, urban housing also varies by income, with the best sections of many Tanzanian cities being occupied by the well-off segments of society. Unsurprisingly, the quality of housing in the cities' upper-, middle-, and lower-class regions closely reflects these income levels. Urban housing in Tanzania therefore varies from the palaces of the wealthy areas to the unplanned and poorly serviced slum and squatter hovels that are occupied by the cities' poor. While housing density is highest in the cities' low-income areas, housing quality, materials, and finish is highest in the well-off sections of these cities.

NOTES

1. John Mack, "Eastern Africa," in Tom Phillips (ed.), *Africa: The Art of a Continent* (Munich/London/New York: Prestel, 1999), 117–78; Monica Blackmun Visoná, "Eastern Africa," in Monica Blackmun Visoná, Robin Poynor, Herbert M. Cole, and Michael D. Harris (eds.), *A History of Art in Africa* (New York: Harry N. Abrams, 2001), 440–71.

2. Augustin Hatar, "The State of Theatre Education in Tanzania," paper prepared for UNESCO, 2001, http://portal.unesco.org/culture/en/files/19603/10814381543hatar .pdf/hatar.pdf, accessed June 13, 2012.

3. Vicensia Shule, "The Role of 'Political Will' in Implementing Arts Education in Tanzania," University of Dar es Salaam & International Drama/Theatre and Education Association (IDEA), Tanzania, http://www.unesco.org/, accessed June 26, 2012.

4. Sidney Littlefield Kasfir, *Contemporary African Art* (London: Thames & Hudson, 1999), 64–101.

5. John Mack, "Eastern Africa."

6. John Mack, "Eastern Africa"; *Time*, "Africa's Ancient Steelmakers," September 25, 1978, http://www.time.com/time/magazine/article/0,9171,912179,00 .html, accessed June 27, 2012.

7. UNESCO World Heritage Centre, "Decision—30COM 8B.36—Nominations of Cultural Properties to the World Heriate List (Kondoa Rock Art Sites)," 1992–2012, http://whc.unesco.org/en/decisions/1002, accessed June 28, 2012.

8. Monica Blackmun Visoná, "Southern Africa," in Monica Blackmun Visoná, Robin Poynor, Herbert M. Cole, and Michael D. Harris (eds.), *A History of Art in Africa* (New York: Harry N. Abrams, 2001), 476; TravelSmart Ltd. World Guides, "Tanzania Landmarks and Monuments," 2012, http://www.tanzania.world-guides .com/tanzania_landmarks.html, accessed June 27, 2012.

9. UNESCO World Heritage Centre, "Decision. . . ."

10. Elias Jengo, "The Makonde Sculpture," *AFRUM: Contemporary African Fine Art*, 2009, http://www.afrum.com/index.php, accessed June 28, 2012.

11. Rand African Art, "Sukuma (?) Figure from Tanzania," http://www .randafricanart.com/Sukuma_figure_Tanzania_1.html, accessed June 27, 2012.

12. The Great Lakes Consortium for International Training and Development and The Arts Council Lake Erie West, *Art—In a Woman's World* (Toledo: The Great Lakes Consortium for International Training and Development & The Arts Council Lake Erie West, 2010); Mwandale Mwanyekwa and Bob Sankofa, "Unapokuwa

Mwanamke Mchongaji [When You Are a Woman Sculptor]," *UDADISI: Rethinking in Action*, September 17, 2009, http://udadisi.blogspot.com/2009/09/unapokuwa-mwanamke-mchongaji.html, accessed June 27, 2012.

13. Mwandale Mwanyekwa and Bob Sankofa, "Unapokuwa Mwanamke . . ."; Mwandale Mwanyekwa, "Mwandale Mwanyekwa," 2008, http://mwandale .blogspot.com/, accessed June 27, 2012.

14. Felix A. Chami and Remigius Chami, "Narosura Pottery from the Southern Coast of Tanzania: First Incontrovertible Coastal Later Stone Age Pottery," *Nyame Akuma* 56 (December 2001): 29–35.

15. Barbara Thompson, "Namsifueli Nyeki: A Tanzanian Potter Extraordinaire," *African Arts* 40, no. 1 (2007): 57.

16. Barbara Thompson, "Namsifueli Nyeki"; S. A. C. Waane, "Pottery Making Traditions of the Ikombe Kisi of Kyela District: An Anthropological Paper," Occasional paper 4, National Museum of Tanzania, 1976.

17. Monica Blackmun Visoná, "Eastern Africa"; AFRUM, "Tingatinga," *AFRUM: Contemporary African Fine Art*, http://www.afrum.com/index.php, accessed June 28, 2012.

18. Africa on Canvas, "Tingatinga," http://www.africaoncanvas.ca/content/ tingatinga, accessed June 28, 2012; Tinga Tinga Art Cooperative Society Tanzania, "Welcome to Tinga Tinga Quality Products," http://www.tingatinga.org.uk/index. html, accessed June 28, 2012; AFRUM and TACS, "What or Who Is Tinga Tinga?" 2009–2011, http://www.tingatingastudio.com/menu_about.html, accessed June 28, 2012.

19. Aadel Brun Tschudi, "Ujamaa Villages and Rural Development," *Norsk Geografisk Tidsskrift (Norwegian Journal of Geography)* 26, nos. 1 and 2 (1972): 27–36; Mboneko Munyaga, "Ujamaa Village Settlement Meant to Spread the Wealth," *Tanzania Daily News* (Dar es Salaam), October 31, 2011.

20. Dean Sinclair, "Memorials More Enduring than Bronze: J. H. Sinclair and the Making of Zanzibar Stone Town," *African Geographical Review* 28 (2009): 71–97; Abdulaziz Y. Lodhi, "Muslims in Eastern Africa: Their Past and Present," *Nordic Journal of African Studies* 3, no. 1 (1994): 88–98; Jacqueline Woodfork, "Cities and Architecture," in Toyin Falola (ed.), *Africa Volume 2: African Cultures and Societies before 1885* (Durham, NC: Carolina Academic Press, 2000).

21. Sarah L. Smiley, "Population Censuses and Changes in Housing Quality in Dar es Salaam, Tanzania," *African Geographical Review* 31, no. 1 (2012), DOI:10.1080/19376812.2012.679451.

22. Alexandra Zavis, "The Roof Is Falling In on a Cultural Legacy in Zanzibar," *Los Angeles Times*, December 25, 2005, http://articles.latimes.com/2005/dec/25/ news/adfg-stonetown25, accessed June 29, 2012.

5

Cuisine and Dress

CUISINE

TANZANIA HAS DIVERSE cuisine or cooking traditions and practices that are influenced by its rich trade, ethnic, religious, racial, cultural, agricultural, and ecological heritage. Moreover, its cuisine varies by socioeconomic class, with the upper echelons of society enjoying the most diverse diet. Besides the various indigenous peoples' diets, Tanzanian cuisine has also over time been influenced by Arab Muslim, Portuguese, Indian, Pakistani, German, and English culinary traditions.

While Tanzania is fairly large, only 11 percent of its land area is suitable for crop agriculture. The country's key food crops include maize (corn), sorghum, millet, rice, wheat, pulses (mainly beans), cassava, potatoes, and a wide variety of fruits (e.g., bananas and plantains, pears, apples, plums, passion fruit, grapes, and avocado), vegetables (cabbages, tomatoes, sweet pepper, cauliflower, lettuce, and indigenous vegetables), and spices.

A significant part of the county's protein comes from poultry, fish, and animal sources. Chicken and ducks are Tanzania's most important sources of poultry meat and eggs. The country has an estimated chicken population of 37 million, and most of them are found in the regions of Shinyanga, Mwanza, Tabora, and Mbeya. Conversely, layer chickens are found near the major egg markets (i.e., cities) of Dar es Salaam, Kilimanjaro, Pwani, Dodoma, Morogoro, and Iringa. Overall, Tanzania is a net importer of poultry meat and eggs.[1]

Tanzania has an abundant supply of fish from its marine (Indian Ocean) and freshwater fisheries, such as lakes (e.g., Victoria and Tanganyika), dams, reservoirs, swamps, and ponds and rivers (e.g., Rufiji, Ruvuma, and Ruaha). Fish consumption is highest near the country's fisheries as well as in the urban areas where higher incomes make this delicacy more affordable. In the country's Indian Ocean coastal zone, a wide variety of fish is available, including kingfish, marlin, dolphin, horse mackerel, sailfish, rock cod, sardines, prawns, and sharks. Seaweed is also produced for the domestic and export market. Nile perch, catfish, and tilapia are the country's most important freshwater fish, though most of its Nile perch catch is exported. Fish are seldom eaten by the country's nomadic livestock communities such as the Maasai, who have traditionally preferred getting their protein from cattle, goats, and sheep. In Tanzania, fish is normally stewed, grilled, or deep fried and eaten alone or with a variety of other dishes.

A major source of the country's meat supply is livestock, especially cattle, goats, sheep, and pigs. Improved cattle constitute a tiny fraction of the country's cattle herd, a factor that contributes to its relatively low milk production and consumption. Two-thirds of the country's milk supply comes from subsistence farmers whose small surplus is sold for cash in local urban centers. The remaining supply of milk (one-third) comes from the country's few modern dairy farms.

Sheep and goats provide about 12 percent of Tanzania's animal protein needs and are mainly produced by local subsistence farmers throughout the country. Although pork is a minor source of animal protein in Tanzania, much of it is produced in the country's north and southwest regions. Increased pig production is limited by poor production methods, lack of research and effective extension services, diseases like African swine fever, poor nutrition, limited breeding stocks, and religious taboos that limit the market for pig products. Wild game meat from buffalos, antelopes, elephants, waterbucks, ostriches, and zebras is also consumed in many rural areas, refugee camps, and tourist resorts. Because of the country's high levels of poverty, meat is for most people a delicacy that is consumed on special occasions.

Tanzania's most important staple foods by daily caloric intake are maize (33%), cassava (15%), rice (8%), wheat (4%), and sorghum (4%). While these staples sustain the country, their importance varies by location and income, with, for instance, rice and wheat being central to the diets of high-income urban residents. On the other hand, cassava and sorghum are central to the diets of the producing regions and low-income urban households. Maize is, however, an important staple food in rural and urban households from all socioeconomic classes. Overall, Tanzania is self-sufficient in cassava and sorghum production, nearly self-sufficient in maize and rice production, and virtually wholly dependent on imports for its wheat needs.[2]

As shown in Table 5.1, there is a distinct geography to the production of food crops in Tanzania, with the tonnage produced being a good indicator (except for wheat and sorghum) of the crops' importance in the country's diet. From the table, it is also clear that Tanzania's "bread basket" is confined to a handful of regions, especially the ones that are leading producers of maize and cassava.

In terms of production trends, maize, cassava, rice, sweet potato, banana and plantain, groundnuts, simsim, pulses, and sunflower have generally increased since the 1990s while sorghum, wheat, millet, Irish potatoes, and beans and other pulses have generally declined slightly. While Tanzania is a potential food exporter, it continues to import some key staples because of poor agricultural policies, limited research and extension services, poor food processing and marketing, the dominance of traditional production systems, and overreliance on rain-fed agriculture.

Although Tanzania's diet is largely based on starches such as maize, millet, sorghum, rice, and cassava, there is widespread regional variation in the

Table 5.1 Production of Food Crops in Tanzania

Food Crop	Leading Producing Regions	Tanzania's Annual Production in Thousands of Tons in 2002/2003
Maize	Mbeya, Morogoro, Rukwa, Iringa, Mwanza	3,444
Cassava	Mtwara, Coast/Pwani, Mwanza, Morogoro, Kigoma, Rukwa, Singida	2,843
Rice	Mbeya, Morogoro, Mwanza, Shinyanga	1,294
Wheat	Iringa, Arusha	45
Sorghum	Mwanza, Singida, Dodoma, Morogoro	461
Finger and bulrush millet	Dodoma, Singida, Rukwa, Mwanza	200
Sweet potatoes	Kigoma, Shinyanga, Mwanza	989
Irish potatoes	Iringa and Mbeya	334
Beans and other pulses	Mwanza, Shinyanga, Singida, Dodoma, Kagera, Manyara, Mwanza	1,038
Bananas	Kilimanjaro, Kagera, Mbeya, Kigoma, Tanga	1,900
Groundnuts	Shinyanga, Tabora, Dodoma	255
Simsim	Lindi, Ruvuma	15
Sunflower	Singida, Rukwa, Iringa	112

Source: Ministry of Agriculture, Food Security and Cooperatives, *Food Crop Production, Area and Yield*, 2002–2003, http://www.agriculture.go.tz/, accessed April 19, 2011.

preparation and consumption of these staple foods. Because of its high population diversity that consists of over 120 ethnic groups and pockets of people from other parts of the world, Tanzania has no national dish. However, *ugali* comes close to being one given its popularity across the country. *Ugali* is a stiff maize/corn flour porridge or bread (similar to Italian *polenta* or unsweetened American cornbread) that is usually eaten with cooked vegetables, beans, or stewed or roast fish, beef, chicken, or goat meat.[3] As *ugali* is also made from cassava, millet, or sorghum flour in some parts of the country, its color varies depending on the flour used.

While cassava, millet, and sorghum are native to Tanzania, maize or corn was, on the other hand, brought to the country by the Portuguese in 1498. Despite its slightly over 500-year history in the country, it did not become a national staple until it was used as a famine- or drought-relief food (what locals call *chakula cha njaa*) by the government and international relief agencies in the 1970s and 1980s. For this reason, some of the last communities to adopt it initially had no taste for *ugali* or the mixed corn and beans (*makande*) meal that is now popular in many parts of the country.[4]

To prepare an *ugali* dish for one, boil two cups of water in a saucepan (a wide variety of pots is traditionally used to cook *ugali* in Tanzania) on high heat; reduce the heat to medium and slowly pour in two to three cups of non-self-raising maize flour (cornmeal) as you stir briskly with a sturdy flat wooden cooking spoon or stick for three to four minutes to arrive at a consistent hot bread. For more flavor, let the *ugali* cook until it emits a slight burning aroma. Depending on the amount of flour used, the *ugali* can be soft or hard in texture. While harder *ugali* is easier to eat by hand, inexperienced cooks often struggle to make it, leading to *ugali* with a stony consistency that is distasteful. Whether soft or hard textured, the *ugali* eaten across Tanzania varies by individual, family, or ethnic community.

A common way of eating *ugali* is to break a small morsel by hand (usually the right one), shape it into a ball at the fingertips, dent the top of the morsel with the thumb, and then use it to scoop a small amount of the vegetable or meat relish that it is eaten with. Outside of the home, *ugali* with vegetables and meat stew is widely available in restaurants across the country. While the less well-off usually eat *ugali* with vegetables, the better-off segments of society tend to eat it with vegetables and stewed or roast chicken, fish, beef, lamb, or goat meat.

Besides *ugali*, other staple dishes, depending on location and means, include plain rice or *pilau* (rice spiced with curry, cinnamon, cumin, hot peppers, and cloves), *chapati* (a flat, unleavened, round-shaped bread that is made of wheat flour, water, and salt and is similar to Indian *naan*), and variously cooked Irish potatoes, sweet potatoes, bananas and plantains, cassava, and mixed corn and beans (*makande*). The latter dish is also common in places like Upale and in boarding schools and prisons throughout the country. *Ndizi kaanga* (fried bananas or plantains) is a common dish in urban areas while boiled bananas or plantains mixed with beans or meat is a staple meal among the Haya of northwest Tanzania. Boiled or roast maize (corn) on the cob is also a popular snack throughout the country.

Nearly all of these main meals are eaten with various vegetable stews, for example collard greens (*sukuma wiki*), spinach (*mchicha*), cassava leaves (*kisambu*), bean soup, or stewed or roast fish, beef, chicken, or goat meat. These meals are commonly washed down with water, tea, coffee, fruit juice, or even the wide variety of traditional or commercial beer (*pombe*). In most cases, onions, tomatoes, cooking oils, coconut milk, peanuts, and a wide variety of spices are used to flavor the various stews and soups used to eat the main meals. In the coastal zone, many of the fish dishes feature coconut milk and a variety of mild to hot spices, with the hotness of the meals generally decreasing with distance from the coast and urban centers. Coconut-bean, plantain, vegetable, and meat soup is popular throughout the country.

Tanzanians also produce and enjoy a wide variety of tropical fruits, such as oranges, coconuts, bananas, pawpaws, watermelons, papaya, mangoes, passion fruit, pears, apples, plums, grapes, and avocadoes. These are often eaten after the main meal or as snacks throughout the day.

Tanzania's developing market economy generally makes it possible for many of the country's staple foods and fruits to be available throughout the country. Nevertheless, urban areas have the richest choice of food because of their higher ethnic mix and incomes. Thus, foods such as rice, wheat bread, *chapati*, *sambusa* (a tasty meat or vegetable pie), and *mandazi* (a puffy donut roll) are ubiquitous in urban Tanzania. Higher incomes also afford many urban Tanzanians higher levels of meat consumption, though even here, as in most rural areas of the country, poor households usually eat meat on special occasions like weddings and Christmas.

The very best of Tanzania's cuisine is more readily abundant in Dar es Salaam, the country's largest, richest, and most cosmopolitan city. Here, one easily finds restaurants that specialize in Tanzanian fare as well as the international cuisine that serves the needs of the city's Arabic, European, and Asian population, tourists, and various local elites.

Most Tanzanians eat three meals a day, though what they eat for breakfast, lunch, and dinner varies widely by income, ethnicity, and location. The many poor Tanzanians often make do with less than three meals a day, and most of their meals are unbalanced. As a result, malnutrition is a common problem in Tanzania, and school lunch programs are being used to combat it in the school-age population.

For most Tanzanians, breakfast is usually a simple affair consisting of hot black tea or coffee with *ugali*, bananas, cassava, sweet potatoes, or some other local starch source depending on the season. Maize (corn) or millet (*ulezi*) porridge (*uji*) is also a popular breakfast item in many rural areas and boarding schools throughout the country. Porridge is made by boiling a mixture of corn flour, water, and sugar. For richer rural and urban households, a breakfast consisting of a cup or two of hot tea or coffee taken with sweet fried rice breads (*vitumbua*), sweet deep fried donut or dinner rolls (*mandazi*), bread (*mkate*), flat bread (*chapati*), and eggs (*mayai*) is common. Many richer households also incorporate local foods like bananas, cassava, and sweet potatoes in their breakfast. Increasingly complicated work schedules mean that many families seldom have time to gather for breakfast. In the busy times of the year (e.g., ploughing, planting, and harvesting seasons), many Tanzanians often eat enough breakfast to keep them going until dinner.

Lunch often consists of *ugali* or some other starch base like plantains and bananas (*ndizi*), rice (*pilau* or *wali*), Irish or sweet potatoes, and cassava, which are eaten with beans (*maharawe*); grilled chicken (*kuku choma*); grilled goat or cow meat (*nyama choma*); wild or bush meat that is either sun dried, grilled, or cooked (*nyama pori*); grilled pork (*kiti moto*); stewed meat (*mishikaki*); grilled or stewed fish (*samaki*); okra (*bamia*); greens such as spinach and collard greens (*mchicha*), peas (*njegere*), and cassava leaves (*kisamvu*); and soup from boiled animal bones and meat or blood (*kisusio*). It is usually washed down with water, tea, coffee, fruit juice, or the country's wide variety of traditional or commercial beer (*pombe*). Because many people seldom have the time or the resources to regularly eat lunch, it is the most skipped meal in the country.

Dinner (supper) is the country's main meal. Aside from usually gathering the whole family, dinner tends to be the country's heaviest and most leisurely meal. It usually features the same meals as lunch except in wealthier households, where a different dish might be served.

Snacks usually vary by income, location, and season. But in general the common ones are tropical fruits, puffy donut rolls (*mandazi*), coconut or groundnut rolls (*visheti*, *kashata*), kabab, samosa (*sambusa*), fried rice cakes (*mkate wa kumimina*, *vileja*, *vitumbua*), *bajia*, grilled gizzards (*firigisi*), dates (*tende*), groundnuts or peanuts (*karanga*), cashew nuts (*korosho*), fried nut-sized fish (*daga*), pan-grilled grasshoppers (*senene*), and pan-grilled flying termites (*kumbikumbi*) as well as select American- and European-style snacks for those who can afford them in the major cities. With increased incomes and better food processing, storage, and distribution, more snacks are increasingly becoming available.

While Tanzanians are generally very good hosts, their mealtime customs vary widely based on ethnicity, income, religious beliefs, or even whether the host is a rural or urban dweller. In many rural and Muslim households, men and women eat separately. By custom, food is usually cooked by women and girls on a wood fire in a three-stone hearth or on a charcoal stove in the kitchen or open courtyard. Although men are usually involved in food production, they are seldom involved in its preparation at home except when working as chefs in hotels, institutions, or when living alone or away from their wives.

Meals are usually served on low tables or floor mats by women and girls. Because food is usually eaten by hand, except for dishes like rice that involve the use of limited cutlery like spoons or forks, diners usually wash their hands before the meal in a bowl that goes around the table with a towel. The main dish and stew are often set in large communal bowls in the middle of the dining table surrounded by each diner's smaller relish (vegetable or stew) bowl. After washing their hands and filling their stew bowls, diners use their right hands to eat. In situations where food is served on individual plates, guests and older males are often served first. In religious households, some sort of prayer precedes the meal. After the meal, guests wash their hands again and are then served with a bowl of fresh fruit or a hot beverage, if available. In the middle of the day when temperatures are high, a glass of cold water or fruit juice is the preferred way of washing down the meal. In upscale urban households, dessert may be also served.

Biomass in the form of firewood, charcoal, and farm residues is the dominant cooking fuel in Tanzania. Thus, it accounts for about 90 percent of the country's rural cooking energy, with the rest coming from petroleum (8%), electricity (1%), and other sources (1%). Because the three-stone wood-burning hearths that dominate rural cooking have very low efficiencies (in the 12–15% range) and are a key factor in the country's high incidence of respiratory diseases due to poor indoor ventilation, there have been attempts to improve or replace them since the 1980s by entities like the nonprofit Tanzania Traditional Energy Development and Environment Organization (TaTEDO).

As part of this effort, new ceramic, metal, and improved clay charcoal and firewood stoves with much higher efficiencies have been developed and disseminated, though their widespread use is fraught with many challenges. These include inadequate policies, strategies, financing, marketing, promotion, awareness, and adoption of the new stoves as well as many producers' lack of adequate technical, production, and quality-control capacity. Nevertheless, the new stoves are slowly becoming popular.[5]

An improved traditional cooking stove in Tanzania. (Per-Anders Pettersson/Getty Images)

In urban areas, biomass (mostly charcoal) accounts for 70 percent of cooking energy needs, with electricity and natural gas accounting for the rest. The latter two are mostly used in wealthier urban households with wood-fuel stoves being used as backups. Thus, the increasing adoption of improved cooking stoves (e.g., ceramic-lined charcoal stoves) is likely to have a positive environmental impact in both rural and urban areas. As electricity and food refrigeration become more widespread, the environmental cost of the country's high food wastage is also likely to decline.

Beverages

Tanzanians consume a wide variety of beverages including milk, fruit juices, tea, coffee, soft drinks, beer, wine, and hard liquors. Of these, milk, juice and other nonalcoholic beverages are the most popular given their suitability for all ages, occasions, and incomes. Tea (*chai*) and coffee (*kahawa*) are also popular among the adults. While tea is consumed throughout the day, often with friends and family, coffee is usually taken in the cool evening with coconut or groundnut rolls (*kashata*) as people chat, relax, and play cards or board games (*bao*) on their front porches.

Practically every Tanzanian ethnic community has a traditional brew derived from its major staple, including bananas, maize, and millet. For instance, the coastal region has coconut beer (*mnazi* or *tembo*) while the Chagga of the Kilimanjaro region have *mbege* (a banana beer) and *wanzuki* (a liquor made of fermented honey and water). The Haya of the western shores of Lake Victoria prefer *lubisi, nkonyagi* and *mbandule* while other parts of the country like pawpaw fruit beer and *gongo*, an illegal distilled cashew-nut drink whose brewed version is called *uraka*. The country's two major breweries, Tanzania Breweries and Serengeti Breweries, also make a variety of alcoholic drinks like beers (e.g., Kilimanjaro, Safari, and Serengeti), spirits like *konyagi*, and wine.

Many of the globally popular soft drinks from the Pepsi-Cola and Coca-Cola conglomerates, such as Pepsi, Fanta, Coca Cola, Stoney, Krest, Mirinda, and Sprite, are widely available in urban areas and in rural shopping centers. There are also many locally produced and imported fruit juices.

Beverage consumption in Tanzania depends heavily on income; with wealthy individuals enjoying the widest selection. Businessmen and other high-income individuals frequently enjoy processed beer, wine, and malts. As in many other countries, alcoholism is a growing social problem in Tanzania, with many people (especially men) increasingly using it to escape the harsh realities of life. The adulteration of many local ethnic brews with chemicals like methanol has increasingly made them highly addictive if not dangerous.[6]

Cuisine and Ceremonies

Food and drink play an important role in Tanzanian social, religious, and political ceremonies, including marriages and funerals. In many communities, weddings are joyous events with plenty of food, refreshments, and dance. Couples and their families try their best to ensure that their wedding guests are well fed with all manner of delicacies. As the success of a wedding is often judged by the amount of food left over, wedding hosts try hard not to run out of food.

In many of Tanzania's African traditional religions (ATRs), food is an essential part of worship as various foods and drinks are part of the sacrifices and libations offered to the ancestors and gods. While Christians and Muslims do not have food and drink offerings, they do use food and drink in various other ways. For instance, the Christian Holy Communion uses food and drink elements to memorialize the death and resurrection of Jesus Christ. On Christmas, churches often fill to the brim with worshippers who afterwards scatter to their homes for sumptuous meals and leisurely evening neighborhood and beach walks, thanks to the country's pleasant warm, tropical climate. Many churches also serve light refreshments to their members on Christmas.

Similarly, the Muslim month-long daytime fast of Ramadan features plenty of food and drink before sunrise and after sunset. During Eid al-Fitr celebrations that mark the end of Ramadan, Muslims feast on stockpiles of food (e.g., rice, bread, fish, chicken, beef, cassava chips), nonalcoholic beverages (e.g., tamarind juice), and fruits (e.g., plantains and dates). Moreover, children dress up in colorful costumes and go from house to house in search of cake, lemongrass tea, and other delicacies.

On secular national holidays like Independence Day, Tanzanians from all walks of life also hold countrywide celebrations that often involve plenty of food, drink, and dance.

Internationalization of Tanzanian Cuisine

While Tanzania has a diverse indigenous cuisine, it has for centuries welcomed the culinary traditions of the Arabian Peninsula, South and Southeast Asia, Europe, the Americas, and other African regions. In recent decades, the breadth of its cuisine has benefitted from its booming global tourism business, the growing presence of many international companies and organizations, and the expanding Tanzanian diaspora. Other important contributors to this effort include the marketing activities of global food companies, supermarkets, television, and rising incomes. For all these reasons, one can enjoy food from all over the world in many Tanzanian cities, especially Dar es Salaam and Arusha.

DRESS

Traditional Dress and Adornments

Traditional Tanzanian dress has evolved over time. In the precolonial era, clothing was made from locally available materials such as bark cloth and domestic and wild animal skins. Thus, besides sex and ethnicity, location was an important determinant of available clothing, with some ethnic groups having fairly elaborate attire while others wore next to nothing. But in general, adults wore grass skirts, bark clothes, and animal skins that at least covered various portions of the lower body. Women also generally wore beads and bangles. Children scarcely wore any clothing until the onset of puberty, although girls were often adorned with colorful necklaces and earrings.

In many traditional Tanzanian societies, personal adornments were widespread, though they varied by community and region. Some of the common ones included tattoos, body marks, beads, earrings, nose and lip ornaments, bracelets, oil, ghee, headdresses, cow dung, and various body paintings.

Among the most elaborate personal adornments in traditional Tanzania were and are those of the Maasai of northern Tanzania. Maasai *morans* (warriors) were and are usually the best adorned, with tattoos and other body marks

A smiling woman in her traditional Maasai female adornments. (Chris Jackson/ Getty Images)

(especially on the cheeks); well-oiled bodies (with animal fat) covered with red clothing; feet protected by animal skin sandals; adornments like necklaces, earrings, and ivory bands on their upper arms (when and where available); intricate head shavings and hair styled with red ochre; and the customary personal weapons of a spear, a club, and a sword. Besides contributing to a warrior's prestige, elaborate dress traditionally played an important role in courtship. Conversely, Maasai women and girls have traditionally worn colorful and elaborate bead necklaces, headbands, and earrings. Since the mid-1900s, many Maasai have increasingly worn Western-style dress even as others have used some Western clothing items (e.g., red cotton sheets) to perpetuate their dress traditions.

In many Tanzanian societies, the removal of some teeth, especially the two lower front ones, was a common aspect of personal adornment, initiation, traditional medical practice that enabled people to feed in the event of their contracting tetanus or lockjaw disease. In nearly all traditional Tanzanian communities, there was special attire for certain ceremonies or functions, such as that worn by dancers, warriors, shamans, traditional healers, and medicine men.[7]

Modern Dress and Adornments

Since the advent of Arabs and Europeans to Tanzania, the traditional African dress styles described above have declined. While contemporary Tanzanian clothing is quite diverse, with African, Asian, Arab, and European elements, most Tanzanians wear loose, gender-specific, European-style clothes.

Therefore, many mainland Tanzanian women wear Western-style tops, t-shirts, blouses, knee-length skirts, dresses, and shoes. They seldom wear trousers, as these are commonly seen as men's clothing. However, in the urban areas, it is increasingly common for women to wear trousers, tight clothes, and skimpy outfits. Women also wear various adornments including necklaces, bangles, hats, watches, earrings, rings, and handbags. Tanzanian women tend to wear short or long braided hair. Hair extensions are also common.

Many of the country's women also wear a colorful wrap-style garment called the *kanga* or *khanga*, which is often complimented by a headscarf. *Kangas* usually feature simple to intricate print designs and printed messages

Tanzanian dancers wear *kanga*, traditional African cloths, bearing the image of President Bush as they perform for him, at a social dinner held at the State House in Dar es Salaam, Tanzania, February 17, 2008. (AP Photo/Charles Dharapak)

of love, caution, warning, reassurance, or anything that the wearer wishes to communicate. Many of the messages are common Swahili proverbs such as *Mwenye nguvu mpishe* (Never fight losing battles) and *Fimbo la mnyonge halina nguvu* (The weak/poor never win; nothing works in favor of the poor). Besides being items of clothing, *kangas* also serve as aprons or shawls that women use to carry young children on their backs.

Tanzanian Muslim women generally follow the Islamic dress code that promotes modesty, privacy, and morality. Thus, long, loose dresses that cover the arms and legs (all the way to the ankles) and a headscarf that covers everything except the face is the norm. In Tanzania, this type of head-to-toe black dress is called a *buibui*. Nevertheless, the extent to which individual Tanzanian Muslim women observe this code is often mitigated by the branch of Islam they belong to as well as their ethnicity, the extent of their devoutness, and the local dress culture.

For Tanzanian men, Western-style trousers, t-shirts, hats, and shirts have been popular since the mid-1900s. Men who work in formal enterprises often wear suits and neckties. Common men's adornments include watches, necklaces, and bangles. In Muslim areas, men also adhere to the Islamic dress code. Accordingly, they often wear *kikoi* wraps and *kanzus*—flowing white robes that are often embroidered and worn with or without jackets.[8]

For formal occasions, weddings, marriage betrothals, funeral ceremonies, national events, church functions, and audiences with dignitaries, Tanzanians wear pricier and higher-quality versions of the clothing items described above. It is also increasingly common for Christian brides and grooms to take their marriage vows in Western-style wedding clothes. School children usually wear uniforms from primary through high school.

Dress Fashion

Tanzanian dress fashion ranges from the traditional to the modern. Traditional attire is common among the less-westernized groups of Tanzania, such as the Maasai. Nevertheless, elements of traditional dress are widespread even among the most westernized groups such as the Chagga. Among all black African groups, aspects of traditional clothing are also worn on ceremonial occasions. However, traditional African adornments such as bangles are common, everyday dress items.

In the more westernized parts of the country, Western fashion trends are common. For instance, many urban elites in Dar es Salaam buy their clothes at the city's high-fashion shopping malls, such as Shoppers Plaza and the Slipway Shopping Center. The malls stock high-end American and European apparel and footwear products. Brands like Nike, Adidas, Dunlop, and Reebok are popular among Tanzania's affluent young people, thanks to

Maasai woman adorned in a mixture of traditional and modern dress. (Spencer Platt/ Getty Images)

Tanzania's liberal economy and the influence of international magazines, music videos, satellite television, and global merchandise firms. Even among low- and middle-income Tanzanians, similar items are popular and available from the country's secondhand clothes and shoes markets that source their products from the United States and Europe. Thus, it is not uncommon for low- and middle-income Tanzanians to wear sports paraphernalia from popular U.S. and European sports teams.

Another important promoter of Western fashion in the country are the many American and European tourists who visit Tanzania annually clad in popular Western fashion items, which are then adopted by locals. In recent decades, the relatively large global Tanzanian diaspora has also become a key conveyor of global fashion to the country.

While Tanzania is not a major center of global fashion, it has a promising local fashion industry that is beginning to have regional and global success. While most of the country's designers practice their craft in obscurity all over the country, its Dar es Salaam–based high fashion industry is beginning to get noticed. Some of the country's major female fashion designers are Khadija Saad Mwanamboka, Doreen Mashika, Vida Mahimbo, Flotea Massawe, Jamilla Swai, Robi Morro, Zamda George, Kemi Kalikawe, Ailinda Sawe, Asia Idarous Khamsin, Christine Mhando, Farha Sultan, Diana Magesa,

Francisca Shirima (Francis), and Farha Naaz. On the male side there are Mustafa Hassanali, Ally Rehmtullah, and Gabriel Sakita Mollel. Many of the major fashion designers in Dar es Salaam are affiliated with the Tanzania Mitindo (Fashion) House. With Kemi Kalikawe's recent launch of the Naledi Fashion Training Institute that offers short courses and master classes in fashion and design, young Tanzanian fashion designers have a place to refine their skills, exhibit their work, and network with established designers and other fashion stakeholders in the country.[9] Below is a brief overview of the work of Khadija Saad Mwanamboka, Flotea Massawe, and Mustafa Hassanali.

Khadija Saad Mwanamboka, who runs the Khadija Collections Fashion Design Studio, was born in 1977. Although she has no formal training in fashion design, she is one of the country's leading fashionistas or fashion icons, having launched her career in 1994 by designing clothes for herself and her mother. She later showcased her designs at local fashion shows, and she has since showcased her work locally, regionally, and internationally and even adjudicated some national and regional fashion events. She has also dressed some local and international music stars.

Because she is a designer activist who seeks to promote the splendor and glamour of Tanzanian and African clothes, designs, and designers, she primarily designs in the local *kanga*, *batik*, and *kitenge* tradition that mostly uses locally available materials. To facilitate her community development efforts as well as promote local designers, she founded the Tanzania Mitindo (Fashion) House, a nongovernmental, nonprofit organization that uses the fashion industry to give vulnerable Tanzanian children, especially those affected by HIV/AIDS, a healthier and higher quality of life. Specifically, the organization takes care of HIV/AIDS orphans and gives them access to education, shelter, food, medical care, and good and safe playgrounds.[10]

Although Flotea Massawe started working in the industry in the early 1990s, she did not have access to global markets until 2005 when the U.S. Agency for International Development (USAID) gave her company technical help in design and marketing. USAID also helped her to attend a number of trade shows in the United States that enabled her to network with buyers there. Since then her company, Marvelous Flotea Company Limited, has created employment for 200 women, who help to handcraft its pillows, bags, runners, and table mats that are now exported to the United States, India, and Japan.

Aside from assisting Massawe, USAID has also supported fashion shows in the country that seek to develop local talent as well as creating avenues for designer-manufacturer cooperation in developing a strong African fashion industry. Moreover, USAID has sought to introduce Tanzanian fashion designers to the U.S. market for apparel, crafts, and home décor by educating

One of Mustafa Hassanali's fashion designs. (Seyllou/AFP/GettyImages)

them on the various U.S. retail channels, brands, and export avenues; equipping them with strategies for tailoring their designs to U.S. buyers and markets; and giving them technical expertise on how to access these markets. As Massawe's experience demonstrates, while the country has plenty of design talent, limited technical exposure, outdated machinery, and poor marketing have undermined its development and global impact.[11]

Mustafa Hassanali is, perhaps, the most accomplished and sought-after Tanzanian fashion designer, whose work has been characterized as elegant, stylish, flamboyant, and glamorous. His designs reflect the styles of Tanzania's multicultural society as well as avant-garde, hip, and contemporary styles. Besides developing his own collection, he is the founder of the Swahili Fashion Week and the *Harusi* (wedding) Trade Fair, both of which have become the premier events of their kind in Tanzania and much of

East Africa. In particular, the Swahili Fashion Week has become a key platform for fashion and accessory designers from Swahili-speaking countries of
East, Central, and Southern Africa to showcase their talent, network with
their clients, and market their products. Moreover, the event is contributing
to the region's cultural and economic development by promoting the Made
in East Africa brand. Hassanali's *Harusi* (wedding) Trade Fair caters to the
wedding needs of the modern Tanzanian bride.

Besides the showcases that Hassanali holds each year, his work has brought
him considerable international acclaim. He has designed clothes for corpo-
rate and television shows such as *Miss Tanzania* and has showcased his work
internationally, including at the India International Fashion Week 2009 and
Naomi Campbell's Fashion for Relief 2009. His success on the runway combined with his medical background has coalesced in his support of health-
related charity events including breast cancer awareness and the Zanzibar
Mental Hospital. His Fashion 4 Health brand seeks to raise funds for these
causes.[12]

A good indication of how far the Tanzanian fashion and design scene has
come is the rise of a local modeling industry complete with models and promoters like Javed Jafferji—a renowned photographer and author of several
books on Tanzania and other East African countries. Some of Tanzania's
top female models are Miriam Odemba and Flaviana Matata. Miriam
Odemba is an international supermodel who won Miss Tanzania (Temeke),
became the Face of Africa finalist, was first runner-up at the Miss Earth
2008 Pageant in the Philippines, and was crowned Miss Earth Air in 2008.
She became the first Tanzanian to finish in the top three positions in the Miss
Earth Pageant, thereby paving the way for other Tanzanians.[13]

Matata represented Tanzania in the 2007 Miss Universe Pageant in
Mexico, where she became one of the top 10 semifinalists, and ultimately
clinched the number 6 spot out of 77 contenders from around the world.
She also made pageant history by being the first Miss Universe 2007 to sport
a bald look. In 2010, *Essence* magazine named her one of the year's standout
models. Later in the year, she featured in the December 2010 issue of *L'Offi-
ciel Paris* magazine besides participating in New York Fashion Week Fall
2010. At the 2011 *Arise* Magazine Fashion Week Awards in Lagos, Nigeria,
Matata won the Model of the Year award.

Matata was born in Shinyanga, Tanzania, in 1987. She lost her mother to
death at an early age and became a surrogate mother to her siblings. After
the 2007 Miss Universe Pageant, Matata worked for a year as a model for
the Ice Model Agency in Johannesburg, South Africa. While there she participated in various fashion shows, notably the Johannesburg and Cape Town
Fashion Weeks. In February 2010, she secured a modeling spot with New

Miss Universe Tanzania and fashion model Flaviana Matata. (AP Photo/Gregory Bull)

York City's Next Models Agency with the help of Russell Simmons, creator of the Phat Farm clothing fashion line. Matata is also a qualified electrical technician. She is the founder of the Flaviana Matata Foundation that memorializes her late mother and seeks to reduce child pregnancy and empower young women and children.[14]

Dress and Identity

Dress and adornment are central aspects of any person's, people's, or country's identity. These elements are often media for conveying, representing, and contesting existing social power relations in Tanzania and elsewhere. Accordingly, the country's leaders and designers have sought to give it a unique dress that enhances its values and culture, but with no success.

In general, Tanzanians love modest or nonrevealing clothing, whether in casual or business settings. Thus, tank tops, short shorts, and ripped or dirty clothing is generally unacceptable. Even casual clothing such as jeans and shorts is expected to be loose fitting and to sensibly balance local and foreign dress codes.

Formal men's and women's business attire is valued and respected in business circles, especially in the major cities. In rural situations, trousers (pants) and nice collared shirts are acceptable for men while long skirts that reach below the knees, dresses, and nonrevealing tops are preferred for women. Because of the country's increasing globalization, Western dress fashions have become part of Tanzania's identity, more so in Dar es Salaam, where Western clothing and consumerism are in full display, especially among the youth.

But perhaps the most Tanzanian dress is the *kanga*, a brightly colored and boldly designed cotton cloth that has a border all around the edge. The material came to Tanzania when cotton textiles from India and Portugal started to be traded at the Zanzibar slave market in the eighteenth and nineteenth centuries. The Portuguese printed textiles, which were initially used as shawls, had square-like patterns and were shipped in half-meter-wide (about 1.6 feet) rolls that were normally sold in one-meter (3.28 feet) lengths. Eventually women started buying six square meters (64.58 square feet), which were then cut into two and sown together to create dresses whose patterns resembled the plumage of the guinea fowl, or *kanga* in Swahili.[15]

The popularity of *kanga* in Tanzania and much of East Africa partly derives from its versatility—it folds, ties, and winds easily. *Kangas* are mostly worn by women, although men also wear colorful *kanga* shirts. Women's *kangas* often have printed slogans, proverbs, or some other educational, informational, or political messages. Women also use *kangas* as shawls for carrying babies on their backs, aprons when cooking or working around the house and farm, and as fashionable throws or wrap-arounds worn over ordinary dresses. *Kangas* can also be used as table cloths or decorative wall hangings.

Local and international politicians also use *kangas* to popularize their messages. For instance, when former U.S. President George Bush visited Tanzania in 2008, he was welcomed with *kanga* dresses and shirts bearing his likeness and pertinent Swahili and English messages like "*Udumu Urafikiki Kati Ya Marekani na Tanzania*" ("Long Live the Friendship between the United States and Tanzania). Similarly, Tanzanians and many East Africans celebrated the historic election of Barack Obama as U.S. president with *kanga* dresses and shirts bearing his picture.

Many Tanzanian designers, including Mustafa Hassanali, Ally Rehmtulla, and Doreen Mashika, have through their Khangalicious designs worked hard to raise the global profile of the kanga.[16] Batik designs for men and women are also common in Tanzania. However, they have especially become popular among men since former South African president Nelson Mandela wore one.[17]

Some Tanzanian ethnic groups such as the Maasai have traditionally had very distinct dress that they still generally use. Other groups, such as the hunter-gatherer "Bushmen" who live in forest caves near Lake Eyasi, prefer to go without clothes and are thus noted for this unique form of "dress." Other Tanzanian communities also had distinct dress styles that enhanced their unique identity, more so in the precolonial era. In the colonial and postcolonial periods, these unique dress and ethnic identities began to crumble as Tanzania abolished its traditional centers of political power in a bid to build a united national identity.

This effort peaked in the late 1960s when Tanzania launched the Operation Dress-Up policy in a bid to preserve its traditional African morality. Thus, it sought to force everyone in the country to wear clothes that covered their arms, necks, and legs. Simultaneously, it started to get rid of certain undesirable aspects of Western fashion, including miniskirts, tight trousers and dresses, wigs, skin-lightening creams, short shorts, sleeveless tops, and long hair for men.[18] As part of its antinudity campaign, the government soon banned traditional Maasai dress for being too revealing, backward, and inimical to the community's modern development. But in the end, the Operation Dress-Up policy failed because it proved impossible to enforce; it required clothing that was unsuitable for Tanzania's hot tropical climate; it infuriated urban women by insinuating that their professional success was through seduction rather than through their hard work and educational qualifications; urban youth used it to embarrass the government by pointing out that the modernization that the government sought was the very reason for their "undesirable" dress code; and because the Maasai steadfastly held to their culture and refused to change their dress style.[19]

While the country no longer legally enforces a modest dress code, such a code is nevertheless enforced by social practice in most parts of the country, especially in the rural areas. Nonetheless, the quest for socially acceptable forms of dress rages on between the young and the old, rural and urban dwellers, religious and secular Tanzanians, locals and tourists, as well as between traditionalists and the modernists. Thus, in much of the country, older generations continue to lament the revealing dress styles of the younger generation while the younger generations disdain the dated or dull dress styles of the older generations.

In the largely Muslim Tanzanian coast and Zanzibar that is also central to the country's tourism economy, the contest between the *hijab*, the bikini, and the miniskirt is as contentious as ever, with occasional reports of scantily dressed women being attacked by some devout Muslims. Ironically, some "twilight girls" now exploit the supposed chastity of *hijab* wearers to charge a premium for their services. Similarly, devout Christians have also condemned the skimpy dress styles of tourists and even some of their own members. As in other African countries, the coming of global television to Tanzania has also brought with it shows and commercials that undermine any local efforts to promote modest dressing as subtle sex messages are increasingly used to sell merchandise in the country.[20]

Meanwhile, Tanzania continues its search for a national dress. A pair of recent national dress design concepts consists of a colorful *kitenge* (*kanga*) wrap-around and matching headscarf for women and a collarless Chou En-Lai suit for men similar to that common in China. Both designs, the former by Agnes Gabriel and the latter by Rose Valentine, seek to promote a Tanzanian national identity by featuring the national flag on the chest. However, neither design has caught on because some see them as unrepresentative of the country's ethnic diversity, and they are seldom worn by the country's leaders, who mostly prefer Western business suits. Additionally, the women's design has been criticized for seeking to impose *kitenge* (*kanga*) on all women while the men's one has been faulted for being foreign inspired. Both concepts have also been criticized for not being based on research as to what is likely to be popular nationally. In light of the foregoing mistakes, the government appointed a committee in 2012 to collect public input on what the country's national dress should look like.[21]

NOTES

1. Halifa Msami, "Poultry Sector Country Review: Tanzania," FAO, 2007, ftp://ftp.fao.org/docrep/fao/011/ai349e/ai349e00.pdf, accessed April 4, 2011.

2. Nicholas Minot, "Staple Food Prices in Tanzania," prepared for the COMESA policy seminar on Variation in Staple Food Prices: Causes, Consequence, and Policy Options, Maputo, Mozambique, January 25–26, 2010, under the African Agricultural Marketing Project, http://ageconsearch.umn.edu/bitstream/58555/2/AAMP _Maputo_24_Tanzania_ppr.pdf, accessed April 4 2011.

3. Embassy of Tanzania—Washington DC, "Tanzania: Food," http://www .tanzaniaembassy-us.org/tzepeo.html, accessed May 4, 2011; Advameg, "Food in Every Country: Tanzania," 2011, http://www.foodbycountry.com/Spain-to -Zimbabwe-Cumulative-Index/Tanzania.html, accessed April 19, 2011.

4. Personal interviews with Tanzanian natives Alvera Byabato and Doris Mrutu, May 10, 2011—July 16, 2012.

5. E. N. Sawe, "Wood Fuels Stoves Development and Promotion in Tanzania: Some Selected Experiences," European Biomass/COMPETE workshop on Bioenergy for Rural Development in Africa and Asia, June 30, 2009, Hamburg, Germany, http://www.compete-bioafrica.net/events/events2/hamburg/Session%202/S2-5 -COMPETE-REImpact-Hamburg-Sawe-090630.pdf, accessed April 23, 2011.

6. Embassy of Tanzania—Washington DC, "Tanzania: Food"; M. N. Kitundu, V. A. E. B. Kilimali, H. B. Maurice, G. I. Kiula, and M. E. Kamwaya, "Presence of Methyl Alcohol in Local Alcoholic Beverages in Tanzania and Its Relationship to Impaired Vision or Death," *Tanzania Journal of Natural and Applied Sciences* (TaJONAS) 1, no. 2, (December 2010), 102–5.

7. J. Mutai, E. Muniu, J. Sawe, J. Hassanali, P. Kibet, and P. Wanzala, "Sociocultural Practices of Deciduous Canine Tooth Bud Removal among Maasai Children," *International Dentistry* Journal 60, no. 2 (April 2010): 94–98.

8. Hassan O. Ali, "Kanga Writings," 2004, http://www.glcom.com/hassan/kanga .html, accessed April 25, 2011.

9. Tanzania Mitindo House, "Designers," 2009, http://www.mitindohouse.org/, accessed April 28, 2011; Hasina Mjingo, "Kemi Kalikwe—Brain behind Naledi Fashion Institute," *Tanzania Daily News*, October 14, 2010, http://in2eastafrica .net/kemi-kalikwe-brain-behind-naledi-fashion-institute/, accessed April 28, 2011; Karisma Fashion Group, "Vida Mahimbo," Karisma Fashion Group, 2009, http:// www.vidamahimbo.com/, accessed April 28, 2011; Swahili Fashion Week, "Designers," 2010, http://www.swahilifashionweek.com/, accessed April 28, 2011.

10. Swahili Fashion Week, "Khadija Mwanamboka—Tanzania," Swahili Fashion Week, 2010, http://www.swahilifashionweek.com/, accessed April 28, 2011.

11. USAID—East Africa, "African Entrepreneur Taps into U.S. Market," April 20, 2011, http://eastafrica.usaid.gov/en/Article.1339.aspx, accessed April 26, 2011.

12. Ogova Ondego, "Tanzanian Fashion Designers Showcase Their Work in Dar es Salaam and Kigali," *Art Matters*, March 18, 2009, www.artmatters.info/?p=1233, accessed April 27, 2011.

13. Majuto Omary, "Tanzania's Miriam Odemba Wins Miss Earth pageant," *Ethiopian Review*, November 11 2008, http://www.ethiopianreview.com/content/ 13112, accessed April 27, 2011.

14. "Catwalk Star," *Standard*, April 27, 2011, http://www.standardmedia.co.ke/, accessed April 27, 2011; Bella Naija, "Klûk CGDT, Deola Sagoe, Flaviana Matata & Tiffany Amber Win at the 2011 ARISE Magazine Fashion Week Awards," *Bella Naija*, March 14, 2011, http://www.bellanaija.com/, accessed April 27, 2011.

15. Bhavna Pandya-Barratt, "Proudly Tanzanian: The Khanga Story," *This Is Bhavna (blog)*, Wednesday, January 14, 2009, http://www.blogger.com/feeds/ 19494422/posts/default, accessed April 29, 2011.

16. Michuzi, "Khangalicious," *Michuzi Blog*, June 12, 2008, http://issamichuzi .blogspot.com/2008/06/khangalicious.html, accessed July 17, 2012.

17. Valentine Marc Nkwame, "Tanzania: Mandela Shirts' Intrigue Kenyan Journalists," *My Africa*, October 28, 2006, http://myafrica.wordpress.com/2006/ 10/28/tanzania-mandela-shirts-intrigue-kenyan-journalists/, accessed May 11, 2011; Dina Ismail, "Maonyesho ya 'Twende' Yamalizika kwa Washiriki Kupata Mafanikio," *Sports Lady*, September 17, 2010, http://dinaismail.blogspot.com/ 2010/09/maonyesho-ya-twende-yamalizika-kwa.html, accessed July 17, 2012.

18. E. G. Gillespie, "Tanzania Border Control," 2008–2012, http://www
.fascinating-travel-destinations.com/tanzania-border.html, accessed April 25, 2011;
Katherine A. Luongo, "Review of Dorothy L. Hodgson. *Once Intrepid Warriors:
Gender, Ethnicity, and the Cultural Politics of Maasai Development,* Bloomington:
Indiana University Press, 2001," *H-Africa,* April 2003, http://www.h-net.org/
reviews/showrev.php?id=7433, accessed May 11, 2011.

19. Leander Schneider, "The Maasai's New Clothes: A Developmentalist Modernity and Its Exclusions," *Africa Today* 53, no. 1 (Fall 2006): 101–29; Andrew M.
Ivaska, "'Anti-Mini Militants Meet Modern Misses': Urban Style, Gender and the
Politics of 'National Culture' in 1960s Dar es Salaam, Tanzania," *Gender & History*
14, no. 3 (November 2002): 584–607; Julius K. Nyerere, "Ujamaa—The Basis
of African Socialism," *The Journal of Pan African Studies* 1, no. 1 (1987): 4–11;
"Tanzania: Dressing Up the Masai," *Time,* November 24, 1967, http://www.time
.com/time/magazine/article/0,9171,844158,00.html, accessed May 3, 2011.

20. Eric N. Shartiely, "The Portrayal of the Tanzanian Woman in Television
Commercials: Is She a Piece of Soap, a House, or Gold?" *Africa & Asia* 5 (2005):
108–41; Rosabelle Boswell, "Say What You Like: Dress, Identity and Heritage in
Zanzibar," *International Journal of Heritage Studies* 12, no. 5 (2006): 440–57.

21. "Time for Tanzania to Consolidate Unity," *The Guardian,* April 23, 2011.
http://www.ippmedia.com/frontend/index.php?l=28383, accessed May 4,
2011;"One More Month for National Dress Committee to Complete Its Work,"
Tanzania Daily News (Dar es Salaam), March 2, 2012, http://allafrica.com/stories/
201203020063.html, accessed July 17, 2012.

6

Marriage, Family, Lineage, and Gender Roles

As IN OTHER COUNTRIES, marriage, family, lineage, and gender roles are central aspects of Tanzanian society. Gender refers to the socially and culturally prescribed attributes, roles, and rules for male and female members of society. Besides influencing individual roles in society, gender is central to the determination of individual identity, self-worth, welfare, occupation, and access to social and productive resources like land.

Consequently, appreciation of gender is critical to an understanding of Tanzania's social organization and its citizens' place in society. The unique roles that gender confers on men and women help society to function and ultimately contribute to the formation a unique Tanzanian culture. Because Tanzania is a largely a patriarchal or male-controlled society, it confers on men many more social advantages than women. Thus, males enjoy most of the country's socioeconomic resources and privileges.

In the country's rural gender division of labor—that is, socially ascribed tasks, roles, and responsibilities for men and women—women and girls are generally responsible for household chores such as fetching water and firewood and preparing food, caring for small children and livestock, and much of the farm work, especially the cultivation of food crops. Conversely, men prepare land for cultivation, care for large livestock, market produce, and make important financial and political decisions for the family. In many parts of rural Tanzania, these gender roles are changing due to increasing female education, the effects of HIV/AIDS, alcoholism, and growing materialism. Moreover, increased rural-urban migration of males in search of better work opportunities has created space for many rural women to perform roles that were traditionally reserved for males. In urban areas, the traditional gender division of labor is less clearly defined.

Marriage and family are critical to the continuation and preservation of society by ensuring the birth, nurture, and training of children into responsible individuals and members of society. Thus, marriage and family play an important role in the cultural and social reproduction of Tanzania because they help to pass on to the next generation society's customs, traditions, classes, morals, habits, behavior patterns, and preferences. In this way, society, and much of what it stands for, is preserved biologically, culturally, socially, economically, and politically. Tanzanians therefore highly esteem marriage and family.

LINEAGE

Lineage refers to a person's ancestry or genealogy and is central to individual, family, and clan identity in Tanzania. Although descent can be patrilineal (through the father's side), matrilineal (through the mother's side), or bilateral (through both parents), the vast majority of Tanzania's ethnic communities are patrilineal. In the past, there were substantial matrilineal communities in the coastal areas of the country, but these have declined since the 1800s.[1] The Makua, Yao, Lugulu, Makonde, and Mwera of southeast Tanzania are some of the country's matrilineal communities while the Zaramo and Ngulu can be both matrilineal and bilineal, depending on context. For instance, the Zaramo are biologically matrilineal and spiritually patrilineal.[2] There are virtually no Tanzanian communities with bilateral descent systems.

Besides contributing to the determination of individual identity, lineage plays a critical role in many Tanzanian communities' social structure, gender relations, land and other property inheritance customs, and the exogamous clan marriage customs (i.e., no marriage between close blood relatives) of many indigenous ethnic communities. Lineage or descent starts with the individual, then goes to the family, clan, and terminates with the tribe. Because most Tanzanian communities are patriarchal, lineage is usually traced along the male line, that is, from son to father to grandfather and so on, until it terminates at the apical male ancestor who is the real or mythical founder of the clan—which is a large extended-family unit. In some cases, ancestry can be traced to the founder of the tribe, which is a combination of several clans that are held together by a common language.

Because clan members regard each other as close relatives regardless of the size of the clan, intraclan marriages are taboo or forbidden because they are considered to be incestuous. This culture of clan exogamy or promotion of marriage outside of a given clan has a good biological basis as the marriage of close blood relatives increases the probability of siring or giving birth to children with certain debilitating genetic diseases.

Good social standing in one's family and clan are highly valued in many Tanzanian ethnic groups because in these communal societies, where collective rights often surpass individual ones, individual misdeeds can easily hurt the reputation of entire clans. Consequently, rejection by one's family and clan is, perhaps, the most severe form of social punishment in many Tanzanian ethnic communities.

In the precolonial era, the history of families and clans was primarily preserved by being passed on orally from generation to generation. But since the advent of colonialism and the associated socioeconomic changes, it has become increasingly difficult to maintain this traditional knowledge system. For instance, the modern school and economic systems, along with urbanization, have disconnected many Tanzanians from their clans and ethnic communities and undermined these groups' ability to maintain their traditional cultures. Moreover, cities not only expose individuals to people from other ethnic communities, they also enable them to marry across ethnic lines, thereby further destabilizing traditional cultures. Additionally, in the first two decades of independence, former Tanzanian president Nyerere vigorously worked to create a national culture that significantly succeeded in undermining loyalty to clan and ethnic group, especially in the younger generations. In the process, many of the country's indigenous cultures lost their vitality.

MARRIAGE

Marriage has always been one of the most important social institutions in Tanzania. Besides helping to perpetuate Tanzanian society, marriage confers on both men and women high social status and qualifies them to serve important leadership roles. Some of the factors that Tanzanians consider when choosing marriage partners are ethnicity, religion, occupation, parental consent, and social class. With increasing urbanization and modernization, adoption of Western courtship and marriage practices, and ethnic mixing, the significance of factors like ethnicity in this process is declining; hence the growing incidence of interethnic marriages.

As marriage is an established means of uniting families and clans, both of these entities have historically played an important role in the initiation and preservation of marriage. Because children (especially males) are many

Tanzanian parents' social and economic security, more so in old age, infertility and childlessness are seen as such major personal tragedies that many communities allow barren couples to save face by borrowing children from their neighbors and relatives. Barren women even go as far as "marrying" other women to bear children for them. But before resorting to such measures, barren couples often go to great lengths to deal with their barrenness. As in many patriarchal African societies, childlessness in Tanzania is often blamed on wives, and some have in fact been divorced for their husbands' impotence. Fortunately, modern medical technology is helping some of these women.

The intense socioeconomic and cultural changes that Tanzania has experienced in the last century have significantly affected marriage and led to less polygamy as well as a higher incidence of divorce (especially in urban areas), cohabitation, and single motherhood.[3] Besides the traditional causes of divorce like barrenness and impotence, failure to bear male children, infidelity, marital violence, and spousal neglect, divorce is also growing due to changing gender roles, greater female independence and assertiveness, the declining stigma of divorce, and the breakdown of the traditional marriage support systems.

The most common marriages in Tanzania are heterosexual monogamous or polygamous (polygynous) unions. Polyandry, or a woman's possession of more than one husband at the same time, is nonexistent in Tanzania. Polygyny, or the practice of men having more than one wife at a time, is the most common form of polygamy in the country, though it is less widespread today than in the past. There are many social, practical, religious, and material reasons for the enduring presence of polygyny in Tanzania.

Materially, polygyny is often widespread in areas with plenty of agricultural or grazing land and low costs of marriage and living. While polygyny is more of a rural than an urban phenomenon, its distribution in the country's rural areas varies widely. Currently, it is probably highest in Maasailand where close to 50 percent of married men are in polygynous marriages.[4]

Socially, many Tanzanian families value children for their role in continuing the family and clan line. Because of the country's high infant mortality rate and short average life spans, many men see polygyny as a means to have more children who can secure the family line and take care of them in old age. The latter factor is also a common reason for high fertility among many Tanzanian women. Polygyny is also widespread because many Tanzanian communities do not allow women to inherit property (especially land). As a result, there is intense economic pressure for single, divorced, and widowed women to get married, even to polygamous men, if only to secure access to livelihood assets like land and livestock.

Practically, polygyny also offers many Tanzanian communities a means of taking care of the usually higher number of females than males in any normal population. In the Tanzanian communities that bar women from owning land and other assets, monogamy would result in many unmarried and destitute women. Polygyny has also long been a means of producing many children who can protect the family from intruders and provide agricultural labor. Although polygyny is often seen as a male prerogative, there are many cases where rural women encourage their husbands to get them cowives who can help them with tedious farm work and household chores. When this happens, the first wife is frequently involved in the selection of her cowives, and she often has as much authority over them as her husband. The concept of the first-wife-as-cohusband is enshrined in Tanzania's marriage act, which allows for polygyny with the consent of the first wife or wives. Moreover, a monogamous marriage may be converted to a polygamous one and vice versa by the free-will declaration of the marriage partners before a judge or magistrate.[5]

Additionally, prior to the advent of modern contraception methods, which are still not widely used in Tanzania due to financial, cultural, and logistical reasons; polygyny promoted family planning and maternal health by enabling the polygamous husband to channel his energies to other wives, thereby allowing a breastfeeding mother to recuperate and to avoid the risk of an unintended pregnancy. Thus, while polygamous families tend to have many children, the number of children per wife is usually lower than that of women in monogamous marriages.[6]

Polygyny is also common in Tanzania for religious reasons. Islam, in particular, permits a man to marry up to four wives as long as he can provide for them and treat them equally. Consequently, there are many polygynous Muslim men in the country.[7]

Overall, polygynous marriages are likely to continue to decline as their practical, material, social and cultural, and religious underpinnings continue to erode. Moreover, in today's increasingly individualistic and materialistic society, it is harder to maintain family harmony in polygynous marriages. Polygyny is also declining because of its contribution to the country's high HIV/AIDS epidemic, as one infected partner can potentially infect more people than is usually the case with monogamous marriages.

Marriage Types

Legally, Tanzanian marriages can be either be traditional, religious (e.g., Christian or Islamic), or civil. Tanzanian law also allows for polygamous and potentially polygamous marriages in the case of traditional and Islamic marriages. While traditional marriages are based on the customary practices of the country's indigenous communities, religious marriages are based on the teachings of its religious groups, while its civil marriages are based on its civil law.

In spite of rapid modernization, traditional marriages are still common in the country's rural areas. Conversely, religious marriages occur all over the country while civil marriages are more common in urban areas. This said, Tanzania's religious and civil marriages tend to be syncretic because they often include certain traditional rites, such as payment of dowry, and most religious marriages use marriage certificates (licenses) from the civil authorities. Tanzanian law also requires all marriages, regardless of how they were initiated, to be registered with the state, though failure to do so does not annul a marriage. Instead, such an omission often attracts a nominal fine when the marriage is eventually registered.

Traditional Marriages

Tanzania's traditional marriage customs are as diverse as its many ethnic communities. Nevertheless, its traditional marriage customs often exhibit significant similarity at the level of the three major people groups in the country: the Bantu (e.g., the Chagga and Haya), the Nilotes (e.g., the Luo), and the Cushites (e.g., the Maasai) because in all three cases marriage is preceded by courtship and the payment of dowry or bride wealth. Historically, marriages were arranged by parents, intermediaries, or close family or clan

A wedding in Zanzibar. (Per-Anders Pettersson/Getty Images)

members, and they often entailed African traditional religious rites. But nowadays, men tend to find their own brides before seeking parental consent for marriage. Moreover, come-we-stay marriages (cohabitation), which seldom observe the dowry prerequisite, have increased in recent decades.[8]

While courtship practices in Tanzania are diverse, it is usually the man or his intermediaries who approach the woman, and not the other way round. Women who approach men risk being seen as immoral because "good" girls have traditionally been expected to respond to, rather than initiate, intimate friendships with members of the opposite sex. In urban areas, women who pursue men have long been thought to be prostitutes, though this perception is changing as women become more empowered and Western courtship practices continue to take root.

In many traditional Tanzanian communities, courtship and marriage come after initiation (usually circumcision) rites that usher children into adulthood and inculcate socially desirable and gender-specific qualities and skills in the initiates. Moreover, the initiation rites and ceremonies provide venues for young people to be schooled in parental matters and the rights, responsibilities, and privileges of adulthood. While in historic times marriage came soon after initiation, this is increasingly rare because modern initiates are usually younger and still in school.[9]

In many traditional societies, courtship was closely supervised by family and society to ensure that the partners were acceptable to each other's families as well as to prevent premarital sex and pregnancy. Thus, among the traditional Makonde, Fipa, Gogo, Zaramo, and Chagga, virginity was highly valued and girls were showered with gifts for being chaste. Among the Zaramo, a girl who had lost her virginity before marriage was liable for divorce on her wedding night besides being ridiculed for disgracing her parents and family. Other communities, especially the Maasai and to a smaller extent the Sukuma, allowed young people to engage in sex before initiation. Nevertheless, a boy who made a girl pregnant was usually fined and forced to marry her. After initiation and marriage, Sukuma and Maasai women were expected to remain faithful to their husbands (and their age mates in the case of the Maasai) while men were generally encouraged to marry as many wives as they could afford. In today's permissive Tanzanian society, virginity is increasingly rare, though it continues to be valued by many communities. Similarly, the social stigma of out-of-wedlock motherhood is much lower even though the marriage prospects of premarital mothers are lower and the poverty rates of single mothers are generally high throughout the country.

While Tanzanian courtship practices have changed over time, some things remain constant. For instance, during courtship, great care is taken by the courting parties and their families to ensure that they are compatible and suitable for each other. Thus, Tanzanians try to avoid marrying from or into families with undesirable qualities such as laziness, witchcraft, gluttony, drunkenness, and barrenness. Tanzanian families have traditionally valued hard-working and responsible spouses because love is often defined as a man or woman's ability to fulfill socially defined gender roles.

Marriage between close relatives has historically been taboo in many Tanzanian communities in order to prevent incest and the congenital or hereditary diseases that are common in the offspring of close relatives. Modern Tanzanian marriage law has validated this exogamy practice by strictly prohibiting the marriage of close blood relatives such as uncles and nieces as well as half-blood relatives, immediate relatives of one's spouse, and even one's adopted children.[10]

Religious Marriages

Religious marriages are those that are conducted according to the teachings and customs of the country's various religions. Christianity and Islam account for most of the country's religious marriages.

Christian marriages are usually conducted in church by priests and pastors using state-issued marriage certificates. The church ceremony usually comes after the satisfaction of traditional marriage requirements like dowry—this being one of the elements of traditional African culture that has been incorporated into local Christian practice. By law and church teaching, Christian marriages are monogamous and are prevalent in areas most influenced by the various Christian denominations of Tanzania. Because Christianity was brought to Tanzania by Europeans, Christian marriages in the country usually feature elements of European or Western weddings like wedding rings, white dresses for brides, maids of honor, best men, flower girls, groomsmen, and bridesmaids. Christian marriage ceremonies also tend to feature local or Western cuisine, dance, and Christian music. Such marriages are usually preceded by premarital counseling sessions, are consummated on the wedding night, and usually include honeymoons, especially for wealthy urban Tanzanians. Because Christian marriages are designed to last a lifetime, they often dissolve through the death of one partner or some other just cause.

Muslim marriages are commonly arranged by parents to ensure marital compatibility. But before marriage, the match has to be agreed to by the potential marriage partners, at which point the girl and the boy exchange engagement rings and the groom gives the bride dowry (*mahr*)—which becomes the irrevocable property of the wife even in divorce. Then the marriage ceremony takes place, usually a simple affair that does not necessarily require the presence of the bride as long as witnesses, usually her

Henna hand etching is popular with many Muslim and Asian brides in Tanzania. (Per-Anders Pettersson/Getty Images)

father and someone else, are present. During the ceremony, brides usually wear cherry-red wedding gowns and decorate their hands and feet with *henna* (a hair, skin, and nail dye derived from the mignonette tree) to enhance their beauty. While Islamic law prohibits Muslim women from marrying outside of their faith and from engaging in polyandry, Muslim men can marry non-Muslim women and can have up to four wives.

The marriage ceremony is usually preceded by a meal, typically dinner. Then the imam (Islamic priest) or some other presiding official is invited to read the relevant sections of the Koran, oversee the signing of a mutually agreed-on contract and the exchange of marriage vows, and declare the couple legally married. Nongolden wedding rings are then exchanged, followed by sumptuous, plenteous food, music, and song. Muslim marriages, like their Christian counterparts, do contain certain local cultural elements. Because the Koran permits men to marry up to four wives as long as they are able to provide for them and treat them equally, Muslim marriages in Tanzania are legally presumed to be potentially polygamous. But because a Muslim man is required to seek the consent of his first wife to be polygynous, and must treat and provide for his wives equally, polygyny is in practice generally the preserve of wealthy Muslim men. Islamic marriages can be dissolved through the death of a partner, the husband's rejection of the wife (i.e., *talaq*), mutual consent of the marriage partners, annulment (*faskh*), or separation by court decree (*tatliq*).[11]

Civil Marriages

Tanzanian civil marriages are conducted by government officials (e.g., magistrates) for those who are irreligious, financially unable, or unwilling to go through traditional or religious marriages. Under Tanzanian marriage law, the minimum age of marriage for males and females is 18 and 15 years of age, respectively. Those who wish to get married must do so freely, must obtain the consent of the girl's father if she is under the age of 18, and must not be close relatives.

Unlike traditional and religious marriages, civil marriages do not require the payment of dowry. Once notice of the imminent marriage is received by the appropriate government official, he or she must publicize it for at least three weeks before the marriage is solemnized and a marriage certificate issued. There is also a civil marriage aspect in Christian weddings because they also have a three-week-notice requirement and their marriage certificates are actually issued by the state.

Cohabitation

Cohabitation is the act of a man and woman living together in a sexual relationship for an extended period of time as if they are married. Though it was virtually unheard-of in many traditional Tanzanian communities, cohabitation is now widespread, especially in urban areas, where it is a common step to marriage. As a mid-1990s survey in Dar es Salaam revealed, 40 percent of respondents in the city were or had been in such a relationship. Because of the growing incidence of cohabitation, the country's Marriage Act of 1971 includes a presumption of marriage for a man and woman based on a two-year or more period of cohabitation. This legal presumption is one of the few legal protections and avenues that cohabiting women and their children respectively have in securing material support from their estranged partners and fathers in the event that such relationships end.[12]

The growing incidence of cohabitation in Tanzania is due to many reasons including the breakdown of social and religious customs that promoted marriage over cohabitation, the high poverty levels that prevent many marriageable people from meeting the upfront costs of marriages (e.g., dowry, weddings, and receptions), and the desire for some people to try out marriage before committing to one another.[13]

Bride Wealth

Bride wealth or dowry is part of many traditional and religious marriages in Tanzania, such as those of the Gogo, Nyakyusa, Nyaturu, Sukuma, and Zanzibari communities. Besides sealing the marriage, dowry symbolically compensates the girl's family for the loss of her labor, unites the groom and bride's families, and establishes the authority of the husband over his wife (e.g., in the case of the Zanzibari Africans) as well as the rights of the father to the children (e.g., among the Sukuma). Dowry usually includes any combination of livestock (especially cows, goats, and sheep), beer, cloth, meat, and money.[14]

Traditionally, the amount of dowry paid depends on a variety of factors including ethnicity or clan, whether the girl is a virgin or not, a divorcee or an unwed mother, and the groom's or his family's socioeconomic status. Whatever the case, the dowry demanded is usually much higher than what the bride's family expects to receive and what the groom's family can or intends to pay. Because dowry payments are never fully paid, the marriage is allowed to proceed once a reasonable amount has been paid. The remainder essentially obligates the groom's family to help the bride's family in hard times even as it gives the girl's family the leverage it needs to ensure that she is treated well in her matrimonial home.

Because in many traditional communities dowry is supposed to be returned in the event of divorce, many wives try to ensure that their marriages work lest they saddle their families with crippling dowry-debt repayments. For this reason, dowry has often been criticized for putting wives in a no-win situation. This said, ongoing socioeconomic changes in Tanzania have left an indelible mark on the custom of dowry.

First, many traditional determinants of dowry, such as virginity, have been replaced by a woman's social status and her educational attainment or earning potential in the modern economy. Second, because it is impractical for urban families to give or receive dowry in the form of livestock, cash has become a common substitute, though the amount exchanged still depends on the bride and groom's socioeconomic status. In many rural areas, dowry is also increasingly given in the form of money, though some communities, for instance the Maasai, still prefer livestock. Third, the quantity of livestock given as dowry in many rural Tanzanian societies has declined because of decreasing livestock herds due to the growing scarcity of pastures. Fourth, because of commercialization of dowry, the amount demanded by many families, especially for educated women, has gone up exponentially over time. As a result, cohabitation is growing as more and young men find themselves unable to afford exorbitant dowry demands. Last, the country's marriage law disallows dowry as a condition of marriage. But because the same law recognizes traditional and religious marriages that often incorporate dowry, the custom endures.

Procedures and Ceremonies

Tanzanian marriages are usually preceded by courtship and payment of dowry, except for those marriages that start with cohabitation, where dowry is paid later. This said, each of the country's many ethnic communities does enrich the general marriage pattern outlined above in its own unique way, with some communities having more elaborate marriages than others. Additionally, the size and elegance of any individual marriage ceremony depends on the couple's socioeconomic status; with richer couples spending fortunes on their weddings.

Moreover, beyond the broad pattern of courtship, dowry, and then marriage, there are also discernible differences in the marriage customs of the country's religions as well as its Bantu, Nilotic, and Cushitic peoples. The following Sukuma and Maasai marriage procedures and ceremonies respectively illustrate these Bantu and Cushitic practices.

Bantu Marriage Procedures and Ceremonies: The Case of the Sukuma

Contemporary traditional Sukuma marriages start either with or without dowry. Dowry marriages are more common in wealthier areas and in seasons of bountiful harvest, with the amount of dowry paid depending on the girl's status, reputation, work ethic, level of education, and whether or not she was married before. With the payment of dowry, the man gets certain rights (including the right to be compensated for his wife's adultery) and secure rights to his biological offspring, who then inherit from him, even as he gets the right to receive his daughters' dowry and the responsibility to provide dowry for his sons.

In marriages that start without dowry, the husband has limited rights to his wife and children. Thus, he gets no compensation for his wife's adultery, and the children belong to their mother's family until the father makes redemptive payments for them. The payments are usually higher for daughters because they bring in dowry and lower for sons because they pay it. As the cost of dowry has increased, it has become increasingly difficult for many Sukuma men to afford dowry marriages. Regardless of the marriage type, the balance of power favors the man, who "marries," while the woman "gets married."

After marriage, the newlyweds commonly establish patrilocal residence, that is, live with or near the husband's parents, though there have been cases in the past when newlyweds have created matrilocal residences, or lived with or close to the wife's parents. Some of the recent changes in Sukuma marriages include the declining incidence of polygynous marriages, the increasing incidence of divorce, and less parental involvement in the selection of their children's marriage partners.[15]

Cushitic Marriage Procedures and Ceremonies: The Case of the Maasai

The Maasai marriage ceremony is quite colorful and elaborate. It starts when a Maasai man, who is circumcised and has fulfilled his *moran* or military duty, which usually runs from age 18 to 30, finds a suitable woman and gives her a chain or *olpisiai* to symbolize his love for her.[16] After ensuring that the girl's family is in support of the union, he sets in motion the following sequence of steps:

- The *engagement* (or *esirit enkoshoke*), which is accomplished by sending the girl's mother a gift of alcohol that is delivered by women from his age set.

- The *identification ceremony*, which starts with the delivery of a gift of alcohol (*enkiroret*) to the girl's father. After he drinks it with his brothers and friends, he then asks the young man to identify the woman he wishes to marry. At this stage, the identification becomes quite humorous, as the lovesick young man is mercilessly teased and humbled.

- The *official engagement*, which starts after the young man's marriage proposal is accepted and continues until the wedding ceremony. During this period, the groom showers the girl's family with gifts to demonstrate his care for them. Once the girl's family is satisfied, the gifts are counted towards the bride's dowry, which essentially legalizes the marriage. At this point, the girl cannot be given to another man. Dowry in Maasai culture is mostly a seal of marriage rather than a wealth-generating venture for the bride's family.

- The *wedding ceremony*, which takes two days. On the first day, the groom brings the official dowry of three head of black cattle (two cows and one bull), a ewe (a female sheep), and a ram (a male sheep). The ram is butchered later in the day and its fat and oil applied to the wedding dress, with the remainder being sent with the bride to her new husband's *kraal*. The groom then takes the ewe and gives it to his prospective mother-in-law, thereby sealing their son-in-law-mother-in-law relationship. She henceforth calls him *paker*, or "the one who gave me sheep." Afterwards, the groom gives a calf to his prospective father-in-law, and they then start calling each other *pakiteng* or *entawuo*. The next day, the bride's head is shaved clean and anointed with lamb fat. She then puts on beautiful beaded decorations and her wedding dress, which is made by her mother and other women to model their sense of community. A group of elders then bless the bride using alcohol and milk. She is then led from her biological home to her new husband's home. On arrival, she gets into her mother-in-law's house and stays there for two days. During the two-day period, the groom is not allowed to eat food in his mother's house (where the bride is staying), nor is the couple allowed to be intimate. At the end of these two days, the bride's head is shaved clean by her mother-in-law, thereby concluding the marriage ceremony. At this point, the groom and his bride become officially married elders who start a new life of building a family and social security through the accumulation of wealth and children.

Traditional Maasai marriages are lifelong unless dowry is not fully paid or one of the marriage partners is a non-Maasai. Besides the Maasai having a permissive attitude toward premarital sex, they also consider wives to be common property among married men of the same age. The rationale for this wife-sharing custom is that it helps to preserve the community by maximizing fertility and guarding against infertility. Moreover, in the event that a couple is prone to certain congenital diseases, wife-sharing ensures that the couple will have some healthy children.

Like many other Tanzanian societies, the traditional Maasai way of life is increasingly threatened by the country's changing socioeconomic conditions. For instance, the age-old custom of wife sharing is increasingly becoming untenable in the face of the HIV/AIDS pandemic. Second, as more and more Maasai youth get educated, they are abandoning their community's culture along with its marriage traditions and customs.[17]

GENDER ROLES

Gender refers to socially created and acquired notions of masculinity and femininity. In Tanzania, these notions are taught by families, communities, and schools. Traditionally, this training was gender specific as boys and girls were segregated from an early age and trained informally by fathers and mothers, respectively.

Tanzanians have historically had distinct gender roles with women mostly being responsible for domestic chores such as cleaning, food production and preparation, taking care of smaller livestock, fetching water and firewood, caring for the sick, and rearing children. Even in the area of trading, women usually engage in petty trades that are related to their domestic chores, including food vending. On the other hand, Tanzanian men play smaller domestic roles, though they are the main breadwinners and shelter providers. They also generally own most of the country's productive assets (e.g., land, livestock, and tools), make most of their family's important socioeconomic decisions, and contribute to household food security through animal husbandry, hunting, and fishing. Yet even in these areas, there is a gender division of labor by which women do most of the milking and fish preparation and marketing.[18]

In agriculture, men are generally responsible for clearing, preparing, and ploughing the farm and crop fields. Nevertheless, women dominate the agricultural sector, providing upwards of 80 percent of the sector's labor as well as producing 60 percent of the country's food. Thus, they overwhelmingly play a central role in sowing, weeding, applying fertilizers and pesticides, harvesting and harvest processing, transportation, and marketing. In the cash-crop sector, they also do most of the production, though existing social conditions do not allow them to control their cash-crop produce. As former Tanzanian president Julius Nyerere once observed, women in Tanzania and elsewhere in Africa "toil on land they do not own, to produce what they do not control and at the end of the marriage, through divorce or death, they can be sent away empty handed."[19]

While many of the core responsibilities of Tanzanian women have changed little since the precolonial era when the male-female division of labor was more equal, men's roles have since changed significantly due to the economic transformations that colonialism initiated in the country. In particular, the introduction of wage labor has increasingly moved men to urban-based modern-sector wage employment. Because these jobs are unsuitable for the typically less educated Tanzanian women, the country's women have over time come to dominate the less lucrative and more labor-intensive rural agricultural sector while men are overrepresented in the well-paying urban wage sector. The lower women's educational attainment has also led to their underrepresentation in the country's decision-making and governance structures, thereby further undermining their socioeconomic success. Because of this and a myriad of other socioeconomic disadvantages, more women than men live in absolute poverty.

Many of the challenges Tanzanian women face are also cultural. In many of Tanzania's patriarchal societies, women mostly access land indirectly through their husbands and sons. They usually do not inherit land from their fathers because they are usually seen as members of their husbands' families. Consequently, unmarried women, who now constitute a significant portion of the country's population, have very limited access to land, which in this largely agrarian society undermines their food and economic security. In some communities such as the Chagga, women who die before marriage are usually buried outside of the family graveyard because, by custom, women's land-inheritance rights rest with their husbands. Consequently, many of the most absolutely poor Tanzanian women are the single or unwed mothers with limited access to land.

Actually, even married women usually have only secondary rights to land and are, as a result, unable to dispose of it or borrow against it when necessary. For this reason, the death of a husband can result in the eviction of his widow unless she has protectors, especially grown-up sons. Even among the communities that allow women to inherit land, a woman can be evicted if her husband dies without male children. And even when she has them, she only gets full rights to the land if there is no male clan member to lay claim to it. Furthermore, such women are often encouraged to keep the land for future generations instead of disposing of it.

Tanzanian men also enjoy more leisure than their women counterparts. For many women, leisure often amounts to doing less arduous work such as household cleaning. Women's limited leisure opportunities are also due to lack of access to labor-saving devices like dish and laundry washing machines. For this reason, many domestic chores take a lot of women's time, thereby limiting both their leisure and personal development. In short, many women work full time in and out of the home.

Another aspect of Tanzanian culture that works against women is their limited access to education throughout life. Because girls are usually seen as outsiders or temporary residents who will soon join their husbands' families, they are usually given fewer educational opportunities than boys by their own families. As a result, the proportion of women in Tanzania declines with educational level from 50 percent at the primary school level to 17 percent at university level. Because of their undereducation, women are underrepresented in the lucrative formal workforce outside the home. Thus, they tend to mostly operate in the domestic sphere and to focus on their historical and cultural domestic roles.

Socialization and Social Change

Socialization is the process of acquiring and passing on a society's norms, customs, and ideologies to the next generation. Tanzanian societies have traditionally sought to socialize their children into successful members of society by seeking to inculcate in them the core values of being disciplined, respectful of elders, moral, honest, and hardworking. They are also trained to avoid antisocial activities such as theft and sorcery, though these are also discouraged by an elaborate system of rewards and punishment.[20]

Socialization has always been gendered and is conducted mainly by family, peers, and the larger community. Accordingly, boys are trained by their fathers and grandfathers through everyday activities and evening fireside chats to be effective fathers, providers, and protectors of their families. Similarly, girls are taught by their mothers and grandmothers to be successful mothers, wives, and nurturers. For this reason, fathers are often blamed for ill-mannered sons and mothers for badly behaved daughters.

While children are socialized throughout their childhood, the responsibilities of adulthood and parenthood are especially taught through the various initiation rites (e.g., circumcision) and ceremonies that mark the transition from childhood to adulthood. Accordingly, the boys' initiation (*jando*, or manhood) curriculum of many communities includes lessons in good manners, bravery, secrets of life, marriage, fatherhood, sexuality, death, male responsibilities, and local customs and taboos. Conversely, the girls' initiation (*unyago*, or womanhood) curriculum is focused on sexuality, pregnancy, childbirth, good wifeliness, motherhood, and local customs and taboos.

Although many modern Tanzanian societies still retain many aspects of their traditional socialization curriculum, rapid socioeconomic change has made certain parts of this curriculum impractical even as other aspects have been supplanted by modern school matriculation. Overall, these social changes have produced a generally inharmonious society that has some calling for traditional cultural revivalism.

Traditionally, children have also been taught various gender-based vocational skills. Thus, boys learn skills like ironwork, carving, pottery, rain-making, divination, and healing through apprenticeship. Conversely, girls learn skills like midwifery, basketry, and the use of various medicinal herbs. In many communities, these vocational skills were often inherited from parents.

Grandparents have long played an important role in socializing children. In some communities, topics like sexuality were or are exclusively taught by grandparents because they are often considered to be the "age-mates" of their grandchildren. Moreover, grandparents can be especially effective in this role because they can illustrate their lessons with material from their long personal life experiences. However, the breakdown of this traditional multigenerational socialization system that ensured the success of virtually every member of society has been partly blamed for the country's growing problem of maladjusted, strung-out, and unproductive youth.

While the breakdown of the traditional social setup started in the colonial era, it has since accelerated and undermined many traditional societies' ability to cope. For instance, the extended periods of time that children spend away from their parents and grandparents has deprived them of critical guidance in their formative years. Moreover, the modern cash economy that often forces fathers to spend considerable amounts of time away from their families has especially weakened the proper socialization of boys in the country.

Increasingly, many of the Tanzanian children who grow up in urban areas seldom spend quality time with their rural-based grandparents and are therefore deprived of this valuable resource. Moreover, many grandparents are rendered useless when it comes to the socialization of their urban grandchildren by language barriers as many young urban Tanzanians continue to lose their ethnic language proficiency.

Socialization through the increasingly dominant modern school system is also flawed because it often teaches skills and behaviors that are irrelevant to local needs (leading to unemployment) and relies on a limited number of adult role models, especially teachers. As a result, the school system creates an environment where students socialize with each other in ways that are not necessarily beneficial to society. The system is also laden with the sexual harassment of girls by older boys and male teachers.[21] Moreover, many Tanzanian students' growing access to global media and the Internet is also complicating their socialization as the technology exposes them to values from other cultures without the benefit of guidance from parents and teachers, many of whom may themselves be unfamiliar with these technologies. The challenges of the country's school system are in many ways emblematic of a society that is changing too fast for its own good.

NOTES

1. Philip Setel, Eleuther Mwageni, Namsifu Mndeme, Yusuf Hemed, and Beldina Opiyo-Omolo, "Tanzania: The United Republic of Tanzania," http://www2.hu-berlin.de/sexology/IES/tanzania.html, accessed August 17, 2011.

2. Sakamoto Kumiko, "The Matrilineal and Patrilineal Clan Lineages of the Mwera in Southeast Tanzania," Utsunomiya University Faculty of International Studies Essays 2008, No. 26: 1–20, http://uuair.lib.utsunomiya-u.ac.jp/dspace/bitstream/10241/6358/1/kokusai26-002.pdf, accessed August 17, 2011.

3. Law Reform Commission of Tanzania, *Inquiry and Report on the Law of Marriage Act, 1971* (Dar es Salaam: United Republic of Tanzania, July 4, 1986); Mark J. Calaguas, Cristina M. Drost, and Edward R. Fluet, "Legal Pluralism and Women's Rights: A Study in Postcolonial Tanzania," *Columbia Journal of Gender and Law* (Summer 2007); "Single Motherhood on Increase in Africa," *Panapress*, October 16, 2003, http://www.panapress.com/Single-motherhood-on-increase-in-Africa—12-493095-25-lang2-index.html, accessed August 26, 2011.

4. Ernestina Coast, "Maasai Marriage: A Comparative Study of Kenya and Tanzania," *Journal of Comparative Family Studies* 37, no. 3 (2006): 399–420.

5. Registration, Insolvency and Trusteeship Agency, "Laws of Tanzania: Marriage Act, Cap 29 RE 2002," http://www.rita.go.tz/, accessed August 26, 2011.

6. Innocent Ngalinda, *Age at First Birth, Fertility, and Contraception in Tanzania*, PhD dissertation, Department of Demography, Faculty of Philosophy III, Humboldt-Universität zu Berlin, 1998, http://edoc.hu-berlin.de/dissertationen/phil/ngalinda-innocent/PDF/Ngalinda.pdf, accessed September 1, 2011.

7. Ibid.

8. Frans Wijsen and Ralph Tanner, *I Am Just a Sukuma: Globalization and Identity Construction in Northwest Tanzania* (New York: Rodopi, 2002), 53.

9. Daniel Mbunda, *Traditional Sex Education in Tanzania: A Study of 12 Ethnic Groups* (New York: The Margaret Sanger Center, Planned Parenthood of New York City, 1991).

10. Tanzania, "Chapter 29, Law of Marriage Act, Part II section 14," 1971.

11. Edward R. Fluet, Mark J. Calaguas, and Cristina M. Drost, *Legal Pluralism & Women's Rights: A Study in Post-Colonial Tanzania*, bepress Legal Series, 2006, Paper 168, http://law.bepress.com/expresso/eps/1683, accessed September 2, 2011.

12. Tanzania, "Chapter 29, Law of Marriage Act, Part II section 160," 1971.

13. Abdulrahman O. J.Kaniki, "What Are the Rights of Concubines?" *The Citizen*, May 15, 2010, http://www.thecitizen.co.tz/, accessed September 5, 2011.

14. Daniel Mbunda, *Traditional Sex Education*; Tanzania, "Chapter 29"; Frans Wijsen and Ralph Tanner, *I Am Just a Sukuma*, 53; Margarita Dobert, "Physical and Social Setting," in Irving Kaplan (ed.), *Tanzania: A Country Study* (Washington, DC: The American University, 1978); Advameg, "Marriage and Family—Nyamwezi and Sukuma," 2011, http://www.everyculture.com/Africa-Middle-East/Nyamwezi-and-Sukuma-Marriage-and-Family.html, accessed September 5, 2011.

15. Ibid.

16. Tepilit Ole Saitoti, "Maasai Wedding Ceremony," 2006, http://www.maasaieducation.org/maasai-culture/maasai-wedding-ceremony.htm, accessed September 5, 2011.

17. Adrian Blomfield, "Aids Threatens Impoverished Masai," *The Telegraph*, December 1, 2004, http://www.telegraph.co.uk/news/worldnews/africaandindianocean/kenya/1477968/Aids-threatens-impoverished-Masai.html, accessed September 6, 2011.

18. Iddi Adam Mwatima Makombe, *Women Entrepreneurship Development and Empowerment in Tanzania: The Case of SIDO/UNIDO-Supported Women Microentrepreneurs in the Food Processing Sector*, Doctoral thesis, Department of Development Studies, University of South Africa, Pretoria, South Africa, 2006; Government of Tanzania, "Gender," http://www.tanzania.go.tz/gender.html, accessed September 8, 2011; Elizabeth Carr, *Community and Land Attachment of Chagga Women on Mount Kilimanjaro, Tanzania*, Master of Science thesis, Department of Geography, Brigham Young University, Provo, UT, USA 2004; Aginatha Rutazaa, "Tanzanian Women and Access to Law," Terry Sanford Institute of Public Policy, Duke University, Durham, NC, 2005, http://sanford.duke.edu/centers/civil/papers/rutazaa.pdf, accessed September 8, 2011.

19. Maureen Kambarami, "Femininity, Sexuality and Culture: Patriarchy and Female Subordination in Zimbabwe," African Regional Sexuality Resource Center in collaboration with Health Systems Trust, South Africa and University of Fort Hare, South Africa, 2006, http://www.arsrc.org/downloads/uhsss/kmabarami.pdf, accessed August 26, 2011.

20. Daniel Mbunda, *Traditional Sex Education*; Joseph Mzinga, "Changing Gender Roles in Tanzania," Sexual Health Exchange 2002–2004, http://www.kit.nl/exchange/html/2002-4_changing_gender_roles_i.asp, accessed September 12, 2011.

21. Zaida Mgalla, Dick Schapink, and J. Ties Boerma, "Protecting School Girls against Sexual Exploitation: A Guardian Programme in Mwanza, Tanzania," *Reproductive Health Matters* 6, no. 12, November 1998, 19–30.

7

Social Customs and Lifestyles

TANZANIA'S RICH CULTURAL milieu consists of many local, regional, and national customs and lifestyles that vary by ethnicity, religion, occupation, income, and educational attainment. This diversity is the product of dynamic interactions between internal (local or national) and external (global) customs, traditions, and lifestyles—interactions that result in the decline and abandonment of some of the country's cultural attributes, the modification of others, and the creation of new ones in light of new information and socioeconomic conditions.

Tanzania's social life revolves around the community, and its people, therefore, have a communal orientation. They thus highly value communal social events like weddings as participation in them is not only enjoyable and fulfilling but is also central to the maintenance of one's social standing. Although Tanzanian society has become more individualistic since the colonial era, its communal orientation is still strong.

Although modern communications and transport are increasingly available, Tanzanians still value face-to-face communication because this is a central aspect of the country's oral culture. Face-to-face communication is richer and more fulfilling than phone calls and, in any event, the country's low literacy levels greatly limit the reach and utility of written communication relative to oral, face-to-face communication. As in other oral societies, Tanzanians frequently use proverbs, idioms, riddles, and stories to enrich their verbal communication. Good use of these oratory devices also demonstrates one's mastery of language.

SOCIAL RELATIONS

Tanzanian social relations are governed by certain age- and gender-based rules. In Tanzania, people who traditionally got initiated together went through life's subsequent stages (e.g., marriage and eldership) together. Even though many traditional initiation systems are weakening and are being replaced by others like schooling, the age-based social organization and interaction system is still important. Thus, one has the most freedom when relating with a person of the same age and sex, and the age mates of one's parents are generally accorded the same respect as one's own parents, with the most respect being given to the elderly, religious and government leaders and others in positions of authority, and the rich.

Respect is conveyed in many ways including the use of official titles, greeting elders with both hands, or deferring to them in various social settings. Respect for elders and religious leaders is usually based on the widespread belief that they have power to confer blessings on those who treat them well as well as curses on those who do not.

As many Tanzanian communities are patriarchal, elderly men, especially those who have good families or are wealthy, command a lot of respect, followed closely by similarly placed elderly women. Thus, all things being equal, one's respect grows with age, social position, and material wealth. Because many Tanzanian communities are communal, values such as mutual help, generosity, friendship, honesty, and hospitality are also highly valued.

When Tanzanians meet for business or social engagements, they usually take time to exchange proper greetings and salutations. While such niceties vary across the country, the salutations usually include inquiries about each other's health and welfare, and those of their respective families. Nevertheless, the type of verbal greeting used is determined by the given community, time of day, occasion, social setting, and the age of the greeter and the addressee; with the most carefree greetings being reserved for ones' close same-sex friends and age mates.

Tanzanian greetings generally involve handshakes, though this may be inappropriate in some situations, such as between unrelated Muslim men and women. Hugs can also be used when greeting close friends and relatives, more so those of the same sex. In some situations, playful wrestling, for instance between grandchildren and grandparents, can be a form of greeting. A typical Swahili-language greeting goes like this:

Person 1: *Shikamoo!* (Hello or Hail!)

Person 2: *Marahaba, Habari?* (Very well, how are you?)

Person 1: *Njema* or *Nzuri tu* (Well, or Just fine)

Tanzanian society has rules that govern male-female relations and interactions. Most important is a well-defined gendered work and interaction system that usually keeps males and females apart for significant portions of their social and working life, especially in rural areas. Even when men and women do work together on the farm, this gender division of labor is present because men tend to be responsible for clearing the farm while the women till, plant, and harvest the crops. This gendered social system often limits the number of close friendships that one can have with members of the opposite sex. At many public social functions, men and women usually sit separately, though in urban areas such restrictions are beginning to erode.

Throughout the country, it is common to use professional and political titles or other honorifics when greeting leaders, elders, and other dignitaries. It is unacceptable for young people to address anybody of their parents' age and above or any other dignitary by name only. It is especially rude for a young person to use an elder's or any other dignitary's first name only in a greeting as this is tantamount to treating them as equals or age mates. Rather, the acceptable practice is to precede the elder's last name with his or her professional, political, or marital title: for instance, *Mr., Dr., Honorable, Mrs.,* or some other honorific like *Mzee* (Swahili for "elder"), *Bi* (Swahili for "lady"), *Uncle,* or *Aunt.* In most cases, it is safe to salute parents other than one's own as *Mama* or *Baba X* (i.e., mother or father of child X). But for one's own parents, *mom* or *dad* is sufficient. It is generally unacceptable to call one's parents by name except when introducing them to an outsider.

Romantic involvements are generally limited to one's age mates, and once married, one generally has to deal carefully with members of the opposite sex. Public displays of romance (e.g., kissing or walking hand in hand with unrelated members of the opposite sex) as well as conversations on sex and other intimate matters are generally unacceptable. However, the country's growing westernization has in recent years somewhat loosened these prohibitions. Thus, revealing clothes like miniskirts and tight jeans are increasingly popular with many urban youth. Moreover, the need to combat the country's relatively high HIV/AIDS epidemic has necessitated the use of relatively explicit public-health outreaches.

In Tanzania's generally patriarchal society, men occupy most of the country's public and private leadership positions and make most of its critical family decisions. Society generally expects women to be subservient to men and to stick with their traditional roles of bearing and raising children, fetching water from nearby streams, preparing and serving food, and washing clothes. In some rural areas, men do not eat with women. Instead, they eat separately with boys while women eat with girls and young children. In the culturally relaxed urban environments where small nuclear families are increasingly common, family members usually eat together.

In many rural areas of the country where communal ties are prevalent, family is often understood in the extended sense. Thus, the rules of mutual support and reciprocity tend to include many people beyond the nuclear family. In some local languages, there is no distinction, for instance, between brothers and cousins.

The perception and place of time in Tanzanian society is complicated because its cultures span the traditional-modern continuum. While Tanzanians generally have a less urgent sense of time than westerners, the degree to which this is true varies widely. Thus, in the traditional communities, time is less important than the preservation of relationships and the completion of the task at hand. It is thus often offensive to interfere with the flow of social events, tasks, or activities in the interest of keeping time. This flexible and cyclical view of time is common in rural areas, where many people do not own watches and many of those who do own them do not run their lives by the clock. With or without watches, many Tanzanians are also like their ancestors in that they can tell time by the position of the sun and moon and by the annual drought and rainfall seasons. Their child-naming traditions also often serve as time-keeping devices because children are often named according to the time of day, season, or local name for the year of their birth. Such children have traditionally served as living memorials of the good or tough times that their families and communities were going through at the time of their birth. Time keeping is however taken more seriously in the urban areas. Yet even here, many Tanzanians operate on "African Standard Time," which is far more tolerant of tardiness than the Western world. Besides many Tanzanians' lax attitude toward time, the poor state of the country's infrastructure makes it virtually impossible for the country to run on time. For instance, unlike the well-known fast, punctual, and efficient Japanese passenger train system, the low integrity of the overall Tanzanian transport system regularly compromises many Tanzanians' ability to be on time even when they want to, such as in cases of medical emergencies.

CEREMONIES

Tanzanians have numerous ceremonies that mark their personal, family, communal, and national milestones, including important historical and spiritual events and the various stages of life: birth, adulthood, marriage, and death. Many of these ceremonies usually feature some combination of food, music, dance, and even drama. As with nearly every aspect of Tanzanian culture, the rites of many of these ceremonies have changed significantly over time.

Marriage Ceremonies

Marriage is often the most socially inclusive and festive of all ceremonies. Tanzanians have long loved good weddings, and this has not changed even in the face of the social and cultural disruptions of colonialism and the country's increased pace of modernization and westernization. The country's marriage ceremonies fall into three classes: traditional, civil, or religious. There are also many "come-we-stay" marriages that start with no specific civil or religious ceremony. Civil marriage ceremonies are usually conducted by government officials while the Christian and Islamic ones follow the tenets of these religions.

The country's traditional marriage ceremonies vary widely. For instance, among the precolonial Chagga of northern Tanzania, marriages were negotiated by a prospective couple's parents. This usually occurred soon after the bride and groom had undergone the customary circumcision ceremony that is now mostly confined to males. After agreeing to a marriage union, the groom's family paid dowry (bride wealth) to the bride's family to symbolically compensate it for the loss of the girl's labor. Although the payment of dowry effectively sealed the marriage, the Chagga followed this event with a sequence of rituals that together amounted to a traditional marriage ceremony. Some of these rituals are still practiced today and are often woven into Chagga Christian weddings. Tanzanian marriage types are described in greater detail in Chapter 6.

Initiation Ceremonies

Initiation ceremonies have long been a central part of traditional Tanzanian societies. While these ceremonies vary by community, they play an important role in ushering people through the various stages of life, such as from childhood to adulthood. They also mark entry into certain social and spiritual groups, as well as serving as individual, age set, and ethnic identity markers. Among the Maasai, Kuria, and other communities that use initiation ceremonies like circumcision to mark the transition from childhood to adulthood, initiation is also a prerequisite for marriage and for participation in many social and cultural rites. Whatever the initiation ceremony, it usually includes the training of initiates on the rights and responsibilities of their new social positions.[1]

Tanzania's colonization, rapid modernization, and globalization have greatly impacted its traditional initiation ceremonies. For instance, intense lobbying by various international entities has in the recent past (1998) prompted the Tanzanian government to ban female circumcision. But because the ban was not accompanied by efforts to preserve the useful social and cultural training that traditionally accompanied this rite, its practitioners

Female circumcision in Tanzania is most prevalent in the Arusha, Kilimanjaro, Dodoma, Singida, Mara, and Morogoro regions. (Jean-Luc Manaud/Gamma-Rapho via Getty Images)

merely took it underground where it has an estimated nationwide prevalence rate of 18 percent. In response, some nongovernmental organizations have tried to come up with alternative initiation ceremonies that feature the training, dance, and singing of their ancient counterparts and some exchange of gifts, as well as creating safe houses for girls and women who do not wish to undergo circumcision. However, these alternatives have a long way to go before they become effective substitutes. The formal school system might also play a greater role in equipping girls with the skills that were formerly gained from the traditional initiation ceremonies.

Conversely, the realization that male circumcision is beneficial in reducing the spread of HIV/AIDS has breathed new life into this traditional practice. Consequently, male circumcision on public health grounds is now growing across the country and has spread to communities that have traditionally not had it. This development will therefore preserve male circumcision well into the future.

Among the communities that practice circumcision in Tanzania, the Maasai probably attach the most significance to it as this is their most important rite of passage. Thus, we here briefly highlight Maasai male circumcision and other initiation ceremonies. While the Maasai have traditionally circumcised both boys and girls, female circumcision is declining due to government and other external social pressures. In contrast, Maasai male circumcision remains popular.

Maasai boys are usually circumcised when they are around 14 to 17 years old, though it is was not unusual traditionally for even much older boys to be circumcised. Before a boy is circumcised, he has to demonstrate enough maturity by, for example, wielding a heavy spear or herding a large herd of livestock. Because age sets are a central feature of Maasai social organization and as the purpose of circumcision is to graduate boys to manhood and to create warriors capable of defending the community, Maasai elders usually wait until there is a large enough population of young men capable of forming an efficient, sufficient, and proficient warrior or military force before they allow them to be circumcised. For this reason, an age group can consist of boys in a narrow or wide age range depending on prevailing birth rates.[2]

Once the community has a sufficient number of boys, preparations begin for their circumcision. The first step in this process is the young boys' participation in the precircumcision ceremony (*enkipaata*), which announces the formation of a new age set and also transitions the preceding age set to senior warriors ready for marriage. The *enkipaata* is usually spearheaded by the fathers of the new age set. As part of the *enkipaata*, a designated group of elders and soon-to-be-initiated boys tour the local region announcing the formation of the new age set for about four months. After this, a Maasai prophet (*oloiboni*) selects a *kraal*, or a cattle enclosure, that becomes the site of certain mandatory preinitiation rituals as well as hosting the 30 to 40 houses that are used to house the initiation candidates. Before this stage, some special-case boys, such as those who have lost a father and need to inherit his property right away, may be circumcised ahead of time. Such boys (or *ilng'eeliani*) are usually seen as the forerunners of any new age group.

During the *enkipaata* ceremony, the chief of the boys (*olopolosi olkiteng*) is selected. But because the *olopolosi olkiteng* is held responsible for the good and bad deeds of his age group, nobody wants this position. The day before the *enkipaata* ceremony, the boys spend a night in the forest. In the morning they stage a mock raid on their *kraal* dressed in loose clothes. They then dance for the whole day to signify their entry into the new age set and then disperse to await their circumcision (*emuratare*) in their individual homes.

About seven days before his circumcision, an initiation candidate is required to pasture his family's cattle for seven consecutive days. On the eighth day before the operation, he spends the night in the cold. Early in the morning, shortly before the operation, he takes a cold shower to cleanse and numb his body. This minimizes the pain of the circumcision operation, which is traditionally carried out without the benefit of painkillers. As he approaches the site of the operation shortly before sunrise, his friends, age mates, and male family members encourage him on. But they simultaneously threaten him with horrible consequences in the event that he lets them down by crying, flinching, kicking the knife, or showing cowardice during the operation.

Such consequences often include threats of social isolation, stampeding of the family cattle herd, and his parents being ridiculed for raising a coward. The gravity of these threats usually stills the initiate long enough for the delicate operation to be done perfectly by an experienced traditional male surgeon. Nevertheless, accidents and infections do occur, with disastrous consequences for the initiates. Moreover, some initiates do wince and force bystanders to pin them to the ground until the operation is over. Many of these "cowards" do nevertheless go on to prove their mettle or courage by serving society in other useful ways.

After the circumcision, the newly minted man or warrior is congratulated for his bravery and given gifts of livestock by his family, relatives, and friends. He then resorts to the customary black clothing as he heals over a three- to eight-month period under the watchful care of his family. Afterwards, he is shaved. Traditionally, the shaving took place in a communal home that the initiates constructed called the home of birds (*enkangoo ntaritik*). Such homes are increasingly rare.

After the initiates are sufficiently healed, they build the warriors' camp (*emanyatta*), which often consists of 20 to 40 houses. They then select the mothers who will live with and cook for them in the camp. This exercise is often quite contentious as the warriors and their fathers haggle over the selection of these women, who might be their fathers' favorite wives. Fathers are also frequently reluctant to let their wives go for fear that they might be taken advantage of in the camp.

It is in these *emanyattas* that the new warriors learn the principles of the Maasai age-set brotherhood system, oratory, and animal husbandry. They also learn the combat skills that enable them to fulfill their 10-year military obligation. At the start of the *emanyatta*, the warriors erect a white-and-blue flag in the middle of the camp. It remains hoisted for the 10-year tenure of the *emanyatta*, during which period the warriors (*morans*) also choose two chiefs to lead, guide, and represent them.

At the end of the 10-year commitment, the warriors attend the *eunoto* ceremony where they graduate into senior warriors and are then allowed to marry and start families. The *eunoto* ceremony takes place in another camp away from the *emanyatta*. The *eunoto* camp consists of 49 houses, one of which is the *osinkira*, or the prophet's (*oloiboni's*) house. As a sign that their combat duties are over, the graduates are not allowed to carry weapons like spears and knives to this ceremony whose other requirements include the distribution of eight bulls (obtained beforehand) to the elders; *a priori* selection of three important leaders, one of which, the *olutono*, is undesirable because the holder is answerable for the transgressions of his age-set members; and a ban on warriors eating alone or outside the *emanyatta* (camp) before this graduation, a prohibition that is meant to teach the warriors self-reliance.

A few months after the *eunoto* graduation ceremony, the warriors undergo the milk ceremony (*enkang e-kule*), in which the warriors' long, ochre-stained hair is shaved by their mothers. Few warriors like this ceremony, as the loss of their highly prized hair often brings them significant emotional stress and loss of dignity. Many shy from women until their hair grows back.

Later on, after the senior warriors have married, the new graduates participate in the meat ceremony (*enkang oo-nkiri*), which, among other reasons, exists to ensure compliance with certain age-set taboos and regulations like adherence to socially prescribed sex customs. A while later, the meat ceremony is followed by the junior elders' initiation ceremony (*orngesherr*), which marks the senior warriors' change of status to junior elders at about age 35. In this ceremony, every initiate gets an elder's chair, which he retains until it is broken or, in the event of his death, is inherited by his eldest son. Early on the day of *orngesherr*, the initiate sits on his ceremonial chair and has his head shaved by his wife, or senior wife if he has more than one. At the end of *orngesherr*, the initiate becomes a full-fledged elder who is fully responsible for his own family. At this point, the junior elder gains the right to leave his father's homestead and build his own, though he can still draw on his father's sage guidance as he needs it.

Like many other communities in modern Tanzania, traditional Maasai society is in a crisis, with modernity rapidly ruining its cultural systems (including initiation rites). However, modernity has not managed to replace what it has destroyed. For instance, no credible initiation systems have arisen in place of the traditional ones. Thus, many of the community's youth are going astray because they are not being properly socialized into productive members of society. To redeem their youth, Maasai and other Tanzanian communities may have to modernize existing rites of passage to make them suitable for contemporary conditions. To do so, they may have to create hybrid initiation rites that combine the best aspects of traditional and modern rites of passage.

Child-Naming Ceremonies

Tanzanian child-naming ceremonies vary by ethnicity, culture, religion, residence, education level, and the worldview of the child's parents. Even in precolonial Tanzania, child-naming traditions varied widely, with some communities naming their children immediately after birth with little fanfare while others did so through elaborate ceremonies that often involved certain religious rituals. Moreover, the sex of the newborn also influenced its naming formalities.

The diverse child-naming traditions of Tanzania's many communities have in many ways been simplified and unified by the child-registration requirements of the modern state. However, while the government requires that children be named, registered, and issued with birth certificates soon after birth for purposes of national planning, extension of health and education services, and protection of children's rights; in reality the country has one of the lowest child birth-registration rates in the world.[3]

All the same, many Tanzanian children's names can be quite informative. First, they convey the sex of the child, for instance, Mariamu (girl) versus Yohana (or John, boy), and the family religion (e.g., Mohammed and Yohana are male Islamic and Christian names, respectively). Second, children are also frequently named after their living or dead relatives, especially grandparents and great-grandparents, in order to connect them to their ancestral heritage. In some cases, it is local ancestral spirits that force the naming of certain children after them. In Sukumaland, for instance, certain deathly ill children have been cured by being named after local ancestral spirits at the recommendation of local medicine men. Third, Tanzanian child names also memorialize the child's features, the circumstances of its birth, the parents' situation at the time of the child's birth or naming, and the season of the child's birth. Thus, many of the country's Swahili names often memorialize desirable qualities, as in Ahadi (female, "promise"), Akili (male/female, "wisdom, intellect"), and Subira (female, "patience"); days and times, as in Alhamisi (male/female, "Thursday"), Alasiri (male/female, "afternoon"), and Alfajiri (male/female, "dawn"); or animals, as in Simba (male, "lion"). Because Tanzania is also a multicultural society, some of its names are also cross-cultural, such as Shabaan Robert, which is an Islamic-Christian name.

Furthermore, as this sampling of Sukuma and Nyamwezi names shows, these communities can name children after natural things, such as Malimi (male, "a lot of suns"), Mabula (male, "a lot of rain"), and Llimi (female, "a lot of suns"); desirable qualities such as Tamu (female, "sweet"), Dashina (male, "the wise one"), and Masanja (male, "bring together people or things"); or even terrifying qualities such as Lupandagila (male, "crusher or one who tramples on things"), and Masaganya (male, "one who stirs up people, or probes into issues").

Death and Burial Ceremonies

Like many other Africans, Tanzanians see life as a continuum, with death being a gateway to a more fulfilling life as an ancestral spirit close to the Supreme Deity or God. Consequently, Tanzanian funeral rites often simultaneously mourn the pain of death and the joy of life. Proper burial rituals are meant to ensure that the dead go in peace while the survivors continue on in peace.[4]

Many Tanzanians believe that one's afterlife is based on one's actions in life. Thus those who lead honorable lives go on to be ancestral spirits that commune with the Supreme Being. For this reason, many Tanzanian practitioners of African traditional religions venerate their ancestors and beseech them for blessings through regular invocations like "ancestors look favorably on us" or, in some cases, through sacrifices. In contrast, it is believed that those who lead dishonorable lives as sorcerers, murderers, and thieves, or who commit suicide or die unnaturally, become ghosts, which, according to local belief, can harm the living unless they are appeased through certain ritual rites.

Burial customs usually vary depending on whether the deceased was female or male, married or unmarried, young or old, Christian or Muslim, or rich or poor. While in the past communities like the Maasai disposed of their dead in the forest to be devoured by animals, such disposal practices have stopped due to the intervention of the government and religions like Christianity. Many Tanzanian Asians, especially those with a South Asian Hindu heritage, cremate their dead. Muslims, to the extent possible, bury their dead within hours of death.

For many non-Muslim Tanzanians, death is followed by an autopsy at a local hospital mortuary. The body is then prepared for burial, with the number of days before the funeral, the quality of casket used, and the grandeur of the funeral ceremony being dictated by the socioeconomic status of the deceased or his or her family. Among the Chagga and other more socioeconomically developed ethnic groups of Tanzania, funerals can be ostentatious and costly affairs.

While not representative of all Tanzanian communities, the following is a review of the fairly similar Sukuma, Jita, Kerewe, and Zinza burial customs for a married man.[5] Among these groups, burial happens the same day as death. The funeral is directed by the *mwesi* (funeral director), who is usually the oldest brother of the deceased. When the funeral ceremony commences, the *mwesi* uses a short-handle hoe to mark the grave site with two parallel lines. He then takes out the first scoops of soil or sand with his short hoe and lets others dig the grave with normal hoes before returning to take out the last two scoops of sand. The deceased's male relatives then kill a cow and skin it to the leg joints, with the bone being left in the skin below the joints. The raw cow hide is then cut into two pieces; with one piece going under the deceased's body while the other covers it. The body is then laid in the grave on its right side (a preferred sleeping position for local men) facing the rising sun, which signifies the source of life in local mythology. The grave is then filled with soil or sand.

The *mwesi* then throws away the short hoe used for the burial ceremony in the forest or down an anthill. He then goes to a river and bathes, followed by the other men in the burial ceremony, the widow (who only bathes below the waist), and other women. Throughout the five- to eight-day mourning period, this group only bathes communally.

After the bathing party returns to the deceased's home, his furniture, personal effects, and food are moved outside the house and are sprinkled with river water by the women in the widow's party. By nightfall, a *mwesha* (sanctifier) is brought from a remote tribe to sleep with the widow and to symbolically cleanse her and her family of the pollution of the dead man, thereby enabling her and his survivors to live on peacefully. Moreover, this custom is designed to break the widow's sexual union with her late husband and to symbolically set her free to move on with her life.

The day after the burial, the official five- to eight-day mourning period starts, with the mourners passing the time talking in subdued tones or playing local checkerboard (*ubao*) games. On the first morning, the sanctifier leaves the house holding his throat as if he is choking while the widow is left in the house sitting with her head bowed and her eyes fixed on the floor. She does not talk to anyone except to her attending widows. At the end of the fifth day the sanctifier returns. He then shaves the heads of the widow and all of her sons and then sleeps with the widow again. The next day, before he leaves in the morning, he instructs the widow to bathe her entire body in the river to cleanse herself of her husband's sweat.

After the bath, the widow returns to the house and bows her head once again as the *mwesi* declares the house to have been overcome. The widow's bed is then lowered to the floor to signify her devastating loss. On the sixth day, all the mourners wash in the river. A white cock is then killed on the threshold of the house, and its blood sprinkled inside the house and its feathers left at the intersection of two local paths. On this day, with her grieving over, the widow emerges with her head up. The *mwesha* then returns and, for the third and final time, spends the night with her in a nearby bush. Afterwards, a short ceremony is held; the widow is inherited by her husband's brother or, for the purposes of ensuring her welfare, by one of her male children. With the mourning concluded, the mourners leave for their own homes.

Like many other cultural practices, the preceding death and burial ceremony is not static but is constantly changing with changing socioeconomic circumstances. For instance, the widow inheritance and cleansing rites are increasingly untenable in the face of deadly diseases like HIV/AIDS. Thus, they are being replaced by symbolic equivalents.

Rainmaking Ceremonies

The communities of modern Tanzania have led agrarian lives for centuries. Thus, the timely receipt of sufficient amounts of rainfall has long been critical to meeting the water needs of its people, animals, and crops. Simply put, rain is life, for without it people, crops, and animals wither and die. It is therefore not surprising that annual rainfall patterns have structured the lifestyle of Tanzanian communities for millennia. As a corollary, Tanzanians have, for equally long periods of time, tried to control the weather through rainmaking and rain-stopping rituals designed to ensure the availability of the right amounts of the life-giving rains at the right time.[6]

Rainmaking in Tanzania is both modern and traditional. Modern rainmaking is a scientific endeavor that involves the use of cloud-seeding technology to induce rainfall. The technique involves firing silver iodide particles into clouds to induce water condensation and its subsequent fall as rain. This method, which involves the use of two aircraft to seed warm and cold clouds at different altitudes, is said to be particularly successful because it can more precisely target areas where the rain is to fall. Tanzania has access to cloud-seeding technology through scientific cooperation agreements with countries like Thailand.[7]

In contrast, traditional rainmaking uses elaborate traditional religious ceremonies to appease the ancestors and the gods in the hope that they will release rain. This technique rests on traditional Tanzanian belief that drought is an unnatural event caused by angry ancestors, gods, or the Supreme Being because of one or more human transgressions. Thus, to end drought, the living have to appease the offended ancestors and gods with offerings and sacrifices. In precolonial Tanzania, rainmaking was widespread, and communities like the Ihanzu of northern Tanzania continue to be celebrated rainmakers.[8]

FESTIVALS

Tanzania has many festivals. The national ones mostly focus on trade and the arts while the local and regional ones usually celebrate things like agricultural harvests. The following is a brief look at the country's main national festivals.

Zanzibar International Film Festival of the Dhow Countries (ZIFF)

This is the largest cultural festival in Tanzania and one of eight such festivals in Africa south of the Sahara. It is also the largest film, music, and arts festival in East Africa. ZIFF is held annually in the first two weeks of July, and it attracts over 100 film entries from the "dhow countries" of the Middle East, Africa, and Asia. Countries in these regions were once connected by wind-driven wooden dhows that crisscrossed the Indian Ocean until the advent of modern engine-powered vessels. Besides film, the ZIFF also promotes, discusses, explores, and rewards the artistic work of artists, musicians, cultural troupes, and photographers from the dhow countries and beyond. In 2010, the festival drew an audience of 150,000, including 45,000 foreign visitors from 52 countries. The ZIFF celebrated its 14th anniversary in 2011.

Zanzibar Cultural Festival (ZCF)

The ZCF is held annually all over the Zanzibar archipelago in July soon after the conclusion of ZIFF. Although the ZCF mainly highlights the archipelago's varied Swahili traditions and customs, arts and crafts, and *taarab* music and dance, it also attracts performers from many other African countries. Zanzibaris celebrate the festival with cultural workshops, events, and performances. In the historical World Cultural Heritage Site of Zanzibar Stone Town, the festival is marked with street carnivals, fairs, and canoe races. On the Zanzibar archipelago's Pemba Island, the festival is marked with the annual bullfight, which was introduced there by Portuguese explorers between the late 1400s and 1600s.

Sauti za Busara (Sound of Wisdom) Music Festival (SBMF)

This festival is held every year in Zanzibar in the second week of February. Popularly known as a festival of African music under African skies, it often attracts about 400 musicians and 40 or so groups from Tanzania and

Performers at the *Sauti za Busara* Music Festival. (Mwanzo Millinga/AFP/Getty Images)

neighboring African countries. This three-day festival usually features concerts on a wide range of traditional, modern, and hybrid music traditions of Africa, Arabia, Asia, and other parts of the world.

Karibu Travel and Trade Fair (KTTF)

The KTTF is Tanzania's and much of East Africa's annual premier tourism-industry festival. It is held in May in the city of Arusha, in the vicinity of Mount Kilimanjaro. Initially designed as a showcase of East African tour operators and destinations, the KTTF has since become an international event that draws exhibitors from all over the world. Many KTTF participants usually take advantage of nearby tourist attractions such as Lake Manyara, Tarangire, Ngorongoro Crater, and the Serengeti. Through KTTF, Tanzania and her neighbors hope to attract more tourists to East Africa by taking advantage of the region's broader diversity of tourist attractions.

Mwaka Kogwa (MK)

This is the customary Shirazi or Persian New Year celebration that is held on the 23rd or 24th of July in Zanzibar. While the festival is based on the Zoroastrian religion, the largely Muslim Zanzibari society has embraced it. The epicenter of the festival is the village of Makunduchi (in southern Unguja or Zanzibar), which holds the main rituals of the festival and where thousands gather to join the celebrations. Besides the singing, dancing, feasting, and drumming, the festival features New Year good-luck rituals. At the start of the festival, all village men engage in a mock fight with banana sticks (in place of real weapons, which were historically used) to vent their frustrations from the past year. Meanwhile, the women of the village put on their best clothes and go through the village and fields singing traditional songs on family, love, and joy. Afterwards, the traditional healer (*mganga*) sets a ritual hut on fire and, on the basis of the smoke's direction, offers a prediction on the village's prosperity in the coming year. Locals and their guests then feast, sing, drum, and dance well into the night.[9]

Other than the preceding festivals, Tanzania also has other festivals in areas like sports. There is also the National Book Week festival that is used by the Tanzanian Publishers Association (PATA) to promote books and a reading culture in the country.

NATIONAL AND RELIGIOUS HOLIDAYS

Tanzania has 14 major national and religious holidays. The secular ones are New Year's Day (January 1), Zanzibar Revolution Day (January 12), Sheikh Abeid Amani Karume Day (April 7), Union Day (April 26), International

Workers' Day/Labor Day (May 1), Maonyesho ya Saba Saba (July 7), Wakulima wa Nane Nane/Peasants' Day (August 8), Mwalimu Julius Nyerere Day (October 14), and Independence Day (December 9).

Of these, Independence Day is the most prominent as it marks the end of British colonial rule of Tanzania's constituent parts of Tanganyika (until December 9, 1961) and Zanzibar (until December 19, 1963). On Independence Day, Tanzanians listen to patriotic speeches from the president and other senior government officials, watch military parades and fly-overs, and enjoy music performances by various dance troupes. The celebrations are usually attended by dignitaries from all over the world. On December 9, 2011, Tanzania held its 50th independence anniversary. It was one of the largest such celebrations.

The country's major religious holidays are linked to its major religions of Christianity and Islam. While the main Christian holidays are Good Friday* (March/April), Easter* (March/April), Christmas (December 25), and Boxing Day (December 26); the Islamic ones are Eid al-Moulid* (January/February), Eid al-Fitr* (July–November), and Eid al-Hajj* (October/November). Because the holidays marked with an asterisk (*) are based on the lunar calendar, their Gregorian (Western/Christian) calendar days vary from year to year, though they occur in the same season of the year. In most cases, celebrations of these religious holidays start on the day before.

While these Christian and Islamic holidays are mainly celebrated by these religions' followers, most of them are now major public holidays because Tanzania has large populations of Christians and Muslims. Below is a brief overview of the country's main religious holidays.

Christmas, which celebrates the birth of Jesus Christ, is the main Christian holiday in Tanzania and in other parts of the world. It is held annually on December 25 and is most heavily celebrated on the Tanzanian mainland, where Christianity is dominant. The day is marked with lively church services that often attract people who rarely set foot in church. Afterwards, worshippers go home to enjoy family feasts, gift exchanges, and visits with family and friends. For some Tanzanians, Christmas is also a day to drink and party heavily. Some affluent families are also beginning to use Christmas as a time for local or foreign family getaways. As in the Western world, Christmas in Tanzania has increasingly become commercialized, to the chagrin of many devout Christians.

Easter memorializes the death and resurrection of Jesus Christ. It consists of Good Friday (crucifixion day) and Easter Sunday (resurrection day). As the dates for this holiday are partially based on the lunar calendar, it occurs on various dates between March 22 and April 25. Easter is the second most important holiday on the Christian calendar. But unlike Christmas, Easter is much less commercialized. Like Christmas, Easter is mostly celebrated on the Tanzanian mainland.

Eid al-Moulid is an Islamic holiday that celebrates the birthday of the Prophet Mohammed, the founder of Islam. On this holiday, Muslims reflect on the significance of Muhammad's life. Although the holiday is celebrated by the main Sunni and Shia branches of Islam, the Wahhabi sect and other fundamentalist Muslims do not celebrate it.

Eid al-Fitr is the Muslim celebration that marks the end of Ramadan—the month-long daytime fast that usually occurs in the ninth month of the Islamic calendar. The holiday is especially celebrated in areas of the country that are dominated by Muslims, such as Zanzibar. It usually lasts four days and features early-morning prayers followed by feasting, gift exchanges, special offerings, new clothes, *taarab* music, singing, and dancing.

Eid al-Hajj (also known as Eid al-Adha or Eid al-Kebir) is a three-day Islamic festival that commemorates Ibrahim's (Abraham in the Christian tradition) willingness to sacrifice his son Ishmael (Isaac in the Christian tradition) at the command of Allah (God). The festival starts after the annual Muslim pilgrimage (or Hajj) to Mecca—the birth place of Islam. Besides honoring the prophet Ibrahim, Muslims see Eid al-Hajj as a holiday of sacrifice and faith. Thus, Muslim families sacrifice cows, lambs, goats, or camels and give one-third of the meat to the poor, another third to family and friends, and keep the remaining third for their own use. During this festival, Muslims offer prayers, attend sermons at nearby mosques, eat sumptuous meals, wear new clothes, exchange gifts, visit with family and friends, and enjoy live Swahili *taarab* music and dancing. Those who managed to make the annual pilgrimage to Mecca in that year are then welcomed home with much jubilation. Like the other Muslim holidays, Eid al-Hajj is most heavily celebrated in coastal and island Tanzania, where there is a large population of Muslims.

AMUSEMENT AND SPORTS

Tanzanians enjoy a wide variety of amusement and sports activities. Examples of these leisure activities, which also serve as important social gatherings, include sports, cinema, beauty pageants, comedy, drama, dance, various traditional games, and the drinking of various beverages like beer, coffee, and tea. Some of these activities are briefly outlined below. Music, drama, and dance are discussed in Chapter 8.

Sports

Tanzania is a sporting nation that is mostly focused on soccer and athletics. However, because of its broad cultural diversity, it has a number of other

Tanzanian soccer players celebrate a goal. Soccer is one of the country's most popular sports. (AP Photo/Rebecca Blackwell)

sports including boxing, basketball, swimming, cricket, golf, motor sports, rugby, tennis, darts, volleyball, badminton, and outdoor camping. Most of these sports have their own national sports associations.

Tanzania's strong sports culture is largely attributed to founding president Nyerere's use of sports (especially soccer/football and *bao*, a local variant of chess) and culture to unite the country. In particular, his school sports development programs through the Tanzania Primary School Games Union (UMITASHUMTA) and Inter-Secondary Schools Games (UMISETA) were a great success. The most popular school sports include football (soccer), netball, volleyball, athletics, basketball, table tennis, and handball. Nyerere also promoted professional sports activities, leading to Tanzania's participation in the African Cup of Nations in Nigeria in 1980; Filbert Bayi's gold medal and world record 1,500-meter win at the 1974 Commonwealth Games in Christchurch, New Zealand; and Bayi and Suleiman Nyambui's silver and bronze medal wins in the 1980 Moscow Olympic Games.[10]

Tanzanian soccer is governed by the Tanzania Football Federation (TFF) which was created in 1930 and has been a Federation of International Football Associations (FIFA) affiliate since 1964. TFF manages the country's major national team, the Taifa Stars (i.e., Nation's Stars), as well as its junior (or under-23) national side, the Ngorongoro Heroes. The Taifa Stars is composed of the best players from the country's Premier League clubs. While the team is a regional soccer powerhouse, it has not done well in the continental Confederation of African Football (CAF) competitions, nor has it ever qualified for the FIFA World Cup. The team has, however, won a few regional FIFA tournaments. In 2011, FIFA rated Tanzania 37th in Africa and 136th in world soccer rankings. When the 2010 FIFA World Cup was held in South Africa, the Taifa Stars were privileged to play a warm-up game with Brazil's national team, the Samba Boys. The Taifa Stars lost 5–1.[11]

The main soccer competition in Tanzania is the TFF's Premier League, which has long been dominated by the country's two main soccer clubs: Young Africans FC and Simba SC—both based in Dar es Salaam. Between 1965 and 2011, Young Africans FC won the Premier League Cup 18 times and Simba SC won it 16 times. Together, they won it 34 times in the 46 years between 1965 and 2011. In the 2011–2012 season, the other national Premier League teams and their home cities were African Lyon (Dar es Salaam), Azam FC (Dar es Salaam), Coastal Union (Tanga), JKT Oljoro FC (Arusha), JKT Ruvu Stars (Dodoma), Kagera Sugar (Bukoba), Moro United (Morogoro), Mtibwa Sugar FC (Turiani), Polisi Dodoma (Dodoma), Ruvu Shooting (Coast), Toto African (Mwanza), and Villa Squad (Dar es Salaam). Besides the country's professional soccer clubs, there are many other local and regional soccer teams throughout the country.

In Zanzibar, soccer is governed by the Zanzibar Football Association (ZFA). In recent years, the ZFA league has been dominated by Miembeni SC, Mafunzi FC, and Mundu FC. While Zanzibar does not have its own national team, its club sides can represent the island in tournaments organized by the CAF.

Over the years, Tanzania has produced many legendary soccer players, including Yassin Napili, Idd Pazi, James Kisaka, Mohamed Mkweche, and Laurence Mwalusako. However, few of them have benefited significantly from their fame because of the country's low income and poor soccer commercialization. Nevertheless, nine Tanzanians are currently playing professionally in other countries. These include Nizar Khalfan from Mtwara, who plays for the Philadelphia Union Club in the United States. Adam Nditi of Zanzibar is also on the roster of the United Kingdom's Chelsea FC Academy, which grooms junior players for the UK premier league side, Chelsea FC.

At the moment, Tanzanian soccer is dominated by males. However, the TFF and the Tanzania Women Football Association (TWFA) are working on a women's national soccer league.

Many Tanzanians enjoy TFF's Premier League soccer games live or on radio and television. But in recent years, the advent of satellite TV coupled with the country's own poor soccer standards have made many Tanzanians avid fans of the English Premier League and the German Football Bundesliga. Thus British Premier League teams like Arsenal, Chelsea, Liverpool, and Manchester United and Germany's FC Bayern München and Borussia Dortmund have hordes of fans in Tanzania. Consequently, watching European Soccer League matches in pay-per-view halls is a popular pastime for males in the country.[12] Unless Tanzanian soccer improves substantially, its live soccer TV broadcasts will not be able to compete with those from Europe. TFF has thus recently sought to improve the quality of soccer in the country by creating the Tanzania Soccer Academy.[13]

Outside of soccer and athletics, Tanzania has also achieved some success in basketball and has one player, Hasheem Thabeet, in the United States' lucrative National Basketball Association (NBA).

Games

Tanzanians play many traditional and modern games including *bao* (a local variant of chess) and cards. The country's traditional games are now managed by the National Traditional Sports Association of Tanzania (*Chama cha Michezo ya Jadi*, CHAMIJATA).

Cinema

Cinema is an elite form of entertainment in Tanzania and is mainly concentrated in the major cities of Dar es Salaam and Arusha. Aside from the theater in Arusha, the country's main cinema theaters are the Century Cinemax at Mlimani City, Dar Es Salaam, which mainly shows Western movies, and the New World Cinema, Dar Es Salaam, which mainly shows Indian movies and is mainly patronized by the country's large Tanzanian Indian population. There are also a number of mobile cinema units that are used by missionary and development organizations throughout the country.

This paucity of movie theaters is a reflection of the fact that cinema never quite became a mass-market commodity in Tanzania because of many factors. First, the country's *Ujamaa* socialist experiment (1960s–1985) discouraged cinema as a purveyor of Western values that were seen as inimical to local culture. Second, in the glory days of cinema, many Tanzanians were too poor to afford movie entertainment. Third, until recently there has been very limited local production of movies that are relevant to local audiences. Fourth, television availability in the country had been quite limited prior to the country's economic liberalization in the mid-1980s. As a result, many Tanzanians had little exposure to cinematic entertainment.

But since liberalization, the local film industry has grown exponentially due to the creation of a more supportive regulatory framework that is overseen by government and industry entities like the National Arts Council of

Tanzania (BASATA), Tanzania Film Federation (TFF), Tanzania Film Commission (TFC), Copyright Society of Tanzania (COSOTA), and the Tanzania Film Censorship Board; greater availability of film-making expertise and technology in the country; and the formation of the ZIFF in the late 1990s that provides a forum for debuting films and for the exchange of ideas among filmmakers.

Two trends are discernible in this industry. First is the *feature film*, which is produced by professional filmmakers and which has not really caught on nor gained much market in the country because of poor distribution, lack of theater facilities, cost, and production standards that make it more suitable for Western audiences. Second is the new *video film* industry, which is produced by amateur video filmmakers and which gets around most of the obstacles noted above in addition to addressing issues that Tanzanians care about. Initially pioneered and imported from Nigeria's Nollywood industry, Tanzanians started imitating this genre, starting with the production of George Otieno's *Girlfriend* (2002), and have since created one of the most productive video film industries on the African continent. It was reputed to be producing 100 films a month by 2010. Video films can be shot in as little as one day and released straight to video DVDs or CDs, which are then sold cheaply on the country's city streets for home use. Some of these video films are also accessible on YouTube and other Internet sites, mobile video trucks, and cheap countrywide pay-per-video halls. The county's film industry is also described in Chapter 3.[14]

Beauty Pageants

Beauty pageants are an important part of Tanzania's popular culture. At the moment, there are two main beauty pageants in the country: Miss Tanzania (MT) and Miss Universe Tanzania (MUT). The former is affiliated with the Miss World Pageant while the latter is linked with the Miss Universe Pageant. Second-place finishers in the annual MT and MUT contests go on to represent Tanzania in the Miss Earth and Miss International pageants, respectively.

Beauty contests started in Tanzania in the early 1960s under the sponsorship of the Kilimanjaro Hotel. At the time, most of the participants were from the city of Dar es Salaam, but the winners could not advance beyond national borders because the contest was not associated with any global beauty competitions. When the country launched *Ujamaa* in 1968, beauty contests were banned because they were seen as being contrary to Tanzania's African culture. Moreover, some members of the public, religious groups, and other pressure groups accused the contests of promoting immorality. The ban lasted until 1994 when the government legalized pageants as part of its economic liberalization.

Nelly Kamwelu, Miss Universe Tanzania 2011. She is the first Tanzanian beauty queen to compete in four Grand Slam pageants (Miss Universe, Miss International, Miss Earth, and Miss Tourism Queen International) in a single year (2011). (Mister Shadow/LatinContent/Getty Images)

Soon after, Lino International Agency organized the first-ever Miss Tanzania Beauty Pageant in 1994, and the winner of that pageant, Aina Linda Maeda, went on to represent the country in the Miss World Beauty Pageant. As in the 1960s, the reintroduction of this art form in the 1990s drew protests that the competitions would degrade the country's morals. However, the organizers have since worked with the government to ensure that the pageants are in line with the country's culture. With greater social acceptance, the competing Miss Universe Tanzania pageant was launched in 2007, and the winner of that competition, Flaviana Matata, has since become a supermodel on the world stage.

Comedy

Comedy is deeply ingrained in Tanzania's oral societies. Nevertheless, professional comedy shows are fairly new to the country and can be traced to the liberalization of the country's media and economy starting in the mid-1980s.

Since then, there has been a significant growth in demand for comedy content, which has in turn led to the gradual commercialization of comedy as well as creating new avenues of comedic entertainment in the country.

As Tanzanian comedy becomes increasingly professionalized and commercialized, it will better serve the changing and emerging needs of the country by, for instance, being used to address touchy subjects like corruption in government. Some of the country's leading comedians are Evans Bukuku, Babu Ayubu, Dogo Pepe, and Falii Mapupa. Bukuku is also the managing director of Vuvuzela Entertainment, which has started to organize and commercialize the country's stand-up comedy talent. Nevertheless, like other artists, many Tanzanian comedians struggle to earn a living from their craft.[15]

OLD AND NEW SOCIAL CUSTOMS AND LIFESTYLES

The Traditional-Modern Lifestyle Continuum

Contemporary Tanzania's social customs and lifestyles lie on a continuum with traditionalists on the left, syncretists in the middle, and modernists on the right. Broadly defined, traditionalists are Tanzanians who, by choice or location, subscribe to the traditional values of the country's various communities. Most traditionalists live in the country's rural areas where contact with the outside world is minimal. But even here, it is more accurate to state that many rural Tanzanians have different levels of traditionalism, and some can even be said to be modernists to the extent that they have relatively high incomes and many modern material possessions such as televisions and cars.

Conversely, Tanzanian modernists are those with a modern worldview that is heavily influenced by European or Western values, such as individualism and materialism, as opposed to the communal values that characterize traditional lifestyles. Many of the modernists are urban based and are in constant contact with fellow modernists from within and outside the country. They tend to have high levels of income, access to local and foreign media, and formal education. However, not all urban dwellers are modernists as some are recent rural-urban migrants with rather traditional worldviews and tenuous access to the conveniences of modern urban living like running water and electricity. For this reason, Tanzanian cities can at once be contradictory scenes of modernity and traditionalism.

In between the traditionalists and modernists are the many Tanzanians who make the best of the country's traditional and modern socioeconomic sectors by selectively using the best aspects of both. The following is a brief overview of the country's largely traditionalist rural lifestyles and the more modernist urban lifestyles.

Traditional Rural-Based Social Customs and Lifestyles

Tanzania's rural areas are dominated by people with traditional lifestyles. Key among these are hunter-gatherers, pastoralists, farmers, and fishermen.

Hunting and gathering are currently mainly practiced by the Hadza of north-central Tanzania. They once led a sustainable nomadic lifestyle in a 4,000-square-mile habitat around Lake Eyasi that is all but gone thanks to the growing population, farms, and livestock herds of surrounding communities such as the Datoga, the Sukuma, and the Iramba. As a result, the Hadza hunter-gatherer way of life is on its way out.[16]

Pastoralism is the practice of primarily deriving one's livelihood from livestock like cattle and sheep. Currently, this lifestyle is dominant among the Maasai of the savanna and semiarid areas of north-central Tanzania. The Maasai, who in the past practiced nomadic pastoralism, are increasingly being forced to shift to ranching and sedentary livestock production by the growing scarcity of the expansive range lands that they once occupied. Many Maasai are now also shifting to crop production as well as continuing to periodically sell their livestock herds to buy food from local markets. While the Maasai have traditionally valued large animal herds, many have been forced by their changing material and cultural conditions to reevaluate that tradition. Some have thus gone to school and become part of the modern Tanzanian economy.

Farming is Tanzania's dominant rural lifestyle. While many Tanzanian farmers are engaged in basic subsistence production, a few are modern commercial producers of crops and livestock. Many Tanzanian farmers hedge against loss by raising both crops and livestock. The average Tanzanian farmer owns a relatively small farm and uses traditional production methods that seldom use mechanization or modern commercial fertilizers and seeds. Depending on their location, some farmers supplement their diet with localized wildlife hunting and fishing. Some irrigation farming is also practiced in parts of the country.

Fishing lifestyles are common near major coastal and inland fisheries such as the Indian Ocean and Lake Tanganyika. There are nevertheless very few Tanzanians who are exclusively dependent on fish for their livelihood.

Most of the preceding rural lifestyles are anchored in villages with intermingled rural towns and markets that, along with schools, health centers, and religious mission stations, also serve as nodes of modernity. Many rural Tanzanians now have widespread access to cell phones and dry-cell-powered radios. Growing access to solar power and electricity is also making it possible for many rural dwellers to operate television sets, which are increasingly contributing to their modernization.

New Urban-Based Social Customs and Lifestyles

As with most urban areas around the world, Tanzanian cities are dominated by people with modern values (e.g., career advancement, individualism, innovation, and materialism) and lifestyles (e.g., doctors and lawyers). Many of the middle- and upper-income individuals work as middle and senior executives in the public, private, and nonprofit sectors. These individuals' high levels of income, education, and access to global media allow them to be at the forefront of their country's growing globalization, mass consumption, and high-life culture. Their low-income counterparts mostly work in low-level public-, private-, and nonprofit-sector positions. However, the vast majority of urban Tanzanians earn their living in the informal sector.

The country's urban dwellers also tend to buy much of their food instead of growing it. They are also more likely to interact frequently with people from other ethnic communities. As a result, most of the country's ethnically mixed marriages are in the urban areas. While rural status symbols include things like livestock, in the urban areas people aspire to own things like cars.

NOTES

1. Daniel Mbunda, *Traditional Sex Education in Tanzania: A Study of 12 Ethnic Groups* (New York: The Margaret Sanger Center, Planned Parenthood of New York City, 1991).

2. Tepilit Ole Saitoti, *The Worlds of a Maasai Warrior* (Berkeley: University of California Press, 1988); Maasai Association, "Maasai Ceremonies and Rituals," http://www.maasai-association.org/ceremonies.html, accessed November 3, 2011.

3. K. Manji, *Situation Analysis of Newborn Health in Tanzania: Current Situation, Existing Plans and Strategic Next Steps for Newborn Health* (Dar es Salaam: Ministry of Health and Social Welfare, Save the Children, 2009).

4. T. Knox, "Funeral Traditions in Tanzania," Mysendoff.com, August 16, 2011, http://mysendoff.com/2011/08/tanzania-funeral-traditions/, accessed July 18, 2012; R. E. S. Tanner, "Ancestor Propitiation Ceremonies in Sukumaland, Tanganyika," *Africa: Journal of the International African Institute* 28, no. 3 (July 1958): 225–31.

5. Don Brown, "The African Funeral Ceremony: Stumbling Block or Redemptive Analogy?" *International Journal of Frontier Missions* 2, no. 3, http://ijfm.org/archives.htm#Volume23, accessed November 12, 2011.

6. Terje Oestigaard, "Traditions in Transitions: Rainmaking in a Changing World in Tanzania," ECAS 2011, 4th European Conference on African Studies, Uppsala, Sweden, June 15–18, 2011, http://www.nai.uu.se/ecas-4/, accessed November 12, 2011.

7. "Tanzania to Get Rain-making Help," *BBC News*, February 16, 2007, http://news.bbc.co.uk/2/hi/africa/6368371.stm, accessed November 15, 2011.

8. Todd Sanders, "Reflections on Two Sticks: Gender, Sexuality and Rainmaking," *Cahiers d'Études Africaines* 166, no. 42–2 (2002): 285–313.

9. Tanzania Tourist Board, "Festival," 2011, http://www.tanzaniatouristboard.com/whats-on/festival/, accessed November 22, 2011.

10. Nasongelya Kilyinga, "Nyerere Is Behind Success Story of Tanzania's Sports," *Tanzania Daily News* (Dar es Salaam), October 13, 2011, http://allafrica.com/stories/201110140785.html, accessed November 24, 2011; Nelly Mtema, "Umiseta Set for Kicks Off," *Tanzania Daily News*, June 13, 2011, http://in2eastafrica.net/umiseta-set-for-kicks-off/, accessed November 24, 2011; Emmanuel Cliff, "Arusha Selects a Regional Umitashumta Team," *The Arusha Times*, June 18, 2011, http://allafrica.com/stories/201106220162.html, accessed November 24, 2011.

11. Emmanuel Muga, "Brazil to Play Tanzania in Pre-World Cup Friendly," *BBC Sport*, Dar es Salaam, May 27, 2011, http://news.bbc.co.uk/sport, accessed November 24, 2011; Stella Nyemenohi, "Stars Mediocre Show Angers Sports Minister," *Tanzania Daily News*, October 13, 2011, http://allafrica.com/stories/201110140112.html, accessed November 24, 2011.

12. "Fans in Tanzania and Kenya Revel in Trophy Tour," *UEFA Champions League*, April 3, 2012, accessed July 18, 2012.

13. James Momanyi, "Tanzania Mainland Face Zanzibar In 'Tie of Legends,'" *Goal.com*, July 17, 2009, http://www.goal.com/en/news/89/africa/2009/07/17/1387728/tanzania-mainland-face-zanzibar-in-tie-of-legends, accessed November 24, 2011.

14. Rosaleen Smyth, "The Feature Film in Tanzania," *African Affairs* 88, no. 352 (July 1989): 389–96; Mona Ngusekela Mwakalinga, *The Political Economy of the Film Industry in Tanzania: From Socialism to an Open Market Economy, 1961–2010*, PhD dissertation, Film and Media Studies, University of Kansas, Manhattan, KS; "Zanzibar International Film Festival, "About ZIFF," 2011, http://www.ziff.or.tz/about/ziff, accessed November 24, 2011.

15. Orton Kiishweko, "Stand-Up Comedy Goes Big in Dar Es Salaam," *Tanzania Daily News* (Dar es Salaam), March 2, 2011, http://allafrica.com/stories/201103030194.html, accessed November 24, 2011; "World Renowned Comedian Bussmann's Holiday Comes to Dar," *Tanzania Daily News* (Dar es Salaam), September 14, 2011, http://allafrica.com/stories/201109150768.html, accessed November 24, 2011.

16. Michael Finkel, "The Hadza," *National Geographic Magazine*, December 2009, http://ngm.nationalgeographic.com/print/2009/12/hadza/finkel-text, accessed December 1, 2011.

8

Music, Dance, and Drama

MUSIC, DANCE, AND drama are central facets of Tanzanian culture and are almost always present in social functions such as marriages, graduations, political rallies, and worship services. However, the extent to which each of these three is utilized varies across the country depending on the occasion, location, and the relevant community's own unique values, culture, and music/dance/drama history. Because Tanzania has over 120 ethnic communities, its music is quite diverse even though it conveys, engages, and celebrates the same general human experiences.

Music, dance, and drama are especially important in Tanzania because much of the country's culture is transmitted orally even though Tanzanians are fairly literate. Like many aspects of the country's culture, its music, dance, and drama are constantly changing.

Because of YouTube, the Internet, and other cheap audio and video recording technologies, Tanzanian music and dance is widely available and popular throughout East and Central Africa. Most of the country's regionally popular music is sung in Swahili, East Africa's most widespread language. Although English is Tanzania's other official language, not many Tanzanian musicians speak or sing well in it. Moreover, it is hard for Tanzanian English singers to break through to global markets because of poor promotion and intense competition from native English-speaking singers from the United States, Britain, and other countries. Tanzanian drama has also not been as successful internationally because of these same reasons, as well as its strong cultural rootedness.

Some of Tanzania's major female musicians and groups include Ray C, Dataz, Judith Wambura (Lady Jaydee), K-Lyinn, Saida Karoli, Bi Kidude, Rose Mhando, Siti binti Saad, and Nakaaya Sumari. On the male side are musicians like Juma Kassim Ally (Juma Nature), Joseph Mbilinyi (Mr. II), the late James Maligisa Dandu (Cool James), Abdul Sykes (Dully Sykes), Joseph Haule (Professor Jay), Hukwe Ubi Zawose, and the late Remmy Ongala.

Tanzania's music, dance, and drama fall into three distinct timeframes: the precolonial, colonial, and postcolonial periods. In the precolonial period, each of Tanzania's ethnic groups largely subscribed to its own music, dance, and drama, with relatively few organized cultural exchanges between them despite their many shared cultural traits.

With colonialism came the creation of a national government, economy, and internal transport and circulation system that soon raised the level of interethnic interaction and exchange even in the area of music, dance, and drama. Moreover, the colonial era witnessed the introduction of music recording technology in the country, which soon spawned a commercial music industry that greatly aided the spread of the country's music within and between its ethnic groups. At the same time, the introduction of music players (e.g., radio and gramophones) and new music genres, instruments, and compositional techniques also greatly aided the development and diffusion of music in the country.

Since independence, the music, dance, and drama trends initiated by colonialism have grown greatly. Moreover, the country's growing modernization, globalization, incomes, population mobility and circulation, and access to modern dance styles and music recording and dissemination technology (e.g., YouTube, the Internet, and cheap digital music and video recorders) have all led to an explosion of the quantity, quality, and variety of music, dance, and drama enjoyed by Tanzanians.

Music

Tanzania's music can be broken down by historical foundation (traditional, modern, or blended), geographic origin (local or foreign), type (vocal, instrumental, or both), performance (group/choir or solo/individual), structure, repertoire, or functional use. This discussion is mainly organized by geographical and historical origin and function.

Contemporary Tanzanian music can be broadly categorized as traditional, modern, or mixed. While traditional music is indigenous and has a much longer history, modern music is of more recent origin and is generally infused with many nonnative influences. In between traditional and modern music is a blended music form that both bridges and has various aspects of these two extremes. Moreover, such mixed music genres are eclectic in their use of instruments and language.

Traditional music is more widespread than its modern counterpart because it is native, is sung in more accessible local languages, and is orally passed down from generation to generation. Considered to be music by and for its people, traditional music is that which is taught by, performed by, and embraced by the country's mostly rural-based ethnic groups and is easily accessible to even the nonliterate population.

Indigenous music is present in nearly all local sociocultural and political functions, festivals, and ceremonies. Specifically, it is used to console the bereaved, praise and memorialize the living and dead, communicate, aid and synchronize work, keep time (i.e., to initiate social functions such as church services). It also aids healing by reviving the spirits of those in tough situations, regulates social behavior by praising good and ridiculing bad behaviors, educates society on gender roles and other things, and entertains.[1]

The traditional music of many of Tanzania's ethnic communities has many shared qualities including song themes, singing and dance styles, costumes, and reliance on the pentatonic (five-note) and diatonic (seven-note) music scales. In general, neighboring groups are more likely to share various music aspects compared to those that live in opposite ends of the country.

Until his death in 2003, Hukwe Ubi Zawose was one of the leading proponents of traditional music in Tanzania. He mainly sang the traditional music of his native Gogo ethnic community, even as Saida Karoli, who is perhaps the country's leading traditional musician, sings songs that are heavily drawn from her northwest Tanzanian Haya ethnic community. The Gogo (Wagogo) live in the Dodoma region of central Tanzania.

Contemporary Tanzanians enjoy music from many geographical sources. In addition to their local music, they have wide access to music from the neighboring and culturally and linguistically similar countries of Kenya, Uganda, Rwanda, Burundi, Mozambique, Zambia, Malawi, and the Democratic Republic of the Congo. American (rap, hip-hop, pop, and gospel), European (pop), Caribbean (reggae), and Indian music are also popular among many Tanzanians. Most of the foreign music comes to Tanzania through commercial channels and the Internet.

Traditional Music Genres

Tanzania has many traditional music genres—those that are firmly anchored in the country's precolonial cultures—including *ngoma* (traditional dance, drumming, and song) and *taarab* (sung Swahili poetry). These genres use a variety of traditional music instruments such as *ngoma* (drums), *nguga* (anklets or ankle bells), *marimba* (a type of xylophone), coconut-shell fiddles, *filimbi* (wooden or bone flutes and whistles), and a variety of traditional trumpets made of ivory and various animal horns.[2]

The basic characteristics of traditional Tanzanian (African) music include its participatory performance (i.e., inclusion of performers and audiences), presence in nearly all aspects of society, widespread association with dance or drama, close relationship with language, percussive nature and use of hand clapping, metronomic or unvaryingly regular rhythm, rare use of modulation, pervasive use of improvised melodies, and the near-universal dualism in melody and instrument.[3]

As in many parts of the world, the future of traditional music in modern Tanzania is a continuing subject of debate. Unlike in the late 1960s to mid-1980s when Tanzania actively sought to preserve its traditional music as part of its socialist policy of self-sufficiency, Tanzania is now an open economy that is modernizing and globalizing rapidly. As a result, many fear that the country will not be able to hold onto its traditional music much longer. Indeed, the flood of foreign music into the country in recent decades, even as the vibrancy of traditional Tanzanian music and dance has seemed to be on decline among the youth, seems to have vindicated these fears. Even "*Muziki wa dansi* [dance music]—a uniquely Swahili blend of jazz, rumba, and traditional music—[that] was born in newly independent Tanzania in the 1960s, on a wave of national pride" appears to be on decline, replaced on the airwaves by Western Top 40 hits.[4]

Yet while rapid modernization continues to be a threat to traditional Tanzanian music, a number of factors continue to keep it alive. First, some discontent with globalization has led to a significant cultural revival in the country that is helping to preserve its traditional music. For instance, the Tanzania Heritage Project is working to keep the country's rich archive of *muziki wa dansi*, tribal dances, and other classics at the country's oldest broadcaster, the Tanzania Broadcasting Corporation, alive by digitizing them and making them available to the public once again. Moreover, some of the country's educational institutions (e.g., the Bagamoyo College of Arts) and its National Arts Council (BASATA) are helping to preserve its music traditions.[5]

A second factor is that while former Tanzanian president Julius Nyerere used the country's music, dance, and drama to achieve his political ends, he simultaneously gave the country a strong music tradition that is being used to revive and preserve its traditional music. Third, the liberalization of the country's airwaves since the mid-1980s has ironically created a market for

Fatuma Baraka, popularly known as Bi Kidude, is a renowned Zanzibari *taarab* and *unyago* music singer. (Mwanzo Millinga/AFP/Getty Images)

traditional Tanzanian music. As a result, there are now many popular traditional musicians in the country including Zanzibar's renowned *taarab* singer Fatuma Binti Baraka (whose stage name is Bi Kidude) who, at nearly 100, is still performing; Kikumbi Mwanza Mpango (popularly known as King Kiki); and Saida Karoli, who has greatly popularized the traditional music of her native Haya community. Fourth, new technologies such as digital music and video recorders and players, the Internet, and YouTube have created an easy way to record and preserve mundane music cultures including those of traditional Tanzania. Moreover, these technologies have made it easy for the global fans of this music to access it, thereby helping to preserve it.

Currently, some of the country's leading traditional musicians are Kikumbi Mwanza Mpango (King Kiki), Fatuma Binti Baraka (Bi Kudude, the Little Granny of Zanzibar), and Saida Karoli. Kikumbi Mwanza Mpango is a naturalized Tanzanian from the DRC who runs Ochestra Le Capital band (also known as Africa Bara Moto Wazee Sugu). He came to Tanzania in the 1970s and became a citizen in 1997. He is known for compositions like "Kesi ya Kanga" (the trial of the guinea fowl) and "Kitambaa Cheupe" (white handkerchief). At the April 2012 Tanzania Kilimanjaro Music Awards, King Kiki was inducted into the organization's Hall of Fame in the individuals category.[6] Fatuma Binti Baraka was born in the early twentieth century in the village of Mfagimaringo to a coconut seller in colonial Zanzibar. At over 100 years old, she is an expert in cultural drumming, classic Zanzibari *taarab* (the music of the Swahili coast, which blends African and Arabic traditions and instruments) and modern Tanzanian *dansi* (dance) jazz. She is also known for her traditional cultural work in *unyago* (the initiation process that young Swahili women undergo before marriage), henna artistry (the elaborate arm and leg wedding decorations of Muslim women), production of *wanja* (the colors used in henna decorations), and traditional healing. In 2007, Bi Kidude became the first artist to receive a lifetime achievement award from the ZIFF.[7] The following is a simple outline of Tanzania's traditional music.

Court Music

Court music (read about singer Habibu Selemani, pp. 70–71) was played in the courts of the country's traditional chiefdoms and kingdoms until their abolition in the early 1960s. Some of these chiefdoms and kingdoms included Karagwe in the Kagera region, Shambaa in the West Usambara mountain range, and the Sultanate of Zanzibar (1856–1964).[8]

Since the proscription of the country's chiefdoms and kingdoms, court music has all but disappeared, though a form of "court music" has since emerged in the country to entertain political dignitaries such as the president. Throughout the country, there are a number of music and dance troupes for this purpose. The Bagamoyo College of Arts is a leading producer and conservator of the country's traditional and other music genres.[9]

Panegyric Music

This music is used to praise the qualities and achievements of individuals (either living or dead), families, clans, regions, objects, or ethnic groups. While many panegyrics suffer no lack of praise for their subjects, the really good ones are the product of careful and honest study of their subjects by experienced panegyrists or eulogists. Panegyrics are often used at birthdays, weddings, retirement ceremonies, or political rallies.

Entertainment and Recreation Music

Music has long played a central role in the recreational life of traditional and modern Tanzanian societies. In many cases, such music is highly participatory and is usually played in the evening at the end of the workday. Besides entertainment, traditional Tanzania's recreational music has long been an instructional vehicle for promoting desirable social values and traits. Many Tanzanian communities still have a vibrant traditional music scene.

Work Songs

In many parts of the country, work gangs or parties use songs to synchronize their effort, while away the work day, and maintain motivation when doing difficult and tiresome work. Work songs often vary widely based on ethnicity, age, gender, and profession. For example, the work songs of the country's fishermen, pastoralists, and farmers are uniquely utilitarian.

Worship Music

Many Tanzanian worship ceremonies, incantations, and ancestral invocations are accompanied by special types of music, dance, and drama. For instance, many traditional Sukuma religious ceremonies feature special music, dance, drumming, and even snake charming. The country's Christian community has built on this tradition and has vibrant Swahili worship music that is popular throughout East Africa.

Ritual and Festival Music

Various social ceremonies such as weddings, initiations (e.g., circumcision), and other rites of passage have their own special music. For instance, wedding songs often pour accolades on the bride and the groom besides advising them on how to lead successful married lives. Similarly, many initiation songs praise the initiates and teach them the rights and responsibilities of their new roles.

Funeral Dirges or Songs

Requiem songs in praise of the deceased, ancestors, and deities are part and parcel of Tanzanian funerals. In traditional funerals, the songs mourn the deceased, encourage the bereaved, and beseech the dead to go in peace and leave the living in peace. While Tanzanian funerals tend to be sad occasions, they can be fairly festive when the deceased happens to be one who lived to a ripe old age. Many Christian denominations' strong belief in the afterlife has also given rise to celebratory funerals as the dead are believed to be in a better place in heaven.

Modern Music Genres

Tanzania's modern music varies widely by source, geography, form, and function. As a coastal country that has long been accessed by foreigners, Tanzania has a medley of music influences including those of the surrounding African countries of Kenya, Uganda, the DRC, Rwanda, Burundi, Mozambique, and Malawi and far-off places like the Arabian Peninsula, India, the United States, Europe, and the Caribbean.

As used here, modern music is that which dates to the twentieth century and is often diverse in its origins, form, and style. In recorded form, the music is sold and marketed through concerts, CDs, the mass media (e.g., radio and television), the Internet (online players and stores), and music stores.

Tanzania's modern music era dates to the early 1900s when European missionaries, traders, and colonial officials introduced modern sound recorders, players, and new music genres. At the same time, the colonial regime's launch of modern transport and communications eventually led to many Tanzanians' introduction to music from across the country and elsewhere, thus aiding the modernization of the country's music landscape.

Tanzanians were first exposed to European music styles and instruments by missionaries who were out to gain converts to Christianity. As part of this effort, Christian missionaries established the country's first Western-style schools that also taught music. While students were initially taught Christian music, it did not take long for the basics of music composition, reading, and recording to start to diffuse to the general marketplace.

As Tanganyika (mainland Tanzania) was a German colony, the German anthropologist Carl Meinhof was the first to record native Tanzanian music in 1902 while on a tour of German East Africa. Unfortunately, there are no known copies of these recordings. By 1912, J. Muir, a His Master's Voice (HMV) Gramophone Company employee noted the potential market for recorded music in contemporary Tanzania and much of East Africa that would satisfy the needs of the emerging European and Indian settler communities that were beginning to have access to gramophones. The recorded music was to be supplied from India. Simultaneously, Alice Werner, an affiliate of the London School of Oriental and African Studies, recorded examples of coastal Swahili *taarab* music that is currently archived in London.[10]

By the 1920s, imported commercial Arabic, Indian, and Western music records (mostly 78-rpm ones) began to be available in coastal East Africa. Among the European music records that were beginning to be available were those from the United States, Britain, France, Germany, Italy, and Portugal, which, along with an increasing availability of Western musical instruments like the guitar, were beginning to play an important role in the creation of the syncretic modern music scene of East Africa. While HMV and other gramophone companies played an important role in popularizing gramophones and recorded music in East Africa throughout the 1920s, it was not until March 1928 that the Indian subsidiary of the HMV company sent a sound engineer to Mombasa (in contemporary Kenya) to record the then leading musicians of the Swahili coast.[11] These were the very popular female singer from Zanzibar Shahir Sitti Binti Saad and her male contemporaries

Maalim Shaban and Subeti Ambar. The three musicians recorded 62 songs, 56 of which were produced on 78-rpm records in August 1928.

The commercial success of the HMV venture led to even more commercially successful recordings in August 1929, which by 1930 had attracted competition from other music companies, notably Odeon and Columbia Records. Of these two, it is Odeon that had great commercial success, not least because it signed Shahir Sitti Binti Saad and more aggressively made new recordings in neighboring Mozambique and Madagascar. At the same time, Odeon recorded the first examples of the less commercially successful examples of Africanized Christian music in contemporary neighboring Uganda. In the end, debilitating competition between HMV, Odeon, and Columbia forced a merger of the three into the EMI Company of Hayes, Middlesex, UK, which distributed its music through its agent, the East African Music Stores in Nairobi. It was EMI, through its Nairobi agent, that oversaw the widespread growth of the music recording industry throughout East Africa, though by the 1940s, distribution of recorded music in Tanzania and much of East Africa was starting to be slowed by the need to censor music for subversive content against British colonialism in Tanzania and her East African neighbors.

While the first and second world wars and the freedom struggle slowed down the commercial development of music in East Africa, another technology was by 1946 salvaging the situation: the growing popularity of local radio broadcasting, cheap individual radio sets, as well as recorded and live music performances that were capable of reaching wider audiences. By the 1950s, EMI was facing intense competition from a number of local and global music labels, which forced it to open recording studios in Mombasa, Nairobi, and Dar es Salaam. This was significant because, for the first time, Tanzanian artists did not have to travel to modern Kenya to record their music. Simultaneously, new technological innovations in music recording and amplified sound blossomed with growing access to electricity. Soon the BBC entered the scene with its English and local vernacular African-language broadcasts that greatly increased demand for local music content.

In mainland Tanzania, local radio broadcasting commenced with the creation of a small radio station, *Sauti ya Dar es Salaam* (the Voice of Dar es Salaam), in the city on July 1, 1951. In the second half of 1955, the British colonial government expanded the station's reach to the provinces by installing more powerful transmitters and changed its name to the Tanganyika Broadcasting Service (TBS) and, a year later, to the Tanganyika Broadcasting Corporation (TBC). The station operated as TBC until the independence government changed its name to Radio Tanzania Dar es Salaam (RTD) in March 1965 and back again to the radio and television broadcaster, TBS in 2002.[12]

By the time of Tanzania's independence in the early 1960s, another seminal event was to shape the country's music: the great influx of Congolese musicians fleeing that country's civil war and other difficulties. These musicians, including the late Remmy Ongala and Kikumbi Mwanza Mpango, not only introduced their Congolese sound into Tanzania but became dominant and eventually helped to create Tanzania's now-dominant syncretic music style, which consists of dry guitar elements fused with the Congolese sound.[13] This influx of Congolese musicians was for a while controversial, and they were often threatened with deportation, but they eventually got assimilated into the country.

Currently, Tanzania has many modern music genres including gospel music (*muziki wa injili*), choral music (*muziki wa kwaya*), dance music (*dansi/muziki wa dansi*), bongo flava or hip-hop (rap, raga, and R&B), reggae, *mchiriku* (electronic *ngoma* or traditional dance, drumming, and song), *zouk*, and *ndombolo* (a fast-paced dance music that originated in the Republic of the Congo and the DRC). Below is quick review of some these more popular genres.

Gospel Music

Gospel or Christian music is quite popular in Tanzania given the country's large Christian population. The music comes in a variety of forms including choir, *dansi*, reggae, and *zouk*, with the first two being the most popular and commercially successful. The success of this music is due to many factors including its popularity with many Tanzanians, and more so the youth, who form the majority of the country's population; its liveliness and heavy use of modern music instruments such as electric guitars, keyboards, and drums; its popularity in the country's dance halls, open-air evangelistic meetings, and popular radio and TV stations; and its fortune in having many star performers (mostly females) who are usually accompanied by energetic dancers. Moreover, the recent liberalization of the country's mass media and growing access to affordable video recording and sharing technology (e.g., YouTube) have all greatly helped to popularize this music as well as make it available to worldwide audiences. Some of Tanzania's leading gospel music artists include female performers like Rose Muhando, Bahati Bukuku, Christina Shusho and male performers such as Solomon Makubwa and Bony Mwaitege.[14]

Choral/Choir Music

This music is performed by religious and secular choral groups. While Muslim choirs, for example the Killimani Muslim School Choir, are a rarity, there are thousands of Christian gospel choirs and a few secular ones. We thus briefly highlight the latter two groups.

Christian choral groups play a very important role in Tanzania's gospel music, and they tend to fall into three groups: the main choirs (*kwaya kuu*), youth choirs (*kwaya za vijana*), and evangelical choirs (*kwaya za uinjilisti*). All have their origins in the various Christian missionary churches and schools that sought to Christianize the country starting in the 1860s. In the preliterate Tanzanian societies of the precolonial and colonial eras, choirs were an effective evangelizing tool that also took advantage of local people's love of music. While most gospel choirs initially relied on translated or adapted European songs, many have over time developed a strong local music-composition tradition.[15]

One of Tanzania's leading gospel choir music composers is Gideon Mdegella, who is also director of the Christian Music Association of Dar Es Salaam that hosts some of the city's major choir competitions. He is also the musical director and conductor of one of Tanzania's major Lutheran choirs, Kwaya ya Upendo (Choir of Love). Mdegella's compositions often draw on his native Hehe as well as broader African and European traditions.

Modern gospel choirs usually practice in the middle of the week for their weekend church performances; have organs, pianos, synthesizers, and traditional or modern drum sets; occasionally record for local radio and TV stations; usually participate in competitions with other choirs; wear uniforms; and are often supported by bands. A key distinctive feature of Tanzanian gospel choirs is that their singing styles often strongly reflect their churches' theology and worship rituals. Thus, while the Seventh Day Adventist and Roman Catholic choirs often use less dance and instrumentation and place more emphasis on the lyrics, the Lutheran, Anglican, and Africa Inland Church (AIC) choirs (whether youth or adult) tend to use more instrumentation, dance, and drama and incorporate more elements of traditional African dance and singing.

Some of the country's major gospel choirs include the Evangelical Lutheran Church in Tanzania's *kwaya ya vijana* (youth choir) KKKT Mlowo and *kwaya kuu* (main choir) KKKT Uyole, the AIC's Mwadui Shinyanga Choir and Makongoro Choir, the Roman Catholic Church's Mt. Cesilia Arusha Choir, the Uvuke Anglican Choir, and the Seventh Day Adventist Kurasini Church Choir. In addition to these mainstream denominational choirs are those that are run by the various nondenominational religious (largely evangelical) groups including the Dar es Salaam–based New Life Crusade Choir and Kinondoni Revival Choir. Music samples from all of the country's major choirs are now available on YouTube.

Secular Choir Music

While choir music had its origins in the Christian church, it had by the mid-1900s expanded into the secular world, where it played an important role in the country's freedom struggle. After independence, the government used various secular choirs as well as comedy and drama groups to promote its political, social, and development agenda. Many schools and cultural groups also had and still have choirs, comedy, and drama troupes that served and continue to serve both educational and other social ends like entertaining local and national leaders. While these choirs have declined throughout the country since the end of socialism in Tanzania in the mid-1980s, their gospel counterparts continue to thrive.

Bongo Flava (Bongo Fleva)

This is an eclectic music genre that encompasses other genres including R&B, rap, raga, and *zouk*. The name *bongo* (brain) *flava* (flavor) means music from Dar es Salaam because survival in the city's streets requires plenty of street smarts. Others suggest that the genre's name salutes Dar es Salaam's role as the country's primate city or main social, cultural, economic, and political center. While *bongo flava* artists often use music to address many everyday life challenges, the mostly young artists that dominate this genre commonly sing about love, relationships, and sex. Next we briefly review this genre's sub-genres of R&B and hip-hop.

Rhythm and blues (R&B) started as an African American music genre that was exported to Tanzania starting in the 1940s. Like the later and closely related styles of rap or hip-hop, R&B originated in inner-city African American neighborhoods and was popularized by U.S. music catalogs in the 1940s through the 1960s. It includes elements of blues, gospel, and soul music and is focused on love and other themes. One the major innovations of Tanzania's R&B is that it is often performed in the local Swahili language and one of its best local singers is Judith Daines Wambura Mbibo, popularly known as Lady Jaydee. She has won numerous awards including the 2004 Tanzania Music Awards—Best R&B Album ("Binti"), 2006 and 2008 Pearl of Africa Music Awards—Best Female Artist (Tanzania), and 2008 Kisima Music Awards—Song of the Year Tanzania ("Anita" with Matonya). In 2012, the best R&B song was "My Number One Fan" by Ben Pol.

Hip-hop or *rap* is a music genre that developed in the 1970s in inner-city African American environments. While it sought to convey the challenges of everyday life in U.S. inner-city environments, it has since diffused to many parts of the world, including urban Tanzania. Wherever the genre has spread, it has tended to take on certain local attributes.

Tanzanian rap emerged in the early 1990s when local youth started aping their African American counterparts' rapping or use of rhythmic and rhyming speech or poetry. Since then, local rap artists have innovated and domesticated the genre and have created a unique rap form that includes local styles of African beats (Afrobeat) and arabesque melodies; dancehall, *taarab*, and Indian film beats; and Swahili and other local-language lyrics.[16] In some cases, the lyrics are a mixture of English and Swahili. Tanzanian hip-hop music can be either secular or gospel.

Despite rap's lower-class U.S. origins, in Tanzania it was first adopted by middle- and upper-class Tanzanian youth with access to Western media outlets. Since then, it has become popular with all urban Tanzanian youth, with the lower-class youth using it to vent their disaffection with tough urban life while their middle-class counterparts use it mainly for entertainment. Tanzanian rap is mostly a male affair because of the genre's initial negative association with supposedly unfeminine qualities like violence, gangs, and promiscuity. Thus, there are very few female rappers in the country, including Florence Kasela (whose stage name is Dataz).

One of Tanzania's leading and founding hip-hop artists is Joseph Mbilinyi (stage name Mr. II, Sugu, or 2-proud). Because of his hip-hop popularity, he was also elected to the Tanzanian Parliament in 2010 to represent the Mbeya Town constituency. Paul Matthysse is one of the country's leading hip-hop producers.

Dansi

Derived from the word *dance*, this music has Congolese, Tanzanian, Cuban, European, and other world influences. *Dansi* music groups vary widely in size, instrumentation (guitars, drums, keyboard, trumpets, horns), and music tradition and can feature low- or high-energy dance music routines. *Dansi* songs often feature a slow lyrical section that is then followed by a danceable section that usually has a faster tempo. Women dancers are a standard aspect of many local dance bands. The lyric sections of their performances usually deal with everything from banal to serious social, economic, and political issues. Some *dansi* band recordings often include panegyric performances or tracks in praise of their patrons, local and national heroes, and politicians, who often use *dansi* bands to promote themselves.[17]

From the 1940s to the mid-1980s, the Tanzanian *dansi* music scene was dominated by Congolese (formerly Zaire, now DRC) bands or those that imitated them. As a result, this music often includes Lingala-language lyrics and Congolese *rumba* dance styles. Moreover, the popularity of Congolese music maestros such as Franco Luambo Makiadi and Tabu Ley has left a lasting impression on contemporary Tanzanian *dansi* music performers.

Since the 1940s, many of Tanzania's popular *dansi* bands have been the various "jazz" bands that are so named because they included many elements of jazz music including saxophones, trumpets, and slow dance styles. Some of these famed bands include DDC Mlimani Park, Dar Es Salaam Jazz Band, and Vijana Jazz and, in more recent decades, Mashujaa Musica Band. While Tanzania gained its own domestic music recording industry in the 1950s, many of these bands preferred to record their music in neighboring Kenya's more modern studios in Nairobi well into the 1980s. In past decades, the list of the country's most prominent *dansi* musicians has included the late Mbaraka Mwinshehe and the late Dr. Remmy Ongala (born Ramadhani Mtoro Ongala wa-Mungamba). Currently, the country's dance scene is dominated by names like Kikumbi Mwanza Mpango (King Kiki) and Queen Darleen, whose song "Maneno Maneno" won the Best Dance Hall Song at the 2012 Tanzania Kilimanjaro Music Awards.

Reggae

Although reggae is not new to Tanzania, it did not really take root in the country until the 1980s when the genre's main performer, Jah Kimbute, returned to the country in 1981. Kimbute, whose style includes elements of jazz, soul, and local Tanzanian influences, encountered reggae in college in Europe. Soon after his return, he launched the Roots & Culture band in 1983 and registered it with the National Arts Council (*Baraza la Sanaa la Taifa*, BASATA) as required by law. Outside Tanzania, Kimbute has played in Trinidad, Zimbabwe, Zambia, Botswana, Haiti, Europe, and Scandinavia.

Some of the reasons for reggae's limited development in Tanzania are its high production costs, as it is recorded with live bands, and its limited airplay. Moreover, the lack of strong copyright protection in Tanzania undermines this and other music genres' growth in the country. Access to global music markets is also a challenge to many Tanzanian reggae musicians. The country's other reggae performers are Innocent Nganyangwa, Alex Kajumulo, and Jamaican-born Everton King-Bailey, alias Zanz B. In 2012, Tanzania's best reggae song was "Warrior from the East" by the Arusha Gold band.[18]

Mchiriku

This is a music genre that resembles and precedes hip-hop, having emerged and become popular in the poor areas of Tanzania's Dar es Salaam, Pwani (coast), and Morogoro regions in the early 1970s. It is derived from a traditional Zaramo dance, or *ngoma*—the Zaramo are the main ethnic group of the Dar es Salaam area. It features fast-paced, repetitive, energetic lyrics and rhythms that are played on small handheld Casio keyboards, drums and whistles, and a bricolage of music instruments from various local materials including old tins that are played with sticks.

Because of its lewd lyrics and erotic dancing, the government twice (in the 1970s and mid-1990s) banned it, though the ban proved all but impossible to enforce. Besides its love themes, *mchiriku* music is also known for its biting social commentaries on youth issues like drug and alcohol abuse, unemployment and other life struggles, and lessons for surviving Dar es Salaam's harsh urban maze, all of which partly explain its exclusion from the country's airwaves and its disapproval by the city's middle and upper classes.

Traditionally, and to some extent now, *mchiriku*-like music was used in the context of weddings and boy-initiation ceremonies, where its bawdy lyrics and dancing were used to teach young people about reproduction. During family occasions, the music was and is often played on the front porches of houses while in urban areas it is mostly played on the streets or in the empty spaces between buildings. Over time, and more so in Dar es Salaam, the music has taken on a more edgy and clandestine entertainment role that has largely consigned it to cassette-tape distribution.

Although a number of *mchiriku* bands, such as Jagwa Music, emerged in Dar es Salaam in the 1990s, the genre has been on the decline in recent years due to the growing popularity of *bongo flava* and hip-hop. Currently, some of its leading artists are Abdalla Gora and Abdul Jolijo, the two band leaders of Jagwa Music. In spite of the genre's apparent decline, recent innovations by groups like Jagwa Music appear to be succeeding in reviving and mainstreaming it as evidenced in Jagwa Music's 2011 performance at the prestigious Roskilde Festival, the largest North European culture and music festival. In 2012, Jagwa Music released their debut CD album, *Bongo Hotheads*, on Brussels' Crammed Discs music label. With this, Jagwa Music seems to be well on its way to mainstreaming *mchiriku* in a manner reminiscent of hip-hop's well-trodden path from the fringe.[19]

Taarab

Taarab is primarily sung Arabic and Swahili poetry that is most popular in coastal and urban Tanzania. *Taarab* started in Zanzibar as court music in the palace of Sultan Seyyid Barghash bin Said and then diffused throughout East Africa. Though originally used for entertainment, it now also informs and educates society on a wide variety of issues including politics, religion, and relationships. Traditionally, *taarab* seldom included dancing, though audience members were free to tip their best performers. *Taarab* has long been recorded and is widely available in recorded form and on the country's airwaves, especially in the coastal zone.

Taarab can either be classical or modern. Classical *taarab*, which is less popular and mainly confined to Zanzibar, usually consists of an orchestra with plucked lutes, violins, goblet drums, tambourines, and one or more vocalists singing in Arabic or Swahili. It mainly communicates through proverbs, riddles, and imagery and is less commercialized.

Unlike classical *taarab*, modern *taarab* is far more commercialized and has many popular bands that perform regularly in Dar es Salaam, Zanzibar, Tanga, Dodoma, Mwanza, Iringa, and other Tanzanian cities. Modern *taarab* is usually performed by modern bands with limited numbers of drummers, guitarists, bassists, keyboardists, and some singers who usually sit at the front of the band and perform sequentially. The smaller modern *taarab* bands are made possible by modern technological advances such as electronic keyboards that can replace several instruments. Unlike its classical counterpart, modern *taarab* is also now quite danceable.

Because of commercial pressures, modern *taarab* has, over time, drifted to more open language. It has also grown corrosive, vulgar, and demeaning to women, who are often the main performers and consumers of its love-themed music. Romantic competitors, such as women in polygynous marriages or those seeking the affections of one man, often use modern *taarab's* cutting poetry to taunt each other's failings as lovers or wives. Predictably, female brawls have become a common feature of modern *taarab* performances. *Taarab* has also long provided safe social spaces for marginalized groups like women and homosexuals. Fatuma Binti Baraka of Zanzibar is one of Tanzania's leading *taarab* singers. At the 2012 Tanzania/Kilimanjaro Music Awards, Mashauzi Classic's (Isha Mashauzi) song "Nani Kama Mama" (Who Is Like Mom) was voted the Best *Taarab* Song.[20]

Cultural/Folk Pop

Cultural/folk pop music is modernized traditional folk music (i.e., the music of traditional Tanzanian societies) that is performed by modern musicians and distributed through commercial channels such as pop concerts, radio stations, music studios, and record stores. Many current Tanzanian pop artists are cultural pop performers to a certain extent because many of them are influenced by their cultural roots. Thus, many are variously engaged in repackaging Tanzanian folk music and dance for modern society by, for instance, incorporating popular traditional dances, attire, instruments, and tunes into their performances or by adapting these tunes for modern music genres, styles, and instruments. Currently, Saida Karoli is one of Tanzania's most popular cultural/folk pop artists. She is not only famous for her modern interpretations of traditional Haya music but also for popularizing these songs across the country through her energetic, entertaining, and highly danceable band rhythms. She is an accomplished singer, composer, dancer, and drummer. Her crisp and unique take on traditional and rural Tanzanian music, society, and life has earned her many fans throughout East Africa. She has been nominated for recognition by the Tanzania Music Awards and the Kora All-African Music Awards.[21]

Patriotic Music

Although Tanzania has many patriotic songs, the most prominent is its national anthem "*Mungu Ibariki Africa*" (God Bless Africa), which is essentially a customized Swahili-language version of the South African Enoch Sontonga's popular 1897 song *Nkosi Sikelel' iAfrika* (God Bless Africa). The song is also Zambia's national anthem (with different words) as well as part of South Africa's national anthem.

Other Modern Music Genres

Besides the preceding review of Tanzania's main music genres, Tanzanians also have wide access to regional East and Central African music genres including Congo's *Lingala*, *takeu* (a new regional popular music genre whose name is derived from the first letters of *Ta*nzania, *Ke*nya and *U*ganda), and foreign music from all over the world, more so that from the Caribbean, the United States, Britain, and India.

Music Promoters and Galas

From 1967 to the mid-1980s, prior to the liberalization of Tanzania's economy, the government played a key role in the promotion of music, dance, and drama in the country as part of its quest to build a cohesive and developed socialist African nation. To achieve these goals, the government created three core art and art-related entities: BAMUTA, BAKITA, and BASATA. While BAMUTA (*Ba*raza la *Mu*ziki la *Ta*ifa, or the National Music Council) was created to preserve, strengthen, and promote Tanzanian music, BAKITA (*Ba*raza la *Ki*swahili la *Ta*ifa, or the National Kiswahili Council) sought to do the same for the Swahili language, even as BASATA (*Ba*raza la *Sa*naa la *Ta*ifa, or the National Arts Council) promoted the arts. Together, the three entities especially promoted Swahili music, dance, and drama because it simultaneously enhanced national cohesion and the national language of Swahili. Yet BAMUTA also sponsored festivals and music galas that promoted all manner of Tanzanian music even as it sought to curtail the "corrupting" influences of foreign colonial and bourgeois (or capitalist-class) music.

Nonetheless, the government's heavy involvement in the country's music industry severely limited its growth in the preliberation era, and commercial distribution of music was limited. Recording opportunities and equipment were also few and far between. All this changed when the country liberalized its economy, politics, and airwaves in the mid-1980s, leading to the proliferation of radio and television stations as well as a flood of entrepreneurs seeking to profit from music production, promotion, and distribution. By 2008, there were 53 radio and 27 television stations in the country, up from one each before liberalization. Similarly, by the mid-2000s, the country had nearly 400 music and other cultural promoters. Besides the airwaves, these promoters also use open-air concerts and the country's many dance clubs to promote their music.[22]

Moreover, the county's main cultural festivals (e.g., Tanzania/Kilimanjaro Music Awards, Zanzibar International Film Festival of the Dhow Countries, Zanzibar Cultural Festival, Karibu Travel and Trade Fair, and *Mwaka Kogwa*) and beauty pageants (Chapter 7) provide important venues for promoting the country's music, as does the continental Kora All-African Music Awards. As is often the case in many other countries, these festivals and pageants often draw the ire of Tanzania's social and religious conservatives.[23]

Musical Instruments

Tanzania's musical instruments closely resemble those of the neighboring countries. Because many of the country's communities have a shared heritage, they also have many of the same musical instruments, especially drums. Nevertheless, these instruments' features, function, tone, quality, timbre or resonance, and social value somewhat varies across the country.

Tanzanian musicians play the *ilimba* or thumb piano. (Jon Lusk/Redferns)

As in other countries, Tanzania's musical instruments fall into five main categories: *membranophones* (percussive instruments that make sound when
struck, e.g., drums); *idiophones* (the various percussive instruments, e.g., rock
chimes and xylophones, that make sound when beaten, scraped, or shaken);
aerophones (wind instruments that are blown into to produce sound, e.g., flutes
and panpipes); *chordophones* (string instruments, e.g., harps, lyres, and guitars); and *electrophones* (those that produce sound by electrical means). Below
is a brief review of the use and distribution of these instruments in Tanzania.

Membranophones

Drums are a central music and communication instrument in most of
Tanzania and Africa. They attend nearly all social, spiritual, and political
ceremonies and occasions including marriage, worship, healing, exorcism,
divination, death and burial, childbirth and naming, political rallies, and
other celebrations. Drums are so central to Tanzanian culture that people
often make do with improvised drums when real ones are unavailable.[24]

The vast majority of Tanzanian drums consist of one or two animal-skin
membranes (usually those of cows or goats) that are attached by leather strips
or some other roping material to one or both ends of a clay pot, gourd, cala-
bash, or hollow wooden or metal frame. The wooden frame can consist either
of a single hollow piece or several strips that are joined and held in place by a
band of sorts. Across the country, the dominant drum material is usually a
factor of what is available in the local environment.

A drum's body shape can be cylindrical, conical, barreled, waisted, goblet-
like, or long. Beyond these general shapes, many Tanzanian communities
variously customize and embellish their drums, with the Makonde of South
Eastern Tanzania making some of the most artistic drums in the country.
Moreover, drums can be single- or double-headed depending on whether
they have one or two playable surfaces. While modern drums are increasingly
available in Tanzania, it is the traditional drums that reign supreme given
their cultural relevance, cost, and easy availability.

While all drums make sound when their membranes vibrate, a drum's
sound varies based on the thickness of its membrane; the size, shape, and
material of its frame; its tuning, which is achieved by varying the tautness
of the membrane on the play head; as well as how it is played—whether by
one or both hands—and with what: straight or padded drumstick(s) or fric-
tion. While the lighter drums can be played while hanging from the player's
neck or shoulder or while held under the arm; the heavier ones must often
be set between the knees, on the ground, or on a stand. The wide variety of
drums in the country translates into an equally wide variety in sound, size,
shape, and function.

In many Tanzanian and African communities, specific drums both send and are the message. Thus they have a meaningful presence that emanates from their shape, type, use, genderedness (whether played by males or females), and sociocultural function. For instance, among the Makonde of southeastern Tanzania, aerophones and other music instruments often serve as masks that represent certain ancestral spirits besides being used for entertainment, divination, or any other purpose. Music instruments can also serve as good-luck amulets or as symbols of fertility and other locally significant attributes. Similarly, many traditional Tanzanian leaders had or have drums (and other music instruments) as part of their regalia (symbols of office), which are central to conveying messages and authority to their subjects. Even modern national celebrations make extensive use of drums.

Moreover, specific drum beats convey specific messages, communal responses, and, in some cases, specific places of assembly. For instance, while a playful drum beat often assembles people for fun, other drumbeats gather and coordinate them for worship, weddings, or mourning, even though the art of "reading" the meaning of various drumbeats has declined somewhat with the country's modernization and urbanization.

During dances, drumming, clapping, dancing, and singing are so intertwined that a change in one leads to a change in the others. Drumming and dance often offer a good basis for telling the country's ethnic groups apart as each has its own drumming styles. Moreover, drums play a central role in the various traditional religions of many Tanzanian communities. For instance, the Sukuma have sacred drums, dances, and songs for their various worship, exorcism, and healing rituals and dances. As spiritual exorcism is believed to occur when both the exorcist and patient dance to specific drumbeats on sacred drums, such ceremonies seldom proceed in the absence of the required drum paraphernalia.

Idiophones

Tanzanians make use of a wide range of idiophones. Human body parts like hands, thighs, and chests are some of the most important idiophones given the wide variety of rhythms they produce when clapped or beaten rhythmically. Outside of the human body are the various sonorous (loud or resonant) instruments made of various natural or manmade materials that are beaten, scraped, or shaken to produce the desired sound or rhythm. Common examples include logs, xylophones (a percussion musical instrument that consists of wooden bars played or struck by mallets), rock chimes, sea shells, gourds full of small stones or seeds, leg rattles, shakers, bells, thumb pianos (*sansa*), wooden or metal lamellophones (e.g., *limba*, 7 notes, and *marimba*, 13 notes), tambourines, and claves (a pair of short, thick wooden sticks, animal bones, or blocks that are rhythmically struck together during singing or dancing sessions). Depending on their construction, these instruments can be permanent or temporary. With increasing contact with the outside world, Tanzanians are also increasingly utilizing a number of modern idiophones.[25]

Aerophones

There are many wind music instruments in Tanzania. Regardless, they are all played by either soft or hard blowing into them with the mouth. Common examples of aerophones in Tanzania include wooden, cane, or gourd-neck flutes (which have anywhere from two to six holes depending on the desired level of modulation); bamboo, wood, metal, or cow or other animal horn trumpets; horns (which differ from trumpets by being curved and conical), and buzzers made of strings and bottle tops. Some of these instruments can also be made of a wide variety of temporary materials depending on the local environment. Thus while agriculturalist groups prefer wooden aerophones, hunter-gatherer and nomadic groups tend to go for domestic and wild animal-horn ones. Harmonicas, accordions, harmoniums, and other modern aerophones are increasingly available in and near cities. In Tanzania, aerophones are especially popular with dancers and children.

Whether an aerophone is soft or hard blown depends on its size and length. Thus, while hard-blown horns are made of large animal horns, their soft-blown counterparts tend to be made of small domestic or wild animal horns. Moreover, while hard-blown instruments have traditionally been used for summoning, entertaining, or communicating with large crowds or dispersed people groups, the soft-blown instruments serve these roles with immediate or small groups of people. Like all other musical instruments, aerophones are played at various social occasions including marriages and religious or political celebrations and can be played alone or in combination with other musical instruments.

Chordophones

Tanzania's chordophones are either single- or multistringed musical instruments such as bows, lyres, harps, lutes, fiddles, and zithers. These instruments are almost as common as drums and range from the traditional (e.g., bows, lyres, harps) to the modern (e.g., guitars, violins, and pianos).

Electrophones

Examples of these instruments that produce sound by electrical means are electric guitars and basses. Most modern Tanzanian bands have one or more electrophones.

Maasai women prepare to meet Prince Charles. Dances are commonly used to entertain dignitaries in Tanzania. (Chris Jackson/Getty Images)

DANCE

Dance is a universal accompaniment to Tanzanian music. In Tanzania, dance is popularly known as *ngoma* (Swahili for dance), though this word can be a verb that means to dance or a noun that refers to a drum, a dance, or a musical event. Thus, one can play a drum (*piga ngoma*); attend or go to a dance or music performance (*enda ngoma*); dance at a ball, disco, club or open-air performance (*cheza ngoma*); or be entertained by a dance troupe (*tumbuizwa na ngoma*).

Like music, dance has many purposes including expressing joy on the occasion of childbirth, courtship, marriage celebrations, visits by relatives and dignitaries, and thanksgiving for good harvests and successful hunts and battles; sadness during mourning and other stressful times; and solemnity at national functions and political transitions. Moreover, dance plays a crucial role in entertainment such as at beer parties, in worship in most religious traditions, in traditional spirit exorcisms, in the socialization of children, and in instilling appropriate behaviors in members of society. Some of Tanzania's well-known ethnic dances include the *lipango* of the Wamalila of Mbeya, *ngongwa* of the Wamakonde of Mtwara, *mgoda* of Wakwere of the coast, *bugobogobo* of the Sukuma of Mwanza and Shinyanga, and *kyaso* of the Unguja (Zanzibar) region.[26]

As African dance is usually communal and functional, Tanzanian social changes have over time undermined certain aspects of traditional dance even as they have spawned new ones. For instance, the dances used to beseech the ancestors and gods for protection in interethnic war have virtually disappeared with the rise of the modern nation state that values unity and peace among its various ethnic groups. Simultaneously, new dances that address modern social challenges such as HIV/AIDS have arisen.[27]

Tanzanian dances are usually expressive and participatory, often involving miming or mimicking, pageant, and various body postures (dances) and facial movements that express diverse individual and communal emotions, attitudes, thoughts, beliefs, and even defensive and aggressive poses. Across the country, much of the variation in dance depends on whether a community emphasizes upper- or lower-body movements. Thus, while the Nguu of Morogoro region have elaborate footwork, other communities rely more on belly, hip, and foot dances.

In many communities, dances that involve many performers have certain rhythms that are used to structure or order them. Thus, a change in rhythm often leads to changes in dance styles as well as the lead performers. Though individual dances may or may not be as structured, good dancers find ways to work with the prevailing rhythm. In certain worship or competition dance routines, the dancer(s) often use various warm-up performances to prepare themselves for the main acts. In either case, the chosen songs must not only set and maintain the right atmosphere and mood for the performance but must also provide the sounds, modulations, and rhythms to be expressed in movement as well as regulating the scope, speed, quality, and dynamics of the dance.

While dance is widespread in Tanzania, it is especially developed among groups like the Sukuma and Makonde that have strong cultural initiation traditions as well as beliefs in divination, magic, and spiritism. Thus, the Sukuma and Makonde have ritual dances that mark all the major stages of the life cycle: birth, puberty, marriage, and death. For the Makonde, the masked *mapiko* dances fulfill this role, and both the Makonde and Sukuma have elaborate dance competitions that use elegant costumes, dance routines, and new song compositions or reinterpretations of existing ones. They also use "dance medicines" that are designed to attract spectators to the performances, protect the dance troupes from the witchcraft of rival groups, and ensure victory over rival groups. In both communities, the dance medicines are secured from trusted medicine men. The performers use the medicines by rubbing them on their bodies like ointment, bathing in them, or absorbing them into their bodies in sauna-like conditions.

A stilt dancer in action. The Makonde are some of Tanzania's most renowned stilt dancers. (Derrick Ceyrac/AFP/Getty Images)

Both groups also have their differences. While the Makonde dances peak at the end of the annual children's initiation ceremonies, for the Sukuma the annual dance competitions are held at the end of the harvest season between June and September. A renowned aspect of Sukuma dance competitions is their innovative dances styles that often involve deadly snakes. For the Makonde, their claim to fame is the *ngongoti* dances that involve masked acrobatic dancers on 6-foot stilts.

Across Tanzania, there are general as well as age-, gender-, occasion-, and occupation-specific dances, each with its own style and attire, which often include sisal skirts, jingles, headbands and headdresses, feathers, shields, spears, rods, necklaces, bangles, special head shavings, and hats made of various materials. Nowadays, many traditional dance implements and clothing are routinely combined with their modern equivalents.[28]

DRAMA

Tanzanian drama, in the sense of a symbolic performance that uses symbolic images and actions to represent life, dates to the precolonial era. It often accompanies music and dance, thereby creating simultaneous musical-dance-drama performances. Thus it not only enhances music and dance but also serves many of the same purposes as these two, namely informing, educating, entertaining, expressing emotion, and communicating. In short, even in the face of the country's relatively high literacy levels, drama, song, and dance continue to be powerful oral and visual mediums of communication as well as being preservers and transmitters of culture in all corners of the country.[29]

There are many facets to Tanzanian drama including music-dance-drama, plays, children's theater, puppetry, acrobatics, and community and development theatre. Not only did all these play an important role in Tanzania's freedom struggle, but they have also been used to enhance its cultural, political, and socioeconomic development since independence starting with the formation of the country's first National Dance Troupe (NDT) in 1965. Soon after, NDT created a repertoire of major Tanzanian songs, dances, and dramas whose popularity spurred the formation of other troupes across the country. Although NDT collapsed in 1967, many of its members went on to establish the influential Bagamoyo College of Arts (BCA) which, along with the University of Dar es Salaam's Department of Performing Arts, the Butimba Teachers College, the Open University of Tanzania, and the Tanzania Theater Center, is a major trainer of the country's dramatists and artists.

Early in the socialist revolutionary period (1967–1985), drama pieces in praise of the country's socialist development path were plentiful. But by the 1970s, critical drama pieces started to appear as the achievement of the country's socialist dream became elusive. Nevertheless, the country's emphasis on the arts in this period saw the emergence of songs, dances, recitations, mimes, and dramatizations that were at the level of and popular with the people. To produce such pieces, playwrights often immersed themselves in the country's communities, identified their problems, and tackled them through drama. Soon, questions emerged about the authenticity of such externally induced drama productions, questions that forced many playwrights to try to be authentic by living in and producing drama with the target communities. As a result, many of the plays from this era were message laden, as traditional African drama has since time immemorial been practical and has seldom been produced just for entertainment or for the sake of it.

While politics dominated Tanzania's dramatic productions in the socialist era, this period's productions also tackled many other issues including family life, marriage, interethnic relations, urban and rural life, corruption, and health issues. Many nongovernmental organizations (NGOs) have also since then used simple drama and theater productions to promote their various development agendas. For example, the Kilakala Unit for the Deaf in Morogoro town has in the 2000s used a drama group of mostly young deaf people to promote its community-awareness program on the needs and rights of deaf children.[30]

With the liberalization of the country's economy in the mid-1980s, many of the cultural troupes that depended on political patronage collapsed even as the competitive multiparty era spawned a few new ones. As radio and television outlets have mushroomed since then, the need for drama production has also increased. Nevertheless, there has been a shift away from the message-laden productions of the socialist era to commercial productions that can sell and attract audiences. Although many Tanzanians lament this trend, it seems set to stay.

Besides the politically and commercially supported troupes, there are many impromptu drama groups across the country. Many of these belong to colleges, schools, churches, and NGOs and are constituted on an as-needed basis, for instance during Christmas, for school competitions, and on other major social occasions. Those that belong to schools are generally permanent because drama competitions are an annual aspect of the Tanzanian primary, secondary, and tertiary school system. Some of the country's largest secular music, dance, and drama troupes are based in Dar es Salaam; they include the Muungano Cultural Troupe and the Tanzania One Theater (TOT). Many of the country's largest church choirs (e.g., Mamajusi Choir) also have active drama programs that support their evangelism through recorded music videos.

Despite Tanzania's rich drama culture, the country has no national theater house, though Dar es Salaam's National Museum and House of Culture is being developed into one. As a result, the country's professional theater development lags behind that of her main East African community neighbors of Kenya and Uganda, which have the National Theatre, the Courtyard Theatre (Kenya), and the Uganda National Theatre and Cultural Center. While the country's National Arts Council (popularly known as BASATA) is charged with the responsibility of developing all aspects of theater in the country, the construction of a national theater has been hampered by lack of funds, forcing many of the country's dramatists to perform in the open or in inadequately equipped halls. While dramatists in Dar es Salaam could use the University of Dar es Salaam's theater, this seldom happens because of its small size, inconvenient location, and the perception that it is unwelcoming to non–university members.[31]

Aside of the paucity of theater facilities, the other key challenges of Tanzanian drama include lack of adequate policy supports, an ongoing colonial hangover or foreign bias in the training of the country's drama artists, lack of drama teachers at the primary and secondary school level, a general disrespect for artists in the country, and inadequate copyright laws to protect the intellectual property of the country's dramatists and other artists.

Among Tanzania's major playwrights are Edwin Semzaba, Penina (Mlama) Muhando, Ebrahim Hussein, Shaaban Robert (dubbed East Africa's Shakespeare), Godwin Kaduma, Emmanuel Mbogo, and Ngalimecha Ngahyoma. Of these, Robert (1909–1962), Muhando, and Hussein are probably the most accomplished and have at one time or another been based at the University of Dar es Salaam's Department of Fine and Performing Arts. The major themes of the playwrights include social justice, education, poverty and challenges of the peasantry, divorce, women's rights, city life, and the challenges of *Ujamaa* (including its villagization policy). Most of these playwrights' works have been in Swahili, something that makes them accessible to the Tanzanian masses.[32]

While most of the country's drama is in Swahili, there is also growing availability of English drama, especially among the elite. English drama has especially grown with the proliferation of Tanzanian English media, more so since the liberalization of the country's economy and airwaves in the mid-1980s. At the moment, most of the country's English drama production occurs in its secondary and tertiary institutions, where English is the medium of instruction and drama is a key avenue for improving students' English proficiency. Some of this drama utilizes English plays from overseas such as Shakespeare. While the growth of English drama is commendable, it is hoped that this will not undermine the country's Swahili drama tradition that is both relevant and accessible to the masses.[33]

NOTES

1. Gregory Barz, *Music in East Africa: Experiencing Music, Expressing Culture* (New York and Oxford, UK: Oxford University Press, 2004), 76.

2. Alex Perullo, *Live from Dar es Salaam: Popular Music and Tanzania's Music Economy* (Bloomington and Indianapolis: Indiana University Press, 2011); Embassy of Tanzania—Washington DC, "Tanzania: People and Culture," http://www.tanzaniaembassy-us.org/?page_id=136, accessed September 29, 2012.

3. Alexander Akorlie Agordoh, *African Music: Traditional and Contemporary* (New York: Nova Science Publishers, 2005), 25–27; Ronnie Graham, *Stern's Guide to Contemporary African Music.* Vol. 2, *The World of African Music* (London: Pluto Press, 1992), 158–62.

4. Hilary Heuler, "Traditional Tanzanian Music Falls in Popularity, but Demands Preservation," *The Christian Science Monitor*, March 23, 2012, http://www.csmonitor.com/, accessed March 29, 2012.

5. Ronnie Graham, *The World of African Music*, 159.

6. Paul Owere, "Remmy, King Kiki Honoured," *The Citizen*, April 16, 2012, http://www.thecitizen.co.tz/entertainment/44-tanzania-entertainment/21507-remmy-king-kiki-honoured.html, accessed July 1, 2012; Mohamed Kazingumbe, "King Kiki and His Music Journey, 1962 to 2012," *Business Times*, June 8, 2012, http://www.businesstimes.co.tz/, accessed July 1, 2012.

7. Zanzibar International Film Festival, "Zanzibar International Film Festival 2007," http://www.youtube.com/watch?v=FchHjxJkUQw, accessed June 7, 2012.

8. Advameg, "Shambaa," 2012, http://www.everyculture.com/wc/Tajikistan-to-Zimbabwe/Shambaa.html, accessed March 27, 2012; Art & Life in Africa, "Karagwe Information," November 3, 1998, http://www.uiowa.edu/~africart/toc/people/Karagwe.html, accessed March 27, 2012; Tanzania Chamber of Commerce, Industry, and Agriculture, Kagera, "Karibu Kagera-Bukoba-Tanzania," http://www.kagera.org/index.htm, accessed March 27, 2012.

9. Ronnie Graham, *The World of African Music*, 159.

10. Lars Fredriksson, "Feast of East: Paul Vernon's Continuing Series of Delvings into the History of World Music Recording Touches Down in East Africa," April 17, 1997, http://bolingo.org/audio/texts/fr145eastafrica.html, accessed April 3, 2012.

11. The engineer went to Mombasa because at the time, contemporary coastal Kenya was part of the Sultan of Zanzibar's domain. It reverted to Kenya at independence in 1963.

12. Tanzania Broadcasting Corporation, "Historical Background," 2012, http://www.tbc.go.tz/~tbcgo/tbc1/historical-background.html, accessed April 3, 2012.

13. Lars Fredriksson, "Feast of East."

14. Alex Perullo, *Live from Dar es Salaam*, 365–66; Kiundu Waweru, "Once a Muslim, Mysterious Disease Drove Muhando to Christianity," *Standard*, September 18, 2010, http://standardmedia.co.ke/?articleID=2000018597&story_title=Once-a-Muslim,-mysterious-disease-drove-Muhando-to-Christianity, accessed May 30, 2012; Rockstar, "East African Gospel Star Rose Muhando Signs Multi-Record Deal with Sony Music," February 24, 2012, http://www.rockstar4000.com/profiles/blogs/east-african-gospel-star-rose-muhando-signs-multi-record-deal-wit, accessed May 30, 2012.

15. Alex Perullo, *Live from Dar es Salaam*, 365–66; Gregory Barz, *Music in East Africa*, 64–65.

16. Peter Jan Haas and Thomas Gesthuizen, "Ndani ya Bongo: Kiswahili Rap Keeping It Real," in Frank Gunderson and Gregory F. Barz (eds.), *Mashindano! Competitive Music Performance in East Africa* (Dar es Salaam: Mkuku wa Nyota Publishers, 2000), 279–94.

17. Werner Graebner, "Ngoma ya Ukae: Competitive Social Structure in Tanzania Dance Music Songs," in Frank Gunderson and Gregory F. Barz (eds.), *Mashindano! Competitive Music Performance in East Africa* (Dar es Salaam: Mkuku wa Nyota Publishers, 2000), 295–318.

18. Alex Perullo, *Live from Dar es Salaam*, 365–66; Svenskt Visarkiv—Centre for Swedish Folk Music and Jazz, "Research Rap, Ragga and Reggae in Dar Es Salaam: Roots & Culture—Jah Kimbute," 2012, http://www.visarkiv.se/en/mmm/media/africa/r&c.html, accessed June 6, 2012; Speciroza Joseph, "Zanz B: Tanzania Reggae Needs Some Fine Tuning," *Business Times Weekly*, November 19, 2010, http://www.businesstimes.co.tz/, accessed June 6, 2012; Kilimanjaro Tanzania Music Awards, "Washindi wa [Winners of the] Kili Music Awards 2011–2012," 2012, http://www.kilitime.co.tz/awards/2009/winners/index.html, accessed June 7, 2012.

19. Alex Perullo, *Live from Dar es Salaam*, 364–65; Roskilde Festival, "Jagwa Music," 2012, http://roskilde-festival.dk/uk/band/singleband/jagwa-music/, accessed June 6, 2012; Clandestino Institut, "Jagwa Music," 2012, http://clandestinofestival.org/2012/en/jagwa-music/, accessed June 6, 2012.

20. Alex Perullo, *Live from Dar es Salaam*, 367; Nathalie Arnold, "Placing the Shameless: Approaching Poetry and the Politics of Pemban-ness in Zanzibar, 1995–2001," *Research in African Literatures* 33, no. 3 (Autumn 2002), 140–66.

21. Busara Promotions, "Festival Artists: Saida Koroli," 2012, http://www.busaramusic.org/database/artists.php?whereartistid=89, accessed March 29, 2012.

22. Alex Perullo, *Live from Dar es Salaam*, 369–88.

23. Issa Yussuf, "Tanzania: Music Festival Draws Mixed Feelings among Zanzibaris," *Tanzania Daily News* (Dar es Salaam), February 15, 2010, http://allafrica.com/stories/201002161015.html, accessed June 7, 2012.

24. Ottó Károlyi, *Traditional African and Oriental Music* (London: Penguin Books, 1998), 1–54; Alexander Akorlie Agordoh, *African Music*.

25. Lois Anderson, "The African Xylophone," *African Arts* 1, no. 1 (Autumn 1967), 46–49, 66, 68–69, http://www.jstor.org/stable/3334364, accessed: June 8, 2012.

26. Cosmas Mlekani, "JKT Arts Troupe Performance Thrills Chinese Ambassador," *Tanzania Daily News* (Dar es Salaam), May 12, 2012, online http://allafrica.com/stories/201205120294.html, accessed July 2, 2012.

27. Ottó Károlyi, "*Traditional African and Oriental Music*, 1–54; Alexander Akorlie Agordoh, *African Music*, 33–35.

28. Elise B. Johansen, "Makonde Mask Dance: Performing Identity," in Frank Gunderson and Gregory F. Barz (eds.), *Mashindano! Competitive Music Performance in East Africa* (Dar es Salaam: Mkuku wa Nyota Publishers, 2000), 255–70; Ottó Károlyi, *Traditional African and Oriental Music*, 1–54; Mohamed Kazingumbe, "Recalling How Makonde Dancers Uplifted Tanzania in 1970," *Business Times— Economic and Financial Times Weekly*, January 20, 2012.

29. Augustin Hatar, "The State of Theatre Education in Tanzania," paper prepared for UNESCO, 2001, http://portal.unesco.org/culture/en/files/19603/10814381543hatar.pdf/hatar.pdf, accessed June 13, 2012; Megan Browning, "Shake It: A Study of Traditional Dance and Drumming in Tanzania With the African Traditional Dance Group," 2009, Independent Study Project (ISP) Collection, paper 648, http://digitalcollections.sit.edu/isp_collection/648, accessed September 29, 2012.

30. Siri Lange, "Rivals on the Urban Cultural Scene," in Frank Gunderson and Gregory F. Barz (eds.), *Mashindano! Competitive Music Performance in East Africa* (Dar es Salaam: Mkuku wa Nyota Publishers, 2000), 67–85; Deaf Child Worldwide, "Raising Awareness through Drama in Tanzania," July 3, 2008, http://www .deafchildworldwide.info/, accessed June 13, 2012.

31. Erick Kabendera, "Why Tanzania Has No Theatre Houses?" *Mwafrika* (blog), December 22, 2006, http://mwafrika-kabendera.blogspot.com/2006/12/ why-tanzania-has-no-theatre-houses.html, accessed June 13, 2012.

32. Martin Banham, Errol Hill, and George Woodyard (eds.), *The Cambridge Guide to African and Caribbean Theatre* (Cambridge, UK: Cambridge University Press, 1994), 115–16.

33. Casmir M. Rubagumya, "Language Promotion for Educational Purposes: The Example of Tanzania," *International Review of Education* 37, no. 1 (1991), 67–85, DOI: 10.1007/BF00598168.

Selected Bibliography

CHAPTER 1: INTRODUCTION

Anonymous. "Africa's Ancient Steelmakers." *TIME*, September 25, 1978, http://www.time.com/time/magazine/article/0,9171,912179,00.html, accessed June 27, 2012.

Mohamed Amin, Duncan Willetts, and Peter Marshall. *Journey through Tanzania.* Nairobi, Kenya: Camerapix Publishers International, 1984.

L. Berry, ed. *Tanzania in Maps.* London: University of London Press, 1971.

James Brennan, Andrew Burton, and Yusuf Lawi, eds. *Dar es Salaam: Histories from an Emerging African Metropolis.* Dar es Salaam/Nairobi: Mkuki na Nyota, 2007.

John Briggs and Davis Mwamfupe. "Peri-urban Development in an Era of Structural Adjustment in Africa: The City of Dar es Salaam, Tanzania." *Urban Studies* 37, no. 4 (2000): 797–809.

Andrew Burton. *African Underclass: Urbanization, Crime & Colonial Order in Dar es Salaam.* Dar es Salaam: Mkuki wa Nyota, 2005.

J. D. Fage and Roland Oliver, eds. *The Cambridge History of Africa: From c. 1600 to c. 1700.* London and New York: Cambridge University Press, 1979.

Abel G. M. Ishumi. *Kiziba: The Cultural Heritage of an Old African Kingdom.* Syracuse, NY: Syracuse University Press, 1980.

Irving Kaplan, ed. *Tanzania: A Country Study.* Washington, D.C.: American University Press, 1978.

J. M. Lusugga Kironde. "Received Concepts and Theories in African Urbanization and Management Strategies: The Struggle Continues." *Urban Studies* 29, no. 8 (1992): 1277–91.

Camillus J. Sawio. "Perception and Conceptualisation of Urban Environmental Change: Dar es Salaam City." *The Geographical Journal* 174, no. 2 (2008): 164–68.

Robert Schroeder. "South African Capital in the Land of *Ujamaa* [Socialism]: Contested Terrain in Tanzania." *At Issue Ezine* 8, no. 5 (September 2008). http://www.africafiles.org/atissueezine.asp, accessed October 1, 2008.

Dean Sinclair. "'Memorials More Enduring than Bronze': J. H. Sinclair and the Making of Zanzibar Stone Town." *African Geographical Review* 28 (2009): 71–97.

Kirsten Strandgaard. *Introducing Tanzania through the National Museum*, Dar es Salaam: The Museum, 1974.

Tanzania. "Country Profile." United Republic of Tanzania National Website. http://www.tanzania.go.tz/profile1f.html, accessed January 19, 2011.

J. B. Webster, B. A. Ogot, and J. P. Chretien. "The Great Lakes region, 1500–1800." In *General History of Africa V: Africa from the Sixteenth to the Eighteenth Century*, edited by B. A. Ogot, pp. 776–827. Berkeley: University of California Press, 1992.

CHAPTER 2: RELIGION AND WORLDVIEW

Allan Anderson. "African Religions." *Encyclopedia of Death and Dying*, 2011. http://www.deathreference.com/A-Bi/African-Religions.html, accessed February 24, 2011.

Richard Cox. "Why Rangi Christians Continue to Practice African Traditional Religion." *GIALens*, 2008, p. 3. http://www.gial.edu/images/gialens/vol2-3/Cox-Why-Rangi-Christians-Practice-ATR.pdf, accessed July 19, 2012.

Bishops of ELCT. "The Dodoma Statement [on Same Sex Marriage]." Evangelical Lutheran Church in Tanzania, January 7, 2010. http://www.elct.org/news/2010.04.004.html, accessed April 1, 2011.

Richard J. Gehman. *African Traditional Religion in Biblical Perspective*. Nairobi: East African Educational Publishers, 2005.

Miranda K. Hassett. *Anglican Communion in Crisis: How Episcopal Dissidents and Their African Allies Are Reshaping Anglicanism*. Princeton, NJ: Princeton University Press, 2007.

Bruce E. Heilman and Paul J. Kaiser. "Religion, Identity and Politics in Tanzania." *Third World Quarterly* 23, no. 4 (August 2002): 691–709.

Philip Jenkins. *The New Faces of Christianity: Believing the Bible in the Global South*. New York: OUP, 2006.

Method M. P. Kilaini. "The Tanzania Catholic Church." RCNet, October 10, 1998. http://www.rc.net/tanzania/tec/tzchurch.htm, accessed March 18, 2011.

Robert Leurs, Peter Tumaini-Mungu, and Abu Mvungi. *Mapping the Development Activities of Faith-based Organizations in Tanzania*. Religions and Development Research Programme, Working Paper 58-2011. Birmingham, UK: International Development Department, University of Birmingham, 2011.

Frieder Ludwig. *Church and State in Tanzania: Aspects of Changing Relationships, 1961–1994.* Boston: Brill, 1999.

Aloysius M. Lugira. *African Traditional Religion.* New York: Chelsea House, 2009.

John S. Mbiti. *African Religions and Philosophy.* London: Heinemann, 1969.

John S. Mbiti. *Introduction to African Religion.* London: Heinemann Educational, 1991.

John S. Mbiti. "The Role of Women in African Traditional Religion." *Cahiers des Religions Africaines* 22 (1988), 69–82.

Amos Mhina (ed.). *Religions and Development in Tanzania: A Preliminary Literature Review.* (Dar es Salaam: Religions and Development Research Program, Philosophy Unit, University of Dar es Salaam, RaD Working Paper 11-2007).

Pew Research Center. *Tolerance and Tension: Islam and Christianity in Sub-Saharan Africa.* Washington, DC: Pew Forum on Religion & Public Life, April 2010. http://features.pewforum.org/africa/country.php?c=216.

Mohammed Saeed. "Islam and Politics in Tanzania." Muslim Writer's Organization, Dar es Salaam, Tanzania. http://www.islamtanzania.org/nyaraka/islam_and_politics_in_tz.html, accessed September 29, 2012.

Michael Westall. "Anglican-Lutheran Relations in Tanzania." Presented at the Anglican-Lutheran Society Annual General Meeting, March 7, 2009. http://www.anglican-lutheran-society.org/Westall%20paper.htm, accessed March 17, 2011.

CHAPTER 3: LITERATURE, MEDIA, AND FILM

Juma Adamu Bakari. "Satires in Theatre for Development Practice in Tanzania." In Kamal Salhi (ed.), *African Threatre for Development: Art for Self-determination.* Exeter, UK: Intellect Books, 1998.

Martin Banham, Errol Hill, George Woodyard, and Olu Obafemi (eds.). *The Cambridge Guide to African and Caribbean Theatre.* Cambridge, UK: Cambridge University Press, 1994.

Lars P. Christensen, Cecilia Magnusson Ljungman, John Robert Ikoja Odongo, Maira Sow, and Bodil Folke Frederiksen. *Strengthening Publishing in Africa: An Evaluation of APNET.* Sida Evaluation 99/2. Stockholm, Sweden: Sida, 1998.

Carol Eastman. "The Emergence of an African Regional Literature: Swahili." *African Studies Review* 20, no. 2 (September 1977): 53–61.

Laura Edmondson. *Performance and Politics in Tanzania: The Nation on Stage.* Bloomington and Indianapolis: Indiana University Press, 2007.

Simon Gikandi. "East African Literature in English." In F. Abiola Irele and Simon Gikandi (eds.), *The Cambridge History of African and Caribbean Literature,* vol. 2, pp. 425–44. Cambridge, UK: Cambridge University Press, 2004.

Johnson M. Ishengoma. "African Oral Traditions: Riddles among the Haya of Northwestern Tanzania." *International Review of Education* 51 (2005): 139–53.

Lonard S. Klein (ed.). *African Literatures in the 20th Century: A Guide.* New York: Ungar, 1986.

Alamin Mazrui. *Swahili beyond the Boundaries: Literature, Language, and Identity.* Athens: Ohio University Press, 2007.

John P. Mbonde. "Gabriel Ruhumbika: Janga Sugu La Wazawa (2002)—Uchambuzi na Uhakika." *Swahili Forum* 12 (2005): 81–93.

Martin Mhando. "Participatory Video Production in Tanzania: An Ideal or Wishful Thinking?" *Tanzanet Journal* 5, no. 1 (2005): 9–15.

Rachel Mkundai. "Journalist Integrity and Press Freedom in Tanzania." Stanhope Centre for Communications Policy Research, April 19, 2005. http://www.stanhopecentre .org/training/EA/mkundai_seminar.shtml, accessed July 16, 2012.

M. M. Mulokozi. "The Last of the Bards: The Story of Habibu Selemani of Tanzania (c. 1929–93)." *Research in African Literatures* 28, nos. 1 and 2 (1997): 159–72.

Mona Ngusekela Mwakalinga. *The Political Economy of the Film Industry in Tanzania: From Socialism to an Open Market Economy, 1961–2010.* PhD dissertation, Film and Media Studies, University of Kansas, Manhattan, Kansas.

Pompea Nocera. "An Interpretation of Said Ahmed Mohamed's Novel *Kiza Katika Nuru* and Some Aspects of Translation." *Swahili Forum* 12 (2005): 63–80.

Oyekan Owomoyela (ed.). *A History of Twentieth-Century African Literatures.* Lincoln: University of Nebraska Press, 1993.

Katriina Ranne. *Drops That Open Worlds: Image of Water in the Poetry of Euphrase Kezilahabi.* Masters thesis, African Studies, Institute for Asian and African Studies, Faculty of Arts, University of Helsinki, Helsinki, Finland, 2006. https://oa.doria.fi/bitstream/handle/10024/4092/dropstha.pdf?sequence=1, accessed July 16, 2012.

Rosaleen Smyth. "The Feature Film in Tanzania." *African Affairs* 88, no. 352 (July 1989), 389–96.

Kelly Swanston. "Tanzania: The State of the Media." Stanhope Centre for Communications Policy Research, May 16, 2005. http://www.stanhopecentre.org/ training/EA/Tanzania.doc, accessed July 16, 2012.

Flavia Aiello Traore. "Translating a Swahili Novel into 'Kizungu': *Separazione*, The Italian Edition of Said Ahmed Mohamed's *Utengano*." *Swahili Forum* 12 (2005): 99–107.

Aili Mari Tripp. *Changing the Rules: The Politics of Liberalization and the Urban Informal Economy in Tanzania.* Berkeley: University of California Press, 1997.

CHAPTER 4: ART AND ARCHITECTURE/HOUSING

Anonymous. "Africa's Ancient Steelmakers." *TIME*, September 25, 1978. http:// www.time.com/time/magazine/article/0,9171,912179,00.html, accessed June 27, 2012.

Felix A. Chami and Remigius Chami. "Narosura Pottery from the Southern Coast of Tanzania: First Incontrovertible Coastal Later Stone Age Pottery." *Nyame Akuma* 56 (December 2001): 29–35.

Great Lakes Consortium for International Training and Development and The Arts Council Lake Erie West. *Art—In a Woman's World.* Toledo, OH: The Great

Lakes Consortium for International Training and Development and The Arts Council Lake Erie West, 2010.

Augustin Hatar. "The State of Theatre Education in Tanzania." Paper prepared for UNESCO, 2001. http://portal.unesco.org/culture/en/files/19603/10814381543hatar.pdf/hatar.pdf, accessed June 13, 2012.

Sidney Littlefield Kasfir. *Contemporary African Art*. London: Thames & Hudson, 1999.

Abdulaziz Y. Lodhi. "Muslims in Eastern Africa—Their Past and Present." *Nordic Journal of African Studies* 3, no. 1 (1994): 88–98.

Tom Phillips (ed.). *Africa: The Art of a Continent*. Munich/London/New York: Prestel, 1999.

Vicensia Shule. "The Role of 'Political Will' in Implementing Arts Education in Tanzania." University of Dar es Salaam and International Drama/Theatre and Education Association (IDEA), Tanzania. http://www.unesco.org/, accessed June 26, 2012.

Dean Sinclair. "Memorials More Enduring than Bronze: J. H. Sinclair and the Making of Zanzibar Stone Town." *African Geographical Review* 28 (2009): 71–97.

Sarah L. Smiley. "Population Censuses and Changes in Housing Quality in Dar es Salaam, Tanzania." *African Geographical Review* 31, no. 1: 2012. DOI:10.1080/19376812.2012.679451.

Barbara Thompson. "Namsifueli Nyeki: A Tanzanian Potter Extraordinaire." *African Arts* 40, no. 1 (2007): 57.

Aadel Brun Tschudi. "Ujamaa Villages and Rural Development." *Norsk Geografisk Tidsskrift—Norwegian Journal of Geography* 26, nos. 1–2 (1972): 27–36.

UNESCO World Heritage Centre. "Decision—30COM 8B.36—Nominations of Cultural Properties to the World Heritage List (Kondoa Rock Art Sites)." UNESCO World Heritage Centre, 1992–2012. http://whc.unesco.org/en/decisions/1002, accessed June 28, 2012.

Monica Blackmun Visoná, Robin Poynor, Herbert M. Cole, and Michael D. Harris (eds.). *A History of Art in Africa*. New York: Harry N. Abrams Publishers, 2001.

Jacqueline Woodfork. "Cities and Architecture." In Toyin Falola (ed.), *Africa Volume 2: African Cultures and Societies before 1885*. Durham, NC: Carolina Academic Press, 2000.

Alexandra Zavis. "The Roof Is Falling In on a Cultural Legacy in Zanzibar." *Los Angeles Times*, December 25, 2005. http://articles.latimes.com/2005/dec/25/news/adfg-stonetown25, accessed June 29, 2012.

CHAPTER 5: CUISINE AND DRESS

Anonymous. "Tanzania: Dressing Up the Masai." *TIME*, November 24, 1967. http://www.time.com/time/magazine/article/0,9171,844158,00.html, accessed May 3, 2011.

Rosabelle Boswell. "Say What You Like: Dress, Identity and Heritage in Zanzibar." *International Journal of Heritage Studies* 12, no. 5 (2006): 440–57.

Dorothy L. Hodgson. *Once Intrepid Warriors: Gender, Ethnicity, and the Cultural Politics of Maasai Development.* Bloomington: Indiana University Press, 2001.

Andrew M. Ivaska. " 'Anti-Mini Militants Meet Modern Misses': Urban Style, Gender and the Politics of 'National Culture' in 1960s Dar es Salaam, Tanzania." *Gender & History* 14, no. 3 (November 2002): 584–607.

M. N. Kitundu, V. A. E. B. Kilimali, H. B. Maurice, G. I. Kiula. and M. E. Kamwaya. "Presence of Methyl Alcohol in Local Alcoholic Beverages in Tanzania and Its Relationship to Impaired Vision or Death." *Tanzania Journal of Natural and Applied Sciences* 1, no. 2 (December 2010): 102–5.

Nicholas Minot. "Staple Food Prices in Tanzania." Prepared for the COMESA Policy Seminar on Variation in Staple Food Prices: Causes, Consequence, and Policy Options, Maputo, Mozambique, January 25–26, 2010, African Agricultural Marketing Project (AAMP). http://ageconsearch.umn.edu/bitstream/58555/2/AAMP_Maputo_24_Tanzania_ppr.pdf, accessed April 4, 2011.

Halifa Msami. "Poultry Sector Country Review: Tanzania." FAO, 2007. ftp://ftp.fao.org/docrep/fao/011/ai349e/ai349e00.pdf, accessed April 4, 2011.

J. Mutai, E. Muniu, J. Sawe, J. Hassanali, P. Kibet, and P. Wanzala. "Socio-cultural Practices of Deciduous Canine Tooth Bud Removal among Maasai Children." *International Dentistry* Journal 60, no. 2 (April 2010): 94–98.

Julius K. Nyerere. "Ujamaa: The Basis of African Socialism." *The Journal of Pan African Studies* 1, no. 1 (1987): 4–11.

Majuto Omary. "Tanzania's Miriam Odemba Wins Miss Earth Pageant." *Ethiopian Review,* November 11, 2008. http://www.ethiopianreview.com/content/13112, accessed April 27, 2011.

E. N. Sawe. "Wood Fuels Stoves Development and Promotion in Tanzania: Some Selected Experiences." European Biomass/COMPETE Workshop on Bioenergy for Rural Development in Africa and Asia, Hamburg, Germany, June 30, 2009. http://www.compete-bioafrica.net/events/events2/hamburg/Session%202/S2-5-COMPETE-REImpact-Hamburg-Sawe-090630.pdf, accessed April 23, 2011.

Leander Schneider. "The Maasai's New Clothes: A Developmentalist Modernity and Its Exclusions." *Africa Today* 53, no. 1 (Fall 2006): 101–29.

Eric N. Shartiely. "The Portrayal of the Tanzanian Woman in Television Commercials: Is She a Piece of Soap, a House, or Gold?" *Africa & Asia* 5 (2005): 108–41.

Embassy of Tanzania—Washington DC. "Tanzania: Food." Republic of Tanzania. http://www.tanzaniaembassy-us.org/tzepeo.html, accessed May 4, 2011.

Chapter 6: Marriage, Family, Lineage, and Gender Roles

Mark J. Calaguas, Cristina M. Drost, and Edward R. Fluet. "Legal Pluralism and Women's Rights: A Study in Postcolonial Tanzania." *Columbia Journal of Gender and Law,* Summer 2007.

Elizabeth Carr. *Community and Land Attachment of Chagga Women on Mount Kilimanjaro, Tanzania.* Master of Science thesis, Department of Geography, Brigham Young University, Provo, Utah, 2004.

Ernestina Coast. "Maasai Marriage: A Comparative Study of Kenya and Tanzania." *Journal of Comparative Family Studies* 37, no. 3 (2006): 399–420.

Edward R. Fluet, Mark J. Calaguas, and Cristina M. Drost. "Legal Pluralism & Women's Rights: A Study in Post-Colonial Tanzania." bepress Legal Series, Working Paper 1683. September 3, 2006. http://law.bepress.com/expresso/eps/1683, accessed September 2, 2011.

Government of Tanzania. "Gender." http://www.tanzania.go.tz/gender.html, accessed September 8, 2011.

Maureen Kambarami. "Femininity, Sexuality and Culture: Patriarchy and Female Subordination in Zimbabwe." African Regional Sexuality Resource Center in collaboration with Health Systems Trust, South Africa, and University of Fort Hare, South Africa, 2006. http://www.arsrc.org/downloads/uhsss/kmabarami.pdf, accessed August 26, 2011.

Sakamoto Kumiko. "The Matrilineal and Patrilineal Clan Lineages of the Mwera in Southeast Tanzania." *Utsunomiya University Faculty of International Studies Essays* 26 (2008): 1–20. http://uuair.lib.utsunomiya-u.ac.jp/dspace/bitstream/10241/6358/1/kokusai26-002.pdf, accessed August 17, 2011.

Iddi Adam Mwatima Makombe. *Women Entrepreneurship Development and Empowerment in Tanzania: The Case of SIDO/UNIDO-Supported Women Microentrepreneurs in the Food Processing Sector.* Doctoral thesis, Department of Development Studies, University of South Africa, Pretoria, South Africa, 2006.

Daniel Mbunda. *Traditional Sex Education in Tanzania: A Study of 12 Ethnic Groups.* New York: The Margaret Sanger Center, Planned Parenthood of New York City, 1991.

Zaida Mgalla, Dick Schapink, and J. Ties Boerma. "Protecting School Girls against Sexual Exploitation: A Guardian Programme in Mwanza, Tanzania." *Reproductive Health Matters* 6, no. 12 (November 1998): 19–30.

Joseph Mzinga. "Changing Gender Roles in Tanzania." *Sexual Health Exchange* 2002–2004. http://www.kit.nl/exchange/html/2002-4_changing_gender_roles_i.asp, accessed September 12, 2011.

Innocent Ngalinda. *Age at First Birth, Fertility, and Contraception in Tanzania.* PhD dissertation, Department of Demography, Faculty of Philosophy III, Humboldt-Universität zu Berlin, 1998. http://edoc.hu-berlin.de/dissertationen/phil/ngalinda-innocent/PDF/Ngalinda.pdf, accessed September 1, 2011.

Aginatha Rutazaa. "Tanzanian Women and Access to Law." Terry Sanford Institute of Public Policy, Duke University, Durham, NC, 2005. http://sanford.duke.edu/centers/civil/papers/rutazaa.pdf, accessed September 8, 2011.

Philip Setel, Eleuther Mwageni, Namsifu Mndeme, Yusuf Hemed, and Beldina Opiyo-Omolo. "Tanzania: The United Republic of Tanzania." http://www2.hu-berlin.de/sexology/IES/tanzania.html, accessed August 17, 2011.

Frans Wijsen and Ralph Tanner. *I am Just a Sukuma: Globalization and Identity Construction in Northwest Tanzania.* New York: Rodopi, 2002.

CHAPTER 7: SOCIAL CUSTOMS AND LIFESTYLES

Maasai Association. "Maasai Ceremonies and Rituals." http://www.maasai
-association.org/ceremonies.html, accessed November 3, 2011.

Don Brown. "The African Funeral Ceremony: Stumbling Block or Redemptive
Analogy?" *International Journal of Frontier Missions* 2, no. 3. http://ijfm.org/
archives.htm#Volume23, accessed November 12, 2011.

Michael Finkel. "The Hadza." *National Geographic Magazine*, December 2009.
http://ngm.nationalgeographic.com/print/2009/12/hadza/finkel-text,
accessed December 1, 2011.

K. Manji. *Situation Analysis of Newborn Health in Tanzania: Current Situation,
Existing Plans and Strategic Next Steps for Newborn Health.* Dar es Salaam:
Ministry of Health and Social Welfare, Save the Children, 2009.

Daniel Mbunda. *Traditional Sex Education in Tanzania: A Study of 12 Ethnic Groups.*
New York: The Margaret Sanger Center, Planned Parenthood of New York
City, 1991.

Mona Ngusekela Mwakalinga. *The Political Economy of the Film Industry in Tanzania: From Socialism to an Open Market Economy, 1961–2010.* PhD dissertation, Film and Media Studies, University of Kansas, Manhattan, KS.

Terje Oestigaard. "Traditions in Transitions: Rainmaking in a Changing World in
Tanzania." ECAS 2011—4th European Conference on African Studies,
Uppsala, Sweden, June 15–18, 2011. http://www.nai.uu.se/ecas-4/, accessed
November 12, 2011.

Tepilit Ole Saitoti. *The Worlds of a Maasai Warrior.* Berkeley: University of California Press, 1988.

Todd Sanders. "Reflections on Two Sticks: Gender, Sexuality and Rainmaking."
Cahiers d'Études Africaines 166, no. 42-2 (2002): 285–13.

Rosaleen Smyth. "The Feature Film in Tanzania." *African Affairs* 88, no. 352
(July 1989): 389–96.

R. E. S. Tanner. "Ancestor Propitiation Ceremonies in Sukumaland, Tanganyika."
Africa: Journal of the International African Institute 28, no. 3 (July 1958):
225–31.

CHAPTER 8: MUSIC, DANCE, AND DRAMA

Alexander Akorlie Agordoh. *African Music: Traditional and Contemporary.* New York:
Nova Science Publishers, 2005.

Lois Anderson. "The African Xylophone." *African Arts* 1, no. 1 (Autumn 1967):
46–49, 66, 68–69. http://www.jstor.org/stable/3334364, accessed: June 8, 2012.

Nathalie Arnold. "Placing the Shameless: Approaching Poetry and the Politics of
Pemban-ness in Zanzibar, 1995–2001." *Research in African Literatures* 33,
no. 3 (Autumn 2002): 140–66.

Martin Banham, Errol Hill, and George Woodyard (eds.). *The Cambridge Guide to
African and Caribbean Theatre.* Cambridge, UK: Cambridge University Press,
1994.

Gregory Barz. *Music in East Africa: Experiencing Music, Expressing Culture*. New York and Oxford, UK: Oxford University Press, 2004.

Megan Browning, "Shake It: A Study of Traditional Dance and Drumming in Tanzania With the African Traditional Dance Group," 2009, Independent Study Project (ISP) Collection, paper 648, http://digitalcollections.sit.edu/isp_collection/648, accessed September 29, 2012

Lars Fredriksson. "Feast of East: Paul Vernon's Continuing Series of Delvings into the History of World Music Recording Touches Down in East Africa." April 17, 1997. http://bolingo.org/audio/texts/fr145eastafrica.html, accessed April 3, 2012.

Frank Gunderson and Gregory F. Barz (eds.). *Mashindano! Competitive Music Performance in East Africa*. Dar es Salaam: Mkuku wa Nyota Publishers, 2000.

Ronnie Graham. *Stern's Guide to Contemporary African Music*. Vol. 2, *The World of African Music*. London: Pluto Press, 1992.

Augustin Hatar. "The State of Theatre Education in Tanzania." Paper prepared for UNESCO, 2001. http://portal.unesco.org/culture/en/files/19603/10814381543hatar.pdf/hatar.pdf, accessed June 13, 2012.

Hilary Heuler. "Traditional Tanzanian Music Falls in Popularity, but Demands Preservation," *The Christian Science Monitor*, March 23, 2012. http://www.csmonitor.com/, accessed March 29, 2012.

Ottó Károlyi. *Traditional African and Oriental Music*. London: Penguin Books, 1998.

Alex Perullo. *Live from Dar es Salaam: Popular Music and Tanzania's Music Economy*. Bloomington and Indianapolis: Indiana University Press, 2011.

Casmir M. Rubagumya. "Language Promotion for Educational Purposes: The Example of Tanzania." *International Review of Education* 37, no. 1 (1991): 67–85.

Embassy of Tanzania—Washington DC. "Tanzania: People and Culture." http://www.tanzaniaembassy-us.org/?page_id=136, accessed March 27, 2012. Tanzania Broadcasting Corporation. "Historical Background." May 13, 2012. http://www.tbc.go.tz/~tbcgo/tbc1/historical-background.html, accessed July 19, 2012.

Svenskt Visarkiv—Centre for Swedish Folk Music and Jazz. "Research Rap, Ragga and Reggae in Dar Es Salaam: Roots & Culture—Jah Kimbute." 2012. http://www.visarkiv.se/en/mmm/media/africa/r&c.html, accessed June 6, 2012.

Index

About the Author

KEFA M. OTISO is associate professor of geography and director of the Global Village at Bowling Green State University, Bowling Green, Ohio. He is the author of *Culture and Customs of Uganda* (Greenwood, 2006) and many book chapters and refereed journal articles. He is a past editor of the *African Geographical Review* and the founding president of the Kenya Scholars and Studies Association.